MAPPING FAITH:
THEOLOGIES OF MIGRATION
AND COMMUNITY

of related interest

Interfaith Worship and Prayer
We Must Pray Together
Edited by Christopher Lewis and Dan Cohn-Sherbok
Foreword by the Dalai Lama
ISBN 978 1 78592 120 9
eISBN 978 1 78450 385 7

People of the Book
An Interfaith Dialogue about How Jews, Christians and
Muslims Understand Their Sacred Scriptures
Dan Cohn-Sherbok, George D. Chryssides and Usama Hasan
Foreword by Marcus Braybrooke
ISBN 978 1 78592 104 9
eISBN 978 1 78450 366 6

Interreligious Dialogue and the Partition of India
Hindus and Muslims in Dialogue about Violence and Forced Migration
Mario I. Aguilar
ISBN 978 1 78592 312 8
eISBN 978 1 78450 625 4

Fortress Britain?
Ethical approaches to immigration policy for a post-Brexit Britain
Edited by Ben Ryan
ISBN 978 1 78592 309 8
eISBN 978 1 78450 620 9

The Role of Religion in Peacebuilding
Crossing the Boundaries of Prejudice and Distrust
Edited by Pauline Kollontai, Sue Yore and Sebastian Kim
ISBN 978 1 78592 336 4
eISBN 978 1 78450 657 5

Mapping Faith

THEOLOGIES OF MIGRATION AND COMMUNITY

Edited by Lia D. Shimada

Jessica Kingsley Publishers
London and Philadelphia

First published in Great Britain in 2020 by Jessica Kingsley Publishers
An Hachette Company

1

Trigger warning: mention of rape in Chapter 17

A CIP catalogue record for this title is available from the British Library and the Library of Congress

ISBN 978 1 78592 387 6
eISBN 978 1 78450 745 9

Printed and bound in the UK by Clays Ltd

Jessica Kingsley Publishers' policy is to use papers that are natural, renewable and recyclable products and made from wood grown in sustainable forests. The logging and manufacturing processes are expected to conform to the environmental regulations of the country of origin.

Jessica Kingsley Publishers
73 Collier Street
London N1 9BE, UK

www.jkp.com

For Rowan and Brecon

Acknowledgements

This book is only possible because of the contributors who gave generously of their time, talent and stories. It has been an honour to work with each of you.

The Susanna Wesley Foundation and the Southlands Methodist Trust allowed me to dedicate my time to this project and created the conditions in which it could flourish. I have the great fortune to work alongside colleagues who value the process as much as the product of any endeavour. Special thanks to Sue Miller, Emma Pavey and Liz Pickett for their support and collaboration.

Natalie Watson was the first person to recognize what this book could be. For her trust in commissioning me, and for her ongoing encouragement, I am deeply grateful. Emily Badger, my wonderful editor, and the team at Jessica Kingsley Publishers carried the project to completion.

My mentor, the geographer Claire Dwyer, was an original contributor. When she was no longer able to write, her friend and colleague Nazneen Ahmed courageously took on the assignment. Although Claire died before she could see this book in print, her lively and empathetic mind is present throughout these pages. We have dedicated Nazneen's chapter to Claire's memory.

Finally, to Jonathan, for his love and companionship through the migrations in our lives: Thank you.

Contents

Part 3: Diaspora

Introduction

Lia Dong Shimada

In the ancient city of Hebron, the Tomb of the Patriarchs rises from the Judaean desert. The walls of this vast shrine, built over two millennia ago, surround caves believed to hold the remains of Abraham and Sarah, Isaac and Rebekah, Jacob and Leah. A family tomb, for three generations, held sacred through the centuries as a place of pilgrimage. As with many families, this burial place is also a source of bitter contestation. Today, separate entrances funnel Muslim and Jewish pilgrims through the grounds of the shrine. At the Muslim entrance, I slipped off my shoes and pulled on the grey cloak that an attendant handed to me. Its hood, made of scratchy fabric, muffled the noises around me. My focus sharpened as I stepped further into the building, towards an encounter with myth made real. Outside, soldiers patrolled the streets and the town crackled with tension – a tinderbox primed to explode.

I went to Hebron as a Christian pilgrim, alongside other members of the Anglican congregation of which I am part. We had travelled from London for a ten-day 'alternative pilgrimage', refracted through the lens of grassroots peacebuilding projects and local Palestinian Christian communities. Jerusalem, Bethlehem, Nazareth: these were places I had only imagined, rendered familiar (or so I thought) through a lifetime of well-known Bible stories. Pilgrimage, though, has a way of turning the world on its head; as we travelled, I was coming to understand that I would never understand what we mean by 'the Holy Land'. In Hebron, in particular, multiple religions converge, spilling forth tangled, overlapping stories of heritage and identity. In the Tomb of the Patriarchs, I glimpsed the possibility of a thrilling conversation.

Avraham. Abraham. Ibrahim. Known by many names, he gave rise to a constellation of faith traditions that revere one God, of which the three largest are Judaism, Christianity and Islam. In lifelong dialogue with God, he travelled widely across the region we know today (in the West) as 'the Middle East'. Abraham's legacy of journey, however, is not confined to 'out there' or 'back then'; it characterizes faith communities to this day. His descendants can be found in every corner of the globe. In Abraham's restless journeying, we find a mirror for contemporary questions about our relationships with God, with each other and with the world. These questions – about movement and ministry, people and places, belief and belonging – bring us into dialogue with ourselves and with one another.

This book offers some routes into this vast conversation about migration, faith and community. The project emerged from a one-day conference that I organized in 2015 at the University of Roehampton, on the theme of 'Migration and Ministry'. Participants, from primarily Christian backgrounds, gathered in London to grapple with the practical implications of migration in their communities. With the British and European media in thrall to the so-called 'migration crisis', punctuated by dramatic headlines and illustrated by photos of weary, anxious refugees, this felt like a prophetic moment for many faith leaders. After the conference, I found myself thinking about the many unanswered questions it had raised. What are the responsibilities of faith communities? How does faith shape migration? How does migration shape our understanding of 'community' in the context of faith? What are the implications? What do we mean, theologically, by words like 'migrant', 'exile', 'refuge'? Where is 'home' for the people of God? And how do we talk about it?

I came to this project as a geographer; my starting point was the slippery nexus of people, place, culture, history and identity. Within geography, the concept of migration is a well-mined seam of thought and research, recognized as a vital aspect of reality. As a person of faith, however, I sought a broader understanding – one that interrogates the presence of God, moving in the world. In other words, I wanted to understand more about the *theology of migration* – as practice, as concept, as experience, as encounter with God. As I grappled with my own learning, I found myself wondering about the ways in which other people, in other parts of the country and from other religious traditions, might approach these questions. I wondered how our different theologies (plural) might generate new ways of understanding the experience of migration in our own lives and faith communities. What might we learn about our understanding of God? This, after all, is where good theology begins – not in the library or the lecture hall, but in the real, grounded experience of God in the everyday.

'Migration' means more than just the physical movement of a person (or object, or population) from one location to another. As the voices in this book reveal, migration in the context of faith and community is a transformative process, one of boundary-crossing journeying that leaves no one untouched or unchanged. 'Migration', to the writers, artists and poets who are featured in these pages, encompasses the heart as much as the body; it challenges our very ideas of God, and from there our beliefs and our practices. At its core is the Greek root '*mei*': to go, to move and (above all, perhaps) to change.

Mapping faith engagements

In the Christian tradition, a triptych is a picture or carving in three panels, typically hinged together to form an altarpiece. Like a triptych, this book contains three sections, although none should be understood as more central than the others. Each section contains a collection of short essays written by practitioners; a contribution by a visual artist; and a handful of poems. The contributors to this book identify primarily (although not exclusively) as Jewish, Muslim and Christian.

The first section, 'Faith Encounters', explores themes of transformation and change. Each essay involves an encounter with a migratory 'other' that deepens understanding of one's own faith.

- In conversation, the artists *Faiza Omar* and *Ric Stott* discuss the challenges and opportunities that arise through their collaborative, interfaith work at 35 Chapel Walk, a community art gallery in Sheffield city centre.
- *Oliver Joseph* offers a beautiful meditation on the image of the tent in Jewish theology. He interweaves reflections on the festival of Sukkot with his experience of volunteering, alongside a group of young adults from his London synagogue, at the migrant camp in Calais.
- As the first Muslim chaplain of Canary Wharf, *Ibrahim Mogra* is part of an interfaith team that serves one of London's busiest commercial centres. He describes the forms of chaplaincy he offers to a diverse, migratory workforce.
- From Belfast, *Katy Radford* reflects on the life of her mother, who as a child travelled on Kindertransport from Nazi-occupied Vienna to England and the Isle of Man, eventually settling in Northern Ireland. Radford considers how her mother's journeying shaped her passion for and commitment to interfaith, ecumenical peacebuilding.
- Anglican priests *Julie Khovacs* and *Ivan Khovacs* describe the process of 'making theology from experience' by reflecting on a ministry of outreach in Julie's central London parish. They interweave their theological reflections with the voices of asylum seekers who have become part of – and transformed – the local congregation.
- *David Mason* reflects on migration as a spiritual experience that can deepen and transform Orthodox Jewish identity, both individual and collective. He recounts his personal journey towards deeper religious observance, alongside his efforts to raise the profile of social responsibility within the United Synagogue.
- *Hassan Rabbani* describes the rich relationship that developed between his Edinburgh mosque and a local parish congregation in the Church of Scotland. By drawing on three historic examples of migration and encounter, he champions the importance of contemporary Christian–Muslim dialogue.

It seems fitting to end this section about faith and encounter with two maps by the illustrator *Katherine Baxter*, who kindly developed one of these images for the cover of this book. The first map depicts the journey of Abraham. The second offers a contemporary view of major holy sites in the Jewish, Christian and Muslim worlds. In her brief reflection, Baxter describes mapmaking as a form of storytelling that can deepen faith and strengthen community. Poems by *Alison Phipps* and *Tawona Sitholé*, in the form of call-and-response, and *Yvonne Green* amplify the theme of transformation through encounter.

In the second section, 'Sacred Texts', we consider the holy writings at the heart of the three religions. The Qu'ran describes Jews and Christians, among others, as 'People of the Book'. Indeed, the contributions in this section never lose sight of the human relationship between text and reader. Collectively, the essays consider how the process of engaging with sacred text becomes a form of migration to a deeper understanding of faith and community.

- *Rachel Godfrey* coordinates a lively Scriptural Reasoning programme in central London. She describes how she brings together participants from different religious traditions to explore each other's sacred texts.
- *Sofia Rehman*, a translator and practitioner, reflects on her efforts to re-centre ʿĀʾisha in the Islamic canon. She describes the wider implications of her work for the Muslim communities of Bradford and Leeds, while also considering translation as a form of personal spiritual migration.
- *Michael Nausner* develops a musical framework, through the metaphor of a multi-voiced orchestra, to examine his encounters with Jewish and Muslim writers and thinkers. As a Christian theologian, he considers how the textual traditions of the 'religious other' inspire him to listen differently to his own holy texts.
- *Robyn Ashworth-Steen* explores exile as a formative theme in Jewish text and identity. She champions the use of reflective

dialogue with Judaism's sacred texts, in order to build 'textured communities that face the darkness in our texts and, therefore, in ourselves.'

- From Ireland, *Sheila Curran* offers a feminist liberationist reading of the encounter between Jesus and the Canaanite woman. She interweaves this well-known Bible story with her Catholic religious ministry of welcoming refugees.
- For *Sayed Razawi*, 'resilience' is a key theological theme shared by Islam, Judaism and Christianity. He considers the importance of migration in Islam's sacred texts, particularly through the life of the Prophet and the foundational story of Abraham, Hagar and Ishmael.
- Though the biblical story of Tamar, *Alison Phipps* discusses the fraught relationship between exile, sexual violence, testimony and silence for migrant women seeking refuge. She closes her essay with a creative retelling – a 'practical theological reading' – of 'The Rape of Tamar'.

The artist *Jacqueline Nicholls*, who comes from an Orthodox Jewish background, delves into her own scriptural tradition with drawings based on her daily reading of the Talmud. In her commentary, she describes the process of encountering this sacred text as a woman, and the 'path of travel' this has involved. Poetry comes from *Aviva Dautch*, who explores the medieval form of the ghazal as a process of re-reading, and Belfast-based writer and theologian *Pádraig Ó Tuama*.

The book's third section is a diverse exploration of 'Diaspora'. The essays raise interlinking questions: Where is home? Where is community? What parts of ourselves are re-made in and through migration?

- *Harvey Kwiyani* incorporates his academic research into a semi-fictional story about a Zimbabwean pastor with a migrant congregation in Birmingham. In his narrative account, he traces the life of this congregation over 20 years and multiple identities.
- Through the Victoria & Albert Museum's collection of Persian

miniature paintings, artist and museum educator *Hajra Williams* reflects on her personal experience of migration. She recounts the challenges of coordinating the museum's South Asian Education Programme, through which she sought to increase dialogue between the museum and the diaspora communities it serves.

- *Sally Style* draws on her extensive translation of the archive of philanthropist Moses Montefiore (1784–1885). Through excerpts from his correspondence, she explores the motivations and experiences of Jewish migrants to the Holy Land in the 19th century.

- Members of *Filipino Community in Harmony, Action, Mobilization and Prayer* (a fellowship group based at Sacred Heart Church in Kilburn, London) discuss their cross-cultural experiences of Catholicism, far from home.

- *Mohamed Omar* recounts his experience of migrating from Somalia to Scotland as a young asylum seeker. He found a sense of community through the local mosque and through football, leading him to create interfaith support networks for other migrants.

- Poet *Jennifer Langer* describes the work of Exiled Writers Ink, the non-profit organization she founded for writers from repressive regimes and war-torn situations. Through the texts and voices of her colleagues, she explores themes of writing, encounter and faith in diaspora.

To reflect visually on the dynamics of diaspora, the Syrian-born artist *Issam Kourbaj* contributed photographs of four art installations, each inspired by or speaking to the experience of contemporary refugees. Together, these images form a narrative of migration as a 'symptom of destruction'. Kourbaj created one of these images, *Lost*, in collaboration with the poet *Ruth Padel*; her poem 'Lesbos 2016' accompanies the photograph. In his commentary, Kourbaj describes his resistance to identity labels such as 'Muslim', 'Arab', 'Syrian'. Instead, he invites viewers to generate their own questions and stories from works of art.

The poetry for this third section comes from *Amir Darwish* and writer and researcher *Nazneen Ahmed*.

An open conversation

This book is, by necessity, incomplete. Although I sought a broad range of contributors, another editor would have gathered a different set of voices, creating another dialogue entirely. In many ways, I produced this book for myself. What was it that I wanted to learn? What piqued my interest? What perspectives would challenge and enhance my burgeoning understanding of 'theology'? And how could this be refracted through the lens of migration? Like every reader, I bring to this book my own migrant identities. As the granddaughter of Japanese and Chinese immigrants to the United States, I moved from Seattle to London by way of Boston (New England) and Belfast. Alongside these physical transplantations, my faith life has migrated through multiple Christian denominations and expressions of worship, to the wing of the Anglican communion where I have made my spiritual home.

Each contribution in this book is one voice in a much larger dialogue about migration, faith and community. The voices in these pages are individual perspectives, offered by people speaking from their own contexts and lived experiences. By no means do they claim to represent formally the faith traditions from which they emerge. Concepts like 'the Abrahamic Religions' may offer a useful framework and point towards common ground, but it is equally important to name the differences that arise – particularly in the context of migration. Moreover, although this book is a dialogue with and between the religions of Judaism, Christianity and Islam, and although many contributors identify as Jewish, Christian or Muslim, others (such as the artist Issam Kourbaj) do not. This book is not 'about' refugees or interfaith dialogue, but about the practical and deeply theological experience of being human. It was written by and for the people who are enmeshed in the day-to-day work of living their faith in the world.

This is not a book to gather dust in a university library, or to enter the academic fray. (The 'Abrahamic Religions' form an exciting, emerging field of scholarship; see Silverstein and Strouma (2015) for a helpful overview.) Nor is this a book to read cover to cover. Instead, I hope you will be guided by curiosity, a desire to reflect on your own faith identities, and a hunger to learn more. No type of faith engagement exists in isolation; this book is just the beginning of a much larger, longer conversation.

I hope that the diversity of perspectives will speak to a broad range of readers, and that the readers of this book will find diverse ways of engaging with its themes and ideas. The range of media includes maps, poems, essays, photographs, interviews and drawings. From individual reflection to group discussion, this book is designed to evoke a response. The final page will direct you to additional materials for further engagement with the living theologies of migration, faith and community.

The people of God are perpetually on the move. So is this conversation.

Reading suggestions

Silverstein, A.J. and Strouma, G.G. (eds) (2015) *The Oxford Handbook of Abrahamic Religions*. Oxford: Oxford University Press.
The Woolf Institute (www.woolf.cam.ac.uk).
The Faith and Belief Forum (www.faithbeliefforum.org).

PART 1

Faith Encounters

---

CHAPTER 1

35 Chapel Walk

Art, Community, Encounter

Faiza Omar and Ric Stott

35 Chapel Walk[1] is a community art space located in the heart of Sheffield, led entirely by artists, curators and creatives. The Revd Ric Stott, a Methodist minister, established the gallery in 2013 in a shop owned by the Methodist Central Hall. Today, 35 Chapel Walk is open seven days a week and hosts a wide range of exhibitions and events that explore spirituality, creativity and community.

This chapter is a conversation between Ric and Faiza Omar, the gallery's manager.

Art as faith encounter

Ric: This is an art space and a community space that is open to everyone. We try to be radically inclusive of all world views and all faiths. It's interesting for me to reflect on what it means to be a Christian minister in the midst of all that. We are embodying a 'faith encounter' as we speak, aren't we?

Faiza: Yes! The thing that made me fall in love with this gallery is my own practice of combining my creativity and my faith. This gallery is

---

1   www.35chapelwalk.com.

a community where you are welcome to be who you are, in whatever creative way you want to be.

I'm a Muslim, from Rotherham. I felt comfortable here, so when the position for centre manager came up, I applied and I got it.

Ric: I think the first time we met, you had a piece in a show here. It was the work that you did on attitudes toward the *hijab*.

Faiza: It was for SheFest, in 2015, around International Women's Day. I submitted one of my art pieces, which is about how women get judged by the headscarf that we wear. I took a twist on that. I just saw the funnier side, the lighter side. I wanted to educate people, but not in a harsh or controversial way. Just to let people know that if you do have a question, come and ask me.

Ric: Well, it worked. That piece changed my view of the *hijab*.

Faiza: Thank you. Yeah, that's what I aim for. I always try to come at it through an easier way or a funnier way. As Muslims, we're not all killers; we're not harsh and hard when it comes to our religion.

The gallery is very welcoming. If you're a creative person, it doesn't matter what background you're from or what faith you are. We're here, all doing the same thing we love.

Ric: I'm curious – before you knew much about the gallery, if you knew that it was run by the Methodist Church and that I'm a Methodist minister, would you have been a bit wary? How would that have changed your attitude?

Faiza: It didn't really phase me. If anything, I think it made me want to come in and learn more.

Ric: Good. And before you started working here, what did you know about the Methodist Church?

Faiza: Nothing. I think I may have heard of it at school, when we did religious studies. Before I started working here, I thought Christianity was all the same. I didn't know there were different backgrounds.

But I am learning how similar our religions are. We have our differences, but in the way our religions work, we're very similar.

Ric: We've curated shows together. We're working together, as we speak, on a Christmas show. We try to curate shows with the rhythm of the church year.

It's far more interesting to co-curate a show on Christmas with someone who isn't a Christian.

Faiza: It'll be good because Muslims have Jesus as well. He's a prophet to us. People forget. So it will be interesting to bring both our sides of Jesus, from two different religions, for the Christmas show.

Ric: I like that phrase, 'We have Jesus as well.' Christianity and the Church do not own Jesus. The more we've talked, the more I realize the commonalities far outweigh the differences. I learn far more from people who have different views and different experiences from me than I ever learn from people who just sit around saying, 'Oh, yeah, we agree.' And the more I live like that, the more I'm just blown away by my experience of God that I see in people.

The life of the gallery

Silent meditation
Faiza: Every single day is different. We do activities and events to get people together. We host art talks, where we get local artists to come in, talk about their artwork, and get our opinion.

Ric: One of the things we do as part of the rhythm of life here is silent meditation on Tuesdays.

Faiza: It's a half-hour session. We invite different people to join.

Ric: We have people of all kinds of faith backgrounds, and atheists.
Silence enables people to really be who they are. So, for me, it might be about prayer and meditation, focusing on the person of Jesus. For you, it holds a different meaning. But we meet in that place.
Every week, we keep that rhythm.

Faiza: When I first came, I had never done anything like that before. I'm an over-thinker and my head just has a mind of its own, so I found the sessions calming for me.

Ric: Actually, you're more disciplined than I am. The rhythm of prayer is embedded in your life, in a way that it isn't for me.

Faiza: In Islam, we have to pray five times a day. I grew up knowing that I have to do a certain thing at a certain time, every single day, at the same time.

Ric: It's almost like digging a well. Disciplined digging. Every week, we just dig a little bit deeper. Holding that space each week somehow changes the nature of a space. There's an idea of 'thin places' in Celtic spirituality. Keeping the rhythm just makes the space different somehow.

Life drawing
Lia: So in terms of what happens in a typical day, you've got silence on a Tuesday. What else might be happening when the gallery is open?

Ric: We do life drawing classes. With models.

Faiza: That's more Ric's thing.

Ric: In Islam, there are sometimes issues with representing people, bodies, and so on. How does that work for you, as an artist who has drawn people?

Faiza: I have trouble drawing from life, because of my faith and background.

With Islam, drawing portraits or figures is seen as *haram*. It's forbidden. It depends how you translate the Qu'ran, but it says in there that if you draw a figure, it's almost like you're trying to recreate God's creation. And so it's not allowed.

In Islam, when it comes to art, the only things you are allowed to draw are plants and patterns. No figures, no faces.

The way I see it, I'm not trying to recreate God's creation. If anything, I'm amazed by it. I'm trying to show love for God's creation – celebrating the beauty of it. Some Muslims would probably kill me for this.

But I think because of my faith and the way I've been brought up, when it comes to seeing naked bodies, it makes me feel uncomfortable. Growing up and studying art, whenever I came to life drawing, I was just: 'No, no, I do not want to go to hell. I can't be seeing naked bodies.'

When I was in art school, I'd make the weirdest excuses to get out of life drawing. Even today, I can't draw from real life. So, even for you to sit there and for me to draw you, I can't do that. I'd have to do it from a picture.

Lia: What was your reaction when you found out: 'Hey, there's going to be a life drawing class today?'

Faiza: I was like: 'I'm going to stay away from that. Going to leave that to Ric!'

Lia: When you say 'life drawing', are you talking full-frontal nudity?

Ric: Oh, yeah. I'm all for a bit of nudity!

This is really interesting, because in the heart of Christianity is the body of Christ. Jesus has a physical body; he's there on the cross, naked. There is a naked body at the heart of Christian faith.

Lia: Listening to both of you talk about life drawing, what I hear is profound reverence, expressed and experienced in different ways.

Ric: Yeah. For me, there's something sensual about drawing a human body. And in my understanding of theology, everyone's body is holy. I'm celebrating this beauty, I'm celebrating the sensuality, because this is all of God.

But you still don't have to come to life drawing.

Faiza: Never! Leave the naked bodies to Ric.

Ric: Happy to oblige.

Actually, it's really respectful. Because there's a big glass window at the front, we have to put a curtain on it. Otherwise the people of Sheffield will get more than they bargained for.

We have plenty of life models. If you've never been to a life drawing class, people have all kinds of weird ideas of what it's like. It's not sexual at all. It's a really interesting space.

Faiza: I feel like I need to be brave enough, and one day just turn up at a life drawing class. I'll probably run away after two minutes.

Ric: It's fair to say there would be plenty of Christians who would be weirded out by it, as well. Because while I think the body is at the heart of Christianity, a lot of the Church is very, very squeamish about the body. That is why we get screwed up about sexuality and relationships and stuff like that. But that's another issue.

Exhibitions

Lia: Sheffield is so diverse. How do you see that manifested in the gallery?

Faiza: Since I started here, I've seen a lot of diversity. With the Black History Month exhibition, I had never seen so many black people in a gallery before. It was a very good experience, because normally black people stay away from galleries. They think, 'That's not for me.'

Ric: In general, art spaces tend to be white spaces with white, middle-class faces. That's true in Sheffield as much as anywhere else. I hope that we've broken that down, here at the gallery.

For the Black History Month show, I was sometimes the only white face in the room. It wasn't an unpleasant experience, but it was slightly disconcerting. It was like: 'Oh, okay. This is what it feels like.' A new experience, and a good one.

Faiza: I think the type of exhibitions we have, and the type of artists that we allow to show their work, has also played a part. With Black History Month, black people see artwork of black people. It makes them comfortable coming in.

With the gallery's birthday show, we had different types of artwork. I had one of my pieces shown. I think Muslim girls seeing an artwork of a Muslim lady wearing a headscarf – that made them comfortable coming in, wanting to see more, wanting to know more.

We do try to have a wide range of different exhibitions that different people can relate to. In return, that has made people comfortable coming in. So the artwork we show has played a big part as well.

Story and sacrament

Lia: Storytelling seems to be a powerful theme in this gallery. A few years ago, we collaborated when I organized a conference on migration and ministry. I commissioned Ric to do some paintings. In our initial conversation, we decided it would be great if you would collaborate with City of Sanctuary,[2] which emerged from the Methodist Church upstairs, here in Sheffield.

---

2   City of Sanctuary is a network that supports and welcomes people seeking sanctuary in the UK: www.cityofsanctuary.org.

Ric: Yes. I painted three portraits [of people going through the asylum process].[3]

In some ways, I found it really unsettling and quite a difficult thing to do. As a white, Christian, middle-class Englishman who's never had to emigrate anywhere, it was like: 'What right do I have to make this work?' I have a lot of white, liberal guilt.

Faiza: But you're very understanding. Unlike a lot of other people, what you've embodied with the culture of the gallery is that you take the time to actually hear people's stories and understand them. Even though you haven't gone through those experiences yourself, by being around people and listening to them and talking to them, you understand their stories. So I don't think you should rule yourself out.

Ric: I still feel ambiguous about it, but that's actually part of it: that feeling, that tension. The conclusion I came to is that I don't need rescuing from that discomfort. What does it mean to serve these stories? This isn't my story, this isn't my experience. So what does it mean to genuinely hear it? And then to somehow transform it into this image that does justice, that isn't about me. It's about enabling a person's experience to be embodied in the canvas.

For me, art-making is a sacramental activity. Sacraments in Christian faith are these physical embodiments of internal experiences. So, we have bread and wine for communion. Or water in baptism, and so on. For me, the physical act of making art, of putting the brush in the paint and smearing it on the canvas, these are not just material things. They are embodying these internal experiences.

So to really hear someone's story, and then somehow attempt to transform that into this physical object, this painting: that's my ministry.

---

3   The paintings can be viewed at www.susannawesleyfoundation.org/paintings-by-Ric-Stott.

Art as migration

Ric: I'm an ordained Methodist minister. The more I exercise my ministry in these spaces that are far beyond the normal boundaries of church life, the more I feel like a Methodist. God seems to be calling me to being in this place.

Methodism emerged from the Church of England in the 18th century. As John Wesley went out into the fields to preach, he went beyond the established religious boundaries. He said that he committed himself to being 'more vile' by preaching in fields. He was eventually thrown out of the Church of England.

Wesley was just going where he felt the Spirit of God was calling him to be. And that's at the heart of what Methodism is. We're not actually meant to be an established, solid church institution. That's not a criticism of the Church of England, but Methodism is more organic, more flexible than that. If the Church of England is like the Asda or the Walmart, then Methodism is that weird, quirky independent little shop. It's a bit clumsy, it's a bit messy, but there's a kindness to it. There's a generosity of spirit to it. And there's an embeddedness – it's got dirty fingernails, properly embedded in communities, doing real, honest work.

The more I've moved beyond the edges of church boundaries, I find Jesus at work in these spaces, saying: 'What took you so long? I've been waiting for you.'

And so the more I do this ministry – out here, in the art world – the more I feel authentically like a Methodist. Artists are just up for exploring, asking questions, taking risks, and pushing comfort. It's a really vibrant place – not only in the practice, but in the ideas.

It's this migration of pushing beyond the boundary of where I am and what I'm doing. It's also a migration of ideas about God. What does it mean when we speak of God?

So when Faiza and I have a conversation, that blows my mind about the possibility that my God was too small. I suppose there are two responses that you can have when you meet someone with a different experience. You can either retreat in fear, and then 'other' that person. You can scapegoat them and say, 'Oh no, that's anathema. You're wrong. I've got the truth.'

Or you can take that encounter as a gift and say: 'Wow, you have something amazing to teach me. And just in meeting you, my vision of the universe and what it means to be human – what it means to know about God – has expanded.'

Faiza: When I started here, I was in my own little bubble. Coming here, working at the gallery with Ric, has shown me how similar we are in our beliefs, and how we live our lives.

In terms of our morals and how we treat other people, I think we're very similar. It comes from our religious background. In a way, working here showed me how we are very similar, despite our different beliefs. And how life is about being kind to people, respecting other people – just being human.

Ric: Can I ask about that? Because I think one of the most problematic boundaries, or migrational crossovers, is 'faith world' and 'art world'. Not necessarily from the faith perspective, but from the art world's perspective. I've found that the art world is very suspicious of faith, God, spirituality and so on.

I've just finished my Masters of Fine Art at the university here in Sheffield. I went as a Methodist minister to do this. I was 'out' in all kinds of ways.

For me, I can't separate my art-making and my faith. That's always going to be part of the conversation. But to talk about God and spirituality in the fine art context is really problematic, if a lot of your work revolves around faith.

Faiza: I'm the same way. At one point, I tried to separate my beliefs and my art. I said, 'I don't want to talk about it.' Because, like you said, religion and politics are very touchy topics. So I tried, but it's hard.

With my artwork, I like the idea of making people a little bit uncomfortable, but then at the same time making them think and talk. I like getting the topic going in a more beautiful way.

Ric: In the art world, there are no taboos about sex and nudity. But, wow, there is a taboo about God. Massive. People are really suspicious. It's one of the last taboos, really, in the art world, to say, 'No, this is about spirituality,' or 'This is about God.'

Certainly, from a Christian perspective, I feel that in making art-work about my faith, I've got to be really careful with the images I use. A crucifix, say, is such a loaded image. It's got so much baggage around it. I'm really aware when I'm using Christian imagery that it's tricky.

Faiza: I agree. With Islam, I'm scared to offend my own people. They're very sensitive, when it comes to the religion itself. The side that I can relate to is Islamic women. I stay on that side of things, rather than religion in whole. I don't want to offend anyone, and I don't want to get on the wrong side of my people.

Ric: I don't mind if my people are offended. I'm doing it right if I've offended them.

In the broader sense of crossing boundaries, that's the nature of art. For me, it's the nature of discipleship, as well. What does it mean for me to follow Christ? It is always about crossing boundaries to meet someone on the other side. Art is a catalyst for that meeting space.

Enabling people to cross boundaries of their own experience, of their own sense of self – that is migration.

CHAPTER 2

Radical Jewish Welcome

A Reflection on Shelter, Sukkot and Calais

Oliver Spike Joseph

Celebrating vulnerability

The Jewish festival of Sukkot usually falls around October. By this point in the calendar, Jewish people will have celebrated Rosh Hashanah (the new year) and marked our most solemn fast day, Yom Kippur. Our year begins with these two festivals. Sukkot, however, marks the change in the agricultural calendar and the seasons: the coming of autumn, when the harvest will be collected.

In the ancient Middle East, like today, the autumn harvest would have included olives, fruits, nuts, dates, pomegranates and perhaps some early citrus fruits. The food collected during this time would sustain whole families all the way through winter. During the harvest, every single hour of daylight matters. Farmers would go out to their fields, sometimes travelling many miles from their village. Instead of returning each night to their homes, they would sleep in the fields, in a temporary structure called *sukkah* (plural: *sukkot*). If you visit the Middle East today, you can still see people sleeping in fields during harvest time – sometimes in a cave, sometimes in a wooden shack with some kind of palm or sheltering leaf on top. Sukkot thus became a festival which pays homage to our reliance on the harvest and highlights the vulnerability which we all face – a central aspect of what it is to be alive.

The harvest in ancient Israel is one of the motifs of Sukkot but, as is often the case in Jewish religious life, we have more than one theological symbol for this festival. The second core historical motif of Sukkot is the Exodus story. This is the story of the Children of Israel, in their wandering. Joseph, son of one of our forefathers, is taken as a slave to Egypt; he is freed and then serves the Pharaoh. His brothers come to Egypt because of famine in the Land of Israel, and they eventually reunite with their lost brother. Generations later, the Israelites become slaves in Egypt. Through Moses's leadership, the Israelites are freed; they leave Egypt and cross the Red Sea. For 40 years, while the Children of Israel wandered in the desert, they lived in temporary structures: *sukkot*.

The *sukkah* connects us to our vulnerability. Without the protection of those temporary structures, the Jewish people would not have survived their years of wandering in the desert. A central question our Rabbis raise is whether the *sukkot* were actual, physical wooden structures, or whether they simply refer to God's presence, and the miraculous protection of the Children of Israel, in the desert.

This adds another layer of understanding of the temporary structure of the *sukkah*. During the festival of Sukkot, we are biblically commanded to build the shelter. On a very basic level, Sukkot is a festival of experiencing vulnerability by being outside our usual, permanent dwellings. At this time of year, we try to challenge our sense of being sheltered. We take away the protective walls which ordinarily shade us from sun, wind and rain, and we acknowledge the true vulnerability that lies at the centre of our lives. For many in our generation, we don't see the harshness of the world and the challenge of the elements, especially as the rain starts to fall and the days get colder and darker. During Sukkot, we have a heightened awareness of nature and the elements. I like taking down the *sukkah* at the end of the festival. There are always a few autumn leaves that have come into the structure. This very real experience of autumn reminds us of our vulnerability as humans and the temporary nature of our lives.

There is a global connection between the story of the Jews and the ancient Israelite people, who travelled and often suffered in their displacement. We read the words from the Bible. *Gerim Hai'eetem*: 'You were strangers in the land of Egypt'. That sense of other-ness has followed the Jewish people throughout history. While Jews have flourished in many parts of the Middle East, in Europe and beyond, our outsider status has caught up with us and, at times, caused great suffering and bloodshed. In this generation of relative prosperity and security for many Jewish communities in Europe, Israel and the United States, it is particularly important that we recall the journeys and struggles of our people.

At this time of year, through our own communal story, we reconnect with our responsibility to care for those who are vulnerable and in need. During the festival of Sukkot, we live in temporary structures by choice. This experience gives us an avenue to look at the world and see those who don't have a place to live – those who, at this very moment, are living in tents. At this time of year, through our own story of displacement and insecurity, we look out to the world and see with clarity the suffering of others.

The journey to Calais

In 2015, when the refugee camp in Calais, France, was big news, one of the leaders from Marom (our young adult community) said, 'Wouldn't it be amazing to spend Sukkot in Calais?'

We jumped on this idea. I worked with three key leaders to organize the project, and one of the Jewish schools lent us a minibus. It was a great trip, a true meeting place of the vulnerability that we mark during Sukkot, with the real experience of thousands of refugees living under canvas, just a few hundred miles from London.

At the time, the camp's infrastructure was struggling to keep up with the demands of more than five thousand inhabitants. Some non-profit organizations had joined together to rent a big warehouse to sort and distribute supplies. News of the refugee camp had captured hearts. Many people had sent donations, as we had from our synagogue in the UK. In Calais, our team helped with stacking and organizing supplies – sorting shoes, socks, T-shirts, jumpers, tents and sleeping bags.

We also went into the camp itself, to help with the clean-up operation. By this time, the camp had existed for over ten years in various forms, without regular waste collection or basic sanitation. This strip of land next to the Calais train terminal had just a few water taps and a small number of portable toilets to serve several thousand people. Most of the toilets had not been emptied and so were unusable. There was rubbish and human waste everywhere.

Those who arrived at the Calais refugee camp imagined they would stay only a couple of days. This was a place of transit, where refugees understood that they could find transport to the UK, where they would meet family or friends and begin a new life. For many, their stay in the 'Jungle', as the camp was known, would be a lot longer. Trying to organize civic life in a place of transit is hard, especially as many refugees had bad experiences as they passed through Europe. The refugee experience of authority (with police, border guards, security officials) was often bullying and aggressive rather than kind and receptive. This environment created suspicion towards the different non-governmental organizations in the camp, even though the services they offered were much needed.

I spoke with people in the camp and listened to their stories. Our work there felt like a drop in the ocean. The people in the camp were getting on with their lives, collecting food and clothes, trying to put another tarpaulin over their tent, sometimes arguing with their neighbours – just trying to survive. It was a very tough place. Towards nightfall, you could feel the energy of the camp changing as people buttoned down for another night. There were often attacks on the camp, as well as inside it. There was sexual violence and violence against children. There was a strong mafia presence – smugglers who were extorting large amounts of money for their services. The rumours and stories inside the camp were of continued violence and struggle.

The young people who went to Calais from our synagogue were moved by this trip. It would have been impossible to not have been changed by this experience.

A refugee identity

At the New North London Synagogue, we are part of a broader community involved in advocacy for refugees. The synagogue's Destitute Asylum Seekers Drop In, an independent charity, is now among the biggest community organizations serving refugees and asylum seekers in the UK. The centre provides services (health, mental health, legal, food and clothing) for approximately 300 people each month. There is a strong desire in our community to care for refugees, but my feeling is that this desire is mixed with a sense of frustration. We know that the little we do is not enough. We went to Calais and we did our little bit. But ultimately, when you read the news, you realize that this story is part of a much bigger, global crisis.

The Jewish community has done very well, both historically and currently, in making its charitable contribution. In recent years, we have worked together with prominent figures, namely Lord Alf Dubs, who was himself saved from Nazi-occupied Czechoslovakia. The Kindertransport, which brought him to the UK, saved almost 10,000 Jewish children from the Nazi occupation of Europe. With many partners, we have promoted provision for refugees, particularly for child refugees, to come to this country as they did during the years of the Kindertransport. The UK Jewish community was at arm's length from the atrocities and tragedies of the Holocaust on mainland Europe. Having said that, many of the members of our community are born of parents who were in Germany, Poland, Ukraine and across Eastern Europe during that time. The Masorti movement's senior Rabbi, Jonathan Wittenberg, is the child of German refugees.

In this generation, the Jewish identity in this country is unique. We have Jews of Eastern European descent, survivors of the Holocaust and, from the other side of the spectrum, Indian, Syrian, Iraqi and Persian Jews who were far from the war in Europe. In my own family, my mother's parents came from Russia and Poland in the late 1800s, in one of the earlier waves of Jewish arrival to the UK. My father's family would have been among the earliest Jews returning to the UK in the 1700s, after the edict of the expulsion of the Jews in the 1290s.

His family owned a *Matzah* bakery in the East End of London. The collective response toward refugees is mixed. In some spaces, there is a sense that we need to protect and take care of ourselves – to focus on our own growth and recovery in the post-war era.

The opposite of this stance is to be a community that remembers, through all the generations, that because we were strangers in the land of Egypt, we should always love the stranger. This knowledge, and the vast literature written about Jewish immigration and Jewish travel, makes it hard to escape the Jewish relationship with being the stranger, the traveller, the refugee. So the response that comes from this awareness is to say: *because of our history, we have a responsibility to have a loving and caring relationship with vulnerable people, including refugees.*

In this particular synagogue community of more than 1000 families, there is a full spectrum of responses to the refugee crisis. But we are open to the question of how we take care of vulnerable people and protect those who are in need. I don't think this is particular to Masorti Judaism (the movement to which the New North London Synagogue belongs). As a Jewish community, we also have our own charitable organizations. World Jewish Relief, for example, looks after the worldwide Jewish community and also does vital work in Syria. We are a community that has a historic relationship with refugees. In Masorti Judaism, our observance and practices are not significantly different from any other religious Jewish community, but we do have a more open-minded relationship with belief and the interface between critical understandings of religion and our religious practice. This nexus – this meeting place of religious life and of a critical understanding of the world – is where our response to the refugee crisis comes from.

When trying to understand 'the Jewish response' to the refugee crisis, the Masorti community urges that ethical and secular political understandings of the world should not be ignored. Our religious lives tell us to love the stranger – to be in relationship with and to care for those who are most in need. Traditionally, in the Torah, this meant the widow, the orphan and the stranger. This religious understanding, combined with our modern political and ethical understandings, is the reason why the New North London Synagogue community, in particular – and the Masorti community, in general – is deeply connected with and committed to the advocacy, care and protection of refugees.

Love more

Calais felt like the Tower of Babel. The mixture of people included Albanians, Eastern Europeans, Roma, Afghanis, Eritreans, Syrians and more. On top of that, there were volunteers who were British, Italian, French and Spanish. We were there as a Jewish community from London. It was a very international and diverse space.

The question of refugees crossing international borders demands so much of our communities – and perhaps more of our minority communities inside Europe. We must decide if we are the ones who will 'pull up the ladder' and 'close the door' to an immigration process which has built many parts of the UK and Europe and welcomed our parents and grandparents. For Jews, this question comes down to how we interpret the biblical imperative: *To love the stranger.*

Our love of the stranger is perhaps the hardest part of our religious lives. One response can be to narrowly understand the phrase: *ahavta le re'acha.* The description of 'stranger' is actually 'neighbour', therefore 'love your neighbour as yourself'. Rabbi Hillel said in the first century that this was one of the founding pillars of Jewish life. In this guise, we can use this biblical imperative to focus our energy internally, to be more loving of those who are like us. Jewish people, like any nation, have the capacity to turn their ethical considerations inwards, to care for your neighbour, relative, friend and family.

Yet there is a more global understanding of 'stranger' that can become part of our communal, ethical portfolio. In this generation, I believe that we are called to go to the furthest, most generous understanding of what it is to 'love the stranger'. Humans are capable of both expansive openness and cruelty. Our minds and hearts can shut down: 'I can't cope with the enormity of this problem', or 'I must protect my own home, my own land.' The alternative response is one of openness towards a religious endeavour: to open your heart to everything we do. Taken to its maximum application, to be truly open of heart means being welcoming of others.

Each year, sometime in November, we will read a part of the Book of Genesis that we call *Va'eira* – the story of Abraham and Sarah welcoming three guests into their tent. *Va'eira* means 'to appear' or 'to be seen'. The image is of Abraham after his circumcision, at the age of 99, sitting in the heat of the day. He is vulnerable as he recovers, but he sits outside, watching for travellers and strangers to invite inside.

Abraham is one of the forefathers of Judaism, fabled to be the first Jew, and a prophet to Islam and Christianity. He becomes *the* example in Jewish faith of how to be hospitable. Abraham shows us that at our most impoverished and ill, we should still be outward-looking and welcoming, always looking for guests. The *Melachim* (messengers) that Abraham brings into his tent are three travellers. But the word *Malach* also means 'angel'. So, Abraham grants us the possibility that when we invite someone in, we are also inviting aspects of God and of godliness into our homes.

This image of Abraham, sitting at the opening of his tent, is also an image of what it means to live in an open community, an open space, where you're always looking outwards, ready to welcome guests. This image connects nicely to two other images of a tent, of shelter, in Jewish life.

One image is the *huppah*, the wedding canopy, which is supported by four poles on four sides but never has any walls. The canopy is a simple piece of fabric on top but open on all sides. This is the canopy under which Jewish couples are married. At that moment of creating partnership – of creating unity, of creating family – you are also entirely contingent and reliant on all the people who are around you. The community that witnesses the wedding commits to supporting the couple as they go forward. And the couple also commits to supporting the people around them. The *huppah* is a representation of an ideal community. Just as we need the support of those around us, so too do we commit to giving back to the world the love that we receive, showing welcome to those furthest from us.

The second image is the *sukkah*, where we started this chapter. During the festival of Sukkot, we also welcome the *Ushpizin*, mystical guests. The *sukkah* becomes open not solely to guests in the present, but also across time and generations. We traditionally welcome different forefathers and foremothers to celebrate in the Sukkot festival with us. In a spiritual capacity, this is an intimate time in which our best selves – our most ethical, dedicated, welcoming, embracing and fearless selves – transcend the parameters of life, death and generations. We are open to all the guests – not just from this world but from *all* the worlds, past, present and future.

The tent holds powerful images: Abraham and Sarah welcoming their guests; ancient Israelite farmers; all of the brides and the bridegrooms coming together. When you get to a place of such broad understanding of *sukkah* – of canopy and protection – it has to be a place that inspires openness and care for others. Our imperative is to offer shelter to others.

CHAPTER 3

The 'God Squad'

Multi-Faith Chaplaincy in Canary Wharf

Ibrahim Mogra

Introduction

As a member of the Canary Wharf Multi-Faith Chaplaincy team, I serve everyone who works within the geographic boundaries of one of London's largest financial centres. We support people who work in banks, law firms, large and small businesses, and retail shops. We serve executives and members of the security staff, maintenance staff and cleaners. All the companies contribute to the chaplaincy costs through the estate's service charge. More than 120,000 people work in Canary Wharf, and our services are provided at no cost to them.

The chaplaincy in Canary Wharf was established in 2004 with just one Christian chaplain, Reverend Fiona Stewart-Darling. It took a lot of hard work on her part to convince the companies that there was a place for God on the estate. In 2012, Rabbi Dr Moshe Freedman became the first Jewish chaplain for Canary Wharf. I followed him a year later to become the first Muslim chaplain. We are assisted by a Catholic chaplain, and our multi-faith team recently expanded to include a retail chaplain and a lay volunteer (both Christian). Each chaplain is here for everyone on the estate, regardless of their religion, faith or world view.

Many times, all people want is just someone to talk to, and to be able to offload. Chaplains are happy to be that listening ear.

Where necessary, we signpost people to providers of specialist, ongoing support. We may not be able to give them any practical help, but we like to think we will have listened without judging or imposing our thoughts. We try to comfort them, reassure them and give them hope. If they want us to pray for them, or with them, we will happily do so.

We are constantly trying to make our presence known through our website, through social media and by visiting different companies. We also have an electronic poster which goes up in the malls and around the estate to create awareness of our presence and what we can offer. In between meetings and appointments, the chaplains will pair up and go on walkabouts. These help us to ensure we are a visible presence. When people see an imam and a rabbi, or an imam and a priest, we notice their delight. Sometimes people do a double-take: here comes the 'God Squad'!

Many people on the estate may not have any religious belief or faith, but they still value our presence. When Rabbi Moshe and I are walking together, we notice people looking. I have sensed that they feel warmth when they see us together – a Jew and a Muslim, two friends chatting away. One day, we were on the Crossrail roof-terrace garden. A lady saw us and said, 'Seeing you two together has just made my day.' She then asked if she could take a photo of us. We duly obliged with broad smiles.

Supporting Muslims in Canary Wharf

As there are approximately 10,000 Muslims working on the estate, it is impossible for me to see all of them. As part of our effort to cater for Canary Wharf's spiritual needs, we have regular religious activities. In the Canary Wharf multi-faith prayer room, there is a weekly Christian service and Mass, while Rabbi Moshe holds weekly 'Lunch & Learn' sessions with Jews. In addition to their daily prayers, Muslims have their main Friday prayer, the *Jumu'ah*, which includes a sermon. The *Jumu'ah* prayer is very well attended, so there are two congregations, one after the other, to accommodate the large numbers. Women join the second congregation and have their own space, which can be curtained off. They also have a separate washroom for ablutions.

When I joined the team in July 2013, there was already an active Muslim society that had been organizing the prayers for many years. As a chaplain, I am here to support and to enable groups to organize their activities. This intentional hands-off approach has resulted in a very healthy relationship between the chaplaincy and the Muslim groups. Prayers are led by bankers, accountants, lawyers, business-men and others who are reasonably well versed in Islam and the rules of prayer. However, with all due respect, they are lay people, not theologians. So I have introduced a *khatib* training programme.

A *khatib* is a Friday prayer leader and preacher. (The *khatib* is always male, so it will be just men attending these training sessions.) I have rolled out this programme in several companies, and we have trained more than 50 individuals so far. I teach them how to prepare the *khutbah* (sermon). I recommend which materials to use, what to include in the sermon, how to choose the subject, how long to speak, and so on. The participants are then better equipped to carry out the role of a *khatib*. They can also hold Friday prayers within their own buildings, as many companies have rooms for quiet and prayer. This is important because it can be challenging to access the estate's multi-faith prayer room. For example, someone working on the 30th floor of a building would have to take a lift down and walk to the room, do their ablutions, offer their prayers and then get back to their desk – all within their lunch break. Organizing prayers within companies saves people time, and it creates camaraderie within the building.

Chaplaincy is not just about pastoral care. It is also about devel-oping and building the capacity of those who access our services. For example, through the *khatib* training programme, we want to enhance confidence through learning basic methods of research and public speaking. These skills also help with work-related presentations, as the participants will be accustomed to addressing large numbers of people through the Friday sermon. I keep in touch with the partici-pants, making sure that they're getting on fine.

Canary Wharf has a diverse population of Muslims, ranging from bankers to shopkeepers, service providers and cleaners. On chaplaincy walkabouts, I make a point of saying 'hello' to the cleaners and security personnel, regardless of their faith or the lack of it. I ask how they are, and their family, and engage in small talk. They always appreciate that the chaplain has stopped by to have a chat. Sometimes it is through these simple conversations that people open up and seek help for any troubles they may be experiencing.

Most of the people who come to see me are office workers. There are some issues that are quite common, such as relationships, pressures of work, deadlines and work–life balance. For those who work in the services sector, an additional challenge is getting time from their shift to pray. They say to me: 'I need to pray but there isn't a suitable place', or 'My shift is a bit awkward and I can't get time to do my prayer.' I suggest that they approach their company's diversity and inclusion team, or I offer to contact the company on their behalf. In most cases, it works out. In my experience, Muslims in Canary Wharf who wish to pray just make the best of what is available.

Ten thousand Muslims sounds like a lot, but not all of them pray. We have a mix of those who pray punctually and regularly, those who pray occasionally and those who don't pray at work. The method of performing a Muslim prayer is really simple. Any clean and quiet place will suffice. Worshippers just pull out their prayer mat, lay it down and pray. The prayer takes about five minutes, at most.

Muslims have to perform ablutions before prayer. The multi-faith prayer room has a washroom designed to enable the washing of feet. Many companies in Canary Wharf have also installed traditional Muslim washing rooms. The companies realize the importance of providing these facilities, and many are happy to do so. They carry out consultations and spend a lot of effort, energy and money to prepare these rooms. Muslim workers are extremely appreciative of these facilities. A happy workforce means a more productive workplace, so there is also a business case to be made. I have observed that in Canary Wharf, companies genuinely want their workers to be happy and content, and to cater for people with faith and religious belief.

When Ramadan comes, there are many awareness programmes on the estate. I go into companies and deliver presentations, so the managers and others understand what a day in Ramadan is like for a Muslim. They will have had just a few hours of sleep. They will get hungry and thirsty and some will become cranky. I suggest that companies make simple adjustments, such as enabling more strenuous work to be done earlier in the day, when people are still energetic. By lunchtime, many will be drained, so I suggest saving simpler and less physical tasks for later. I also suggest that companies consider flexible hours for fasting Muslims during this period. On walkabouts during Ramadan, I come across Muslim security guards. They should not be out in the sun for too long, as the fasting does not permit them to drink water. When the rota is prepared, Ramadan is taken into account, enabling Muslim guards to be in the shade or inside buildings for a few hours. Muslims on the security team appreciate the concessions, but they also know that part of the challenge of Ramadan is to go through your day as you would normally. I think that Canary Wharf has managed to find the right balance of support.

Chaplaincy and community

As chaplains, we attend many events. One of my most memorable was the commemoration of the centenary of the First World War. We joined veterans and others on a platform, and each chaplain offered prayers in their own faith tradition. It was wonderful to remember our ancestors – on all sides – who lost their lives in such a tragic and brutal war.

We also offer our multi-faith chaplaincy team as a panel for discussions. We go into companies and discuss issues like faith and finance, religion and money, and ethics and spirituality in the workplace. In some companies, the interest in these panel discussions is so huge that the room is packed. Afterwards, people interact with us and ask us questions. These events also help the companies to understand the people who work for them. For many believers, faith is what makes them tick. This understanding, in turn, helps companies to cater for their needs.

Sometimes we are invited to events for religious festivals or receptions. Not long ago, I went to a company that was celebrating the Jewish holiday of Shavuot. There were over 200 guests, including Jews from old people's homes around London and a choir of schoolchildren. It was a lovely day, with some of the best cheesecake you will ever have.

During Ramadan, some of the companies will have *Iftar* (the breaking of the fast meal); they invite non-Muslim friends to come and enjoy the food with them. There are also carol services during Advent for Christians. Jesus (peace be upon him) is special also to Muslims and is a major prophet in Islam. He is regarded as one of the 'big five', along with Noah, Abraham, Moses and Mohammed (peace be upon them all). These festivals and activities help to create a sense of togetherness and of being one family.

From time to time, we also reach out to the local community around Canary Wharf. We engage with the local schools and run an annual competition for the children to design Christmas cards. The collection at the chaplaincy carol service is shared with local charities to provide them with much-needed funds, particularly those that work with refugees or the homeless. This is a wonderful way of improving our connections with the local community.

Being part of the multi-faith chaplaincy team has been an amazing journey. I have learned so much about Christianity and Judaism. At the same time, I've also shared so much about Islam. My Christian and Jewish colleagues are sometimes blown away by the things that I have shared with them. With Rabbi Moshe, we see similarities between our jurisprudence and our laws regarding food, marriage, ritual cleanliness, and so on. It's amazing to see the similarities and to learn together.

Once a month, we do scriptural reasoning together. This involves sharing our scriptures (from the Hebrew scriptures, the New Testament and the Qur'an) on a particular theme. We read each other's scriptures and share what we understand from the passages. It has been an amazing opportunity to learn and grow, and develop myself.

More than ever before, I appreciate Jewish and Christian teachings, and I have an even better understanding of my colleagues' way of life and how they look after their flock. I've learned much from observing them look after their fellow believers. It has been very enriching. I feel so grateful to be part of this team.

Reflections on migration

Migration lies at the very heart of Islam's early history. When Muhammad (peace be upon him) began to preach about the one true God, 15 centuries ago in Makkah, his message was not welcome. Muhammad and his followers were persecuted, and the situation became unbearable. They were forced to flee Makkah and seek safety elsewhere. They arrived in the oasis of Yathrib, later to be called Madinah, to start a new life. They had lost their homes and had to leave everything behind to save their families and themselves, and to be able to freely practise their newfound religion. This migration, known as the *hijrah*, was such a significant event in Islam that when the early Muslims were contemplating how to date their calendar, they decided to date it not from Muhammad's birth date or death date, but from the date he became a migrant.

This story, about migration and Islam, has a message for the people who work on the Canary Wharf estate. There is tremendous potential in Canary Wharf for people to improve their financial circumstances. Companies here could offer jobs to those who are struggling and could help them to get back on their feet. I have observed that people in Canary Wharf are generous and donate their hard-earned money to charitable causes. Every month, one well-known store collects significant sums of money from customers' donations, which are then distributed to local community charities that are based around the estate. Those of us who work in Canary Wharf are commuters, migrants for the day, but we spend as much time here as we spend at home. This is also our home, and the communities around the estate are our neighbours. We need to support them.

All of us who work in Canary Wharf could regard ourselves as immigrants on a micro level. We 'migrate' here to work to earn a living so that our families can have a better life. None of us lives on the estate; it is all banks, businesses, offices and shops. When the day ends, we go back home. I myself 'migrate' from Leicester. There are people who 'migrate' from many different parts of the country, from across the Channel, and from across the 'pond'. Those from other countries come in on a Monday, for example; they work a few days, and then go back home. The commuters are what make this place what it is.

Plans to build residential apartments and tower blocks on the estate may change the status quo. We will most likely have settled communities on the estate. 'The only way is up', is what is said in these parts. A lovely piece of land on one end of the estate will be developed with offices, apartments, gardens and open spaces. As a chaplaincy team, we have already started to think about how our roles may change once people live on the estate. Will we be able to extend our services to the residents, or just limit them to those who work here during the day? It's going to be new territory for the chaplaincy team. Exciting times lie ahead.

When people come to work at Canary Wharf, there may be upheaval in their lives. While here at work, there might be issues back home: maybe an ill child, or an elderly parent who needs looking after. We may be struggling to fit all that in. When people migrate, they will have had to leave behind their place of birth, the homes they built with hard work, their friends, family, neighbours and jobs. They will have had to uproot their children from school and from friends. They may be troubled people who need somebody to counsel them. This is where chaplaincy can be of help.

Serving as a chaplain, I have undergone huge transformation myself, appreciating what people do for their families to put food on the table. People in Canary Wharf work long, hard hours, often at the expense of their health and their social life. It has made me appreciate the need to find a balance. I wish I could say to people: 'Look, there's more to life than earning lots of money. It's nice to provide your family with all the luxuries, but you've got to think about what your children would appreciate more, such as having you for a little longer. Reading a bedtime story and tucking them away at night? Or having that toy or that luxury item which you're going to buy them because you've earned a lot of money?'

I feel privileged to have a glimpse into the lives of these very busy people. I see how they're trying to do the right thing for their loved ones, and how easily they could get it wrong. If I can be a source of moderation for them, and just help them to recognize other, important things that they could be focusing on, then I will feel I have been of service to them.

As a Muslim, I believe in all the things that Islam teaches in terms of God and the angels and the scriptures, and the prophets and the afterlife, and judgement day and fate, and all the rest of it. But at the core is my belief that as human beings we are all equal. We are God's family, and we must give respect to every single individual. So, it doesn't matter to me whether it's a Muslim who has come to see me, or a Christian, or any other person. As a chaplain, I try to see a human being, who may be in pain or in difficulty. If I can be of some help to them, then I have fulfilled the requirements of my faith.

CHAPTER 4

Interfaith, Interchurch, InterTidal

A Jew(ish) Tribute to Resilience

Katy Radford

Between 1968 and 1998 in Northern Ireland, over 3500 people died, of whom over 50 per cent were civilians. The conflict (known by some as 'The Troubles') began by raising awareness of historical inequalities, but before long erupted in pro- and anti-state violence. On one side, commitment to Northern Ireland's union with the monarchy of a United Kingdom; on the other side, to the republican ideals of an all-island Ireland. The legacy of that conflict is a divided society; the trans-generational impact of trauma remains acutely alive today. In some areas, it is marked by segregated residential and educational patterns, enabled and bolstered by regional and local schooling, housing and governmental infrastructures. These, in turn, are overseen by a democratically-elected elite, on both sides. Within this mix, however, are growing numbers of people disenfranchised from traditional 'sectarian' politics – many of whom are drawn from minority ethnic and faith-based communities.

North Belfast is home to a synagogue, a gurdwara and a Hindu temple. These places of faithfulness, distinct from the two major religious communities (Protestant and Catholic Christians, including their many offshoots, denominations and churches), sit on a chequerboard of interfaces. These areas are frequently decorated with national flags and painted kerbstones: red, white and blue in unionist areas; green, white and gold in nationalist areas. These are not displayed solely as celebrations of ethno-political identity; they are also perceived as markers of territorial exclusivity. Their presence is, by some, interpreted as a provocative assertion of superiority over, and lack of respect for, the 'other's' ideological and political opinion about the identity of Northern Ireland.

In Belfast, much of the material culture which might represent its Jewish heritage is either hidden or has disappeared. At the Jewish burial ground in Belfast City Cemetery, graves and the former *tahara* (the ritual house used for preparing bodies for burial) are routinely desecrated. A 'new' synagogue, consecrated 50 years ago, now serves the community. The remains of the *mikvah* (ritual bath used for purification) and the former synagogue at Annesley Street (built by Sir Otto Jaffe, twice Lord Mayor of Belfast) are now a leaking, dilapidated storage space for the records of a hospital physiotherapy department. Furthermore, after a developer's oversight of a preservation order, the facade of an earlier synagogue, built in 1871 on Great Victoria Street, was replaced; it now houses an apostolic church. In the Linen Hall Library, which holds significant collections of Northern Ireland's social and political history, there is no mention of the Weinberg and Lowenthal families – to name but two mid-19th-century Jewish merchants who exported Irish linen across the world from that building.

Even a commemorative plaque, installed by a local heritage charity, was prised off a property in Cliftonpark Avenue, North Belfast. Community workers and activists, who are based in the building, allegedly did so at the wishes of the local community and elected representatives. The plaque had marked the birthplace of Chaim Herzog, former President of Israel and son of Rabbi Dr Isaac Herzog, the first Chief Rabbi of both Ireland and the state of Israel after its independence in 1948. In Northern Ireland, actions by the Palestinian Boycott, Divestment and Sanctions support movement have resulted in several Jewish historical casualties with connections to Israel, such as those contained in the Herzog family legacy. It is perhaps surprising that Herzog's extensive contributions to public life are not treated with more pride and respect in a city so mindful of its past and so focused on diversity and equality.

Some see the disappearing legacy of Northern Ireland's Jewish past as an inevitability of demographic change. According to the 2011 census, the Jewish community (which at the turn of the 20th century was 2500 souls strong), now comprises just over 300. The Orthodox synagogue struggles to form a *minyan* (the quorum required for certain prayers and religious obligations) from its 80 members. Other commentators suggest a more orchestrated removal occurring within the context of growing anti-Semitic hate crimes in Europe. The conflation of anti-Zionism with anti-Semitism is an issue that, at the time of writing, dominates politics and the media. The 'disappearance' is interpreted by some to be an example of how anti-Semitism plays out, particularly in areas where a secular, rights-based lens draws on an oppression narrative based on contemporary Middle Eastern politics. Some predominantly Republican-Catholic areas now fly pan-Arabic colours and the flag of the Palestinian territories, indicating empathy and solidarity with oppression imposed by an external, colonial government. Conversely, in Loyalist-Protestant areas, the Union Flag can be found alongside the Israeli Magen David flag. This indicates allegiance with those who support and draw on state defence services when facing violent guerrilla insurrection by their neighbours.

Middle Eastern politics aside, the questionable value placed on Northern Ireland's Jewish legacy contrasts with the experience recorded by those Jews who came in the 1930s, prior to making *Aliyah* (Hebrew for 'going up', referring to those who emigrate to Israel). In 1939, North Belfast's Cliftonpark Avenue housed an organization providing support to the Aid of Jewish Refugees. As their building became overcrowded, the president of the local Jewish community, Barney Hurwitz, leased 70 acres of farmland, previously used for flax bleaching, at the seafront at Millisle on the Ards Peninsula – a landmass 15 miles east of Belfast, extending into the Irish Sea. The disused farm was taken over by idealist agronomists, engineers and *chalutzim* (agricultural pioneers) who converted stables into a dining room, cowsheds into dormitories and, based on a *kibbutz* model, created a self-sufficient farm. Several hundred people worked there, until its final residents left nine years later, in 1948. At any one time, it housed up to 80 people. All the children who came on Kindertransport from Vienna were integrated and educated at the local primary school. Older children travelled on foot or by bike to the next village, Donaghadee, to attend the technical college. While all left the area eventually, many of the young people retained friendships and fond memories of their time in Millisle.

The local Ards and North Down Council continues to draw on the subject as a valued aspect of the area's shared social history. A tourist trail includes public artworks, commissioned by local artists and poets, relating to the Kindertransport narrative. Other cultural expositions include the annual production of plays and performance arts. At Millisle Primary School, where the Holocaust is an integral part of the curriculum, parents and teachers commissioned a 'Safe Haven' garden and a large public sculpture. Both the garden and the sculpture (by Ned Jackson Smyth) are reminders of the welcome refugees received from the villagers. They commemorate those who found friendship, safety and purpose through the kindness of strangers in a small, seaside village.

My father still lives in the cottage where he and my mother retired to. It overlooks the former location of the Millisle Kindertransport farm. The unpublicized nature of the story, along with the owner's reluctance to preserve the remaining building, meant that my parents only became aware of it when they had been living there for a decade. As they began to learn about the history of the place, the story emerged of children whose resilience had been tested and built in this strange environment. Their story echoed that of my mother, Inge.

As an unaccompanied 7-year-old, Inge had travelled on Kindertransport. By sheer coincidence, 30 years later she found herself living where many other Jewish children from Austria had resided, and with whom she may well have shared similar experiences and memories. Millisle gave Inge an opportunity to reflect on her own extraordinary, lifelong interfaith journey.

Family: Reduced and extended

In 1938, in an increasingly unsafe Vienna, Inge's widowed mother endeavoured to find safety for her 11 children. An older sister found her way to the United States; some say their mother played cards professionally in street cafés to save money for the passage. Inge, another sister and two brothers were sent to an orphanage. Subsequently, Inge was fostered by the family of a policeman, where she was separated from her siblings and her religious background. Was this was done by design, to help her assimilate and 'pass'? Or was it a process of proselytizing? Inge's memories of this period were fractured, and she understood only too well that they were, perhaps, falsely mediated by the few photographs she retained of that period. She never knew for certain whether her recollection of being taken to a parade, where Nazi salutes to Hitler were commonplace, was the same occasion as the picture taken of her wearing a flowered garland in her hair, which she felt might have been connected to Easter. What she did remember, however, was the kindness and warmth she received from the Catholic Brindel family, who provided her with a home and sought to help her at a time when others wanted to expose her to harm.

Inge's last memory of Austria was of boarding a train, as a nun pressed a miraculous medal into her hands. The medal, a small piece of 'worthless' aluminium, has been cherished ever since. (Stored in an organza bag with a purple ribbon, it has become a treasured amulet in our family, bringing symbolic comfort as we embark on long journeys.) Vienna station was the last time Inge saw her mother and five of her brothers. In turn, they were taken on their own train journey. Theirs ended in Maly Trostinec, an extermination camp outside Minsk, where they were either shot or perished in the mobile gas chambers.

Inge made her way across Europe with a smoked cheese sandwich, a ball and a little brown suitcase, whose ubiquitous image has come to symbolize the journey undertaken by those who escaped from or perished at the hands of the Nazis. Her passage had been enabled by devout Church of England women living in Kent. A local family adopted her and brought her up; their values and faith shaped her understanding of religious ritual. Inge spent her youth on the Isle of Man, equidistant between Northern Ireland and England, where she would live as an adult. Given her exposure to a range of identities, cultures and faiths, my father (brought up as a Methodist Christian) would refer to her as a 'one-woman ecumenical movement'. This marked the thin end of the comedic wedge, which my parents used regularly to deal with the complexities of an interfaith marriage and the tragedies in their families' lives. Like many survivors and optimists, they preferred black humour to mawkish sentimentality or victim status. It was a trait shared by Inge's remaining siblings, with whom (thanks to the Red Cross and her older sister's relentless searching) she was eventually reunited. Her two older brothers had settled in Israel after their youth in Denmark, and both sisters were now together and married in the United States.

Inge was a woman of faith, grateful for the generosity of those who shone a clear light of reconciliation between differences. By her bed, she had a book of daily reflections on principles, conscience and ethics – some liturgy, some poetry – which accompanied her on overnight visits away from home. Each day, she would find renewal in these contributions. One of her last pieces of work was a series of interviews that she conducted for Northern Ireland's Community Relations Council (Radford 1993). Inge endeavoured to find light in the stalemate that marked relationships between churches, clergy and congregations prior to the signing of the peace accords (commonly known as the Good Friday Agreement). To stay positive, she drew on her little red book and shared aspirations from the different traditions of her religious background. She often heeded both the Jewish philosopher Solomen ibn Gabriol ('At the head of all understanding is realizing what is, and what cannot be – and the consoling of what is not in our power to change') and the American theologian Reinhold Niebuhr, whose similar serenity prayer draws on St Francis of Assisi: 'God, give me Grace to accept with serenity the things that cannot be changed, Courage to change the things which should be changed, and the Wisdom to distinguish the one from the other.'

Faith, hope and clarity

A decade before her death, Inge and I took part in a BBC Radio 4 programme, *From Victim to Survivor* (Hall 2007), which explored the resilience and pragmatism of people who thrive after overcoming adversity. Trauma specialists, oral historians and those committed to the study of the Holocaust and Northern Ireland will, no doubt, have a range of theories that rationalize or critique my mother's 'flash-bulb' memories. Inge's recollections relied on the testimony of an unaccompanied child and were being prompted by her adult daughter. In subsequent interviews, filmed for various Holocaust commemorations, Inge referenced her reluctance and feelings of pressure by me to discuss these issues publicly. This is no doubt a classic case study for considering the trans-generational impact of trauma and loss. And it is, of course, further food for thought – that the context for us thinking about these issues was taking place between two people (my mother and I) who had both experienced and explicitly chosen to work with others whose lives were impacted by the legacy of loss and violence in Northern Ireland. But there were, and are, more pressing concerns than unpacking such motivations. Actions, for example: one of my lasting memories of my mother was of her making an hour-long bus journey, with her wheeled walking frame, to the centre of Belfast, where she stood in the rain at an Amnesty International rally to support Syrian refugees coming to the UK.

The Beth Din and other ecclesiastical courts make judgements about the birth, marriage and burial rights of people like my parents. My parents, however, did not see interfaith marriage as rejection, defection, abandonment or sinful. They taught their children to see their religious journeying as choices made thoughtfully and together, and as a process of augmentation and spiritual growth. These choices enabled faith encounters to be addressed with a value base that served all people with kindness, generosity, reciprocity and intellectual exchange, along with a large, hopeful spoonful of good humour.

A *mitzvah* is a commandment, a religious duty, of which there are 613 in the Hebrew Bible. It is often interpreted as a 'good deed', which is as much a privilege to undertake as it is an obligation of religiosity. When my mother died, and contrary to Jewish observance and taboo, her wish to be cremated was upheld. It was the family's privilege, if not a *mitzvah*, to scatter her ashes in a way that made sense of her life's extraordinary, resilient journey. Inge's ashes were scattered – by three generations of her family, drawn from three continents – in the Garden of Gethsemane, in the Danube...and in the sea at Millisle.

References

Hall, A. (2007) *Something Understood: Victimhood and Survival*. BBC Radio 4, Falling Tree Productions.

Radford, I. (1993) *Breaking Down Divisions: Possibilities of a Local Church Contribution to Improving Community Relations*. Belfast: Community Relations Council.

CHAPTER 5

Beauty for Ashes and the Oil of Gladness

God in Exile, Asylum Seekers and the Journey to Hope

Julie Khovacs and Ivan Khovacs

A group of young Muslim asylum seekers from Sudan, recently settled in the UK, enrolled in an English language course that met in a local Anglican church. The instructor invited the church's priest to give an impromptu presentation on Christian worship.

The conversation turned to their experience of life in the UK. Amid observed: 'People in England don't care about other people. When you walk down the street in Sudan, people talk to you. If you see fighting, you go and stop the fight. If someone is sick, you help them. If you see a married couple arguing, you get involved. But it is different here. No one speaks to me on the street here in England. People look away when I pass them. People only care about themselves.'

This led to a discussion about showing care and compassion, based on Jesus's parable of the Good Samaritan. We asked: Suppose this were set in Sudan. Who would you say you are in the story?

In this chapter, we outline a theology of welcome, in the distinctly Christian language of the self-giving God who journeys among humanity. This chapter is an exercise in practical theology, through the lens of ministry with refugees and asylum seekers. The terms we use require some explanation. *Asylum seeker* refers to people currently petitioning for asylum status in the UK. *Refugees* are people who have been granted asylum status and who now reside in the country (see also Travis 2015). The term 'stranger' is a theological interpretation of the Hebrew word *ger*, denoting a person of foreign origin, separated from a particular community. The people at the heart of the stories that follow are rooted deeply in the life of the church. While not everyone involved identifies as Christian, all are directly or indirectly in touch with the church community.

We locate the welcoming ethos in the biblical theme of God's faithful companionship with those in displacement and exile. The experiences we relate are those of migrants in London taking part in the Welcome Boxes project at St Peter's Church, Eaton Square. Their stories invariably relate a sense that God is with the refugee and asylum seeker. With this 'theology from below' as our starting point, we explore the story of Jesus's 'migratory' journey among humanity.

Welcome Boxes

Welcome Boxes is a national charity, part of the Upbeat Communities project, serving recently arrived migrants whose status in the country is under legal review by the UK Home Office. The charity aims 'to inspire and equip the church to demonstrate God's love for refugees and asylum seekers through the building of welcoming communities'.[1] This appeal resonates with a distinctly Anglican understanding that the parish church serves *everyone* – regardless of church attendance, faith background or personal convictions. This broad ascription of 'church' is also inscribed in the Church of England's particularity as the legally 'established' church. This, in its turn, underwrites the commitment to put faith into action in the heart of every congregational community. The Welcome Boxes project is simply another open door

---

1   www.welcomeboxes.org; www.upbeatcommunities.org.

to a friendly, non-judgemental, helpful encounter with people in the community.

On a typical visit, trained volunteers deliver a box of household gifts to families or individuals referred through London's Housing Justice network. A church like St Peter's then offers a visit and, through conversation, extends an invitation of companionship, pastoral care or practical help. Volunteers might be asked for prayer and conventional spiritual care, but they could also be asked for help making contact with community or government agencies. Invitations to social gatherings in the church usually follow, which help individual migrants to connect with a mutually supportive, multi-faith, multicultural community. The success of these pastoral encounters speaks of the church's ability to be a safe, supportive, listening space. At St Peter's, we count it a privilege to have these ongoing pastoral links, and to be invited, as often happens, into indescribably painful aspects of someone's migration story.

Each person we meet invariably has experienced great upheaval, but each also has an account of fashioning resilience from tears, separation and silence. This is something which neither church clergy nor the middle-class professionals, who represent the majority of our congregation, can easily imagine.

Jonathan is a vibrant young man and a gifted artist. As a teenager, he fled the Congo, fearing credible threats against him and his family. On his journey through Africa and Europe, Jonathan experienced detention and the terror of torture. Of his arrival in Britain, he says, 'I was made to feel like a criminal and put into detention. I was terrified and alone.' Agents of the UK Border Agency questioned his account of violence and the experiences that had pushed him into exile; they accused him of lying. Jonathan felt little hope for his asylum claim.

While his case went under review, Jonathan came into contact with Housing Justice. This was his first experience of welcome. Jonathan says it was Christians who first offered companionship and practical help, and Christians who continue to stand with him today.

It would be wrong to make hasty claims about transformed lives, either on behalf of volunteers or the migrant people we have visited. It is apparent, however, that the effect is reciprocal and mutually appreciated on a purely relational level. 'Befrienders' speak of a growing empathy for the people they come to know in these social, albeit carefully managed, pastoral settings. Refugees and asylum seekers speak of the rare sense of 'belonging', which human contact and a measure of companionship can offer as they face the complex demands of the asylum system.

This is not to say that the relationship is symmetrical; the balance between volunteers and the people we serve is patently uneven. The inequality rhetoric of 'haves' and 'have-nots' applies with embarrassing accuracy. Nevertheless, individuals on either side of the equation remain the authority on whatever meaning they might derive from the pastoral relationship. As volunteer befrienders, we do this partly by allowing our reading of Scripture to be conditioned and, when necessary, challenged by the plainly human nature of these encounters. Our care of refugees, no less than any Christian ministry of compassion, reflects Christ's journey to become human and to suffer with humanity. Vulnerability of heart is a necessary condition for enabling theological practices of healing and hope.

However, we simply cannot take for granted the risks of being entrusted with the stories of people in vulnerable conditions. Does telling someone else's story, and making it the focus of our theological reflection, compromise that person's sense of dignity (not to say 'agency')? Or does it amplify a voice which resonates theologically – precisely because it comes from a position of vulnerability?

Making theology from experience: 'Who do you say that I am?'

A pivotal point in the Gospel's retelling of the Jesus story is the question: *Who do you say that I am?* The question entails an act of vulnerability on Jesus's part; entrusting one's story and sense of identity to someone else's retelling risks being reduced to the scope of their interpretation. In some way, migrants ask people in their host country: *Who do you say that I am?* We are conscious not to impose a theological perspective on already fragile lives. To be clear, the people at the heart of our story are vulnerable because their conditions make them so. Declared consent, and no small amount of expectation, simply leaves them further exposed, for it is always possible to bias the conversation towards our own ends. The answer, though, is not to deny the power inequalities in the conversation, but to face and surmount the potential for misrepresentation.

We do this by borrowing from the contemporary equality rights ethic, summarized in the slogan 'Nothing about us without us.' In his book by that title, James Charlton (2000, pp.3–5) notes 'the revelational claim' in South Africa's disability empowerment movement which, as early as the 1990s, determined that no legislation or public policy should fail to include the voices of the people and communities whose interests they claim. Representations made on behalf of vulnerable people clearly demand such a levelling stance. In our own attempt to flesh out a theological notion of welcome, this implies assuming a posture of deep listening and learning. In practice, this means including representative voices of refugees and asylum seekers, whose lives verge between rebuilding from and surrendering to the hardships of forced migration and exile. Our purpose in placing their migratory journey in theological perspective, therefore, is both to affirm the individuals we have come to know and to uphold *their* agency in piecing together what, in the end, must be a narrative of hope.

Over the past few years, refugees and asylum seekers – Christian or otherwise – have become an identifiable part of our community at St Peter's Church, sharing a common journey to redemption and wholeness. Migrants in our midst have changed us. For the congregation of St Peter's, Eaton Square, there is simply no going back. We now look different: this is who we are; their story is our story.

Our theology of pastoral welcome includes the stories of migrants because human empathy is a Christian, methodological necessity. We journey, so to speak, with someone like Jonathan by allowing ourselves to imagine his middle-of-the-night escape, leaving everything behind to face an unknown future. Doing so, we hope, accords our conversation partner equal priority in making theology from experience. This ethical priority sharpened our focus on the stories of migrants who agreed to personal interviews as part of a research project. Each person was asked to comment on three questions:

1. What brought you to Britain?
2. In what ways have you felt welcomed/unwelcomed?
3. What has been your personal experience of welcome in the church?

On what basis, though, do we press the resulting discussion into theological themes and ministerial reflection on what it means to be a welcoming church? Who, after all, is the stranger?

The border-crossing God

It may seem like an overstatement to claim, as Snyder (2012, p.129) has done, that the Bible is the ultimate story of migration, written by, for and about migrants. Rhetorically, however, Snyder is alluding to the biblical emphasis on God's presence in migration and sojourn, not only in the 'numerous stories about people "on the move"', but beginning in Genesis with the Spirit's 'migration' over unformed creation. From the outset, the Bible 'grapples extensively with what it means to live as outsiders and among strangers' (*ibid.*). This grappling crystallizes in Genesis chapter 12, in the calling of Abraham and Sarah: a theology dominated by a sense of travel and of the God who is on the diaspora journey.

Abraham sets off as an alien on a quintessential pilgrimage from desert to sea.[2] He and Sarah are summoned to leave behind all that

---

2   See also Genesis 23.4: 'I am a stranger and an alien residing among you' and Leviticus 17.8: 'sojourner in the land'.

defines them: their country, their people and their household 'for the sake of only vague promises of a new vision and abundant life' (Snyder 2012, p.130). At stake is God's faithfulness revealed, in displacement: 'this new history requires a wrenching departure, an abandonment of what is for what is not' (Brueggemann 2002, p.17). Abraham and Sarah will come to know God in their wandering; indeed, as Brueggemann concludes, God's faithful and 'decisive intrusion' will become most evident 'at the point where the promises are greatest and the risks the highest' (Bruggemann 2010, p.126).

The motif of the God-accompanied journey thus becomes the defining identity of the liberation tradition in the book of Exodus. Israel's drive through the desert, and delivery from slavery into the sanctuary of God's justice, follows a pattern of displacement, deliverance and the presence of the journeying God. This begins in creation's crossing from chaos to order, in the change from divine act to Sabbath rest, and in the promise embedded in the expulsion of Adam and Eve from Eden: That they shall return 'to the soil from which you were taken' (Genesis 3.19).

This theology of exile and return is perpetuated in the preaching tradition of the prophets. So, for example, Isaiah's vision to know God in the adversity of exile, both in the promise of deliverance and in the confirmation that they are not alone: *He has sent me to bring good news to the oppressed, to give them beauty for ashes, the oil of joy and the garment of praise for the spirit of oppression* (Isaiah 61.1–3, abbreviated.). This healing, reconciling, liberating motif underpins the span of the biblical drama. Humanity, along with creation itself, is drawn through a journey of redemption to the final restoration of all things. This is the central theme of the New Testament, in which the God-on-the-journey whom we meet in Genesis, Exodus and the Prophets is the same relational, incarnate, liberating God we meet in Jesus.

In the Gospels, Jesus is born, lives and dies as one of us. His final passage from death to Resurrection life then writes the definitive chapter of the Exodus liberation story. The Christian faith, marked by the empty cross and beginning by passing through the waters of baptism, is itself cast as a journey. The Church's sacraments trade on notions of passage, transformation, movement and change. The act of communion, as the pinnacle of Christian worship, is premised on everyday bread and wine crossing from the world of the profane into the realm of the sacred. This retelling of Christ's self-offering for humanity entails also a passage across time, culture, geography and place. The very name of Jesus, Immanuel, means 'God with us': the border-crossing God.

> *Sylvia, who fled violence in Kenya, describes her first year in England as a time of upheaval, disorientation and isolation. Although grateful for the life-changing possibility of refugee status in the UK, she nevertheless feels public hostility, sensing that her mere presence is an affront to others. These feelings were exacerbated by the experience of becoming homeless, when Sylvia felt pushed to the edge between life and death. The most damning uncertainty, however, was whether God, whom Sylvia believed had faithfully been with her in her journey into exile, had turned away from her suffering.*
>
> *Yet in her despair, Sylvia felt that God had gone ahead of her, to the depths of social and emotional desolation, precisely to be there and enfold her: 'I had hit the bottom. I had sunk to a place of such shame, a place I never would have imagined myself to be. All I wanted to do was die. And yet, I found something unexpected in this place. In the midst of the shame, the cold, the humiliation, God was there. Somehow God had come down to this place of death and was already there, waiting to welcome me when I arrived.'*

We began this chapter with Amid's reflection on the parable of the Good Samaritan, prompted by the question: *If this were set in present-day Sudan, which of the characters in the story would you identify with?* Looking at the fuller context, Amid's answer is unsurprising. He knows what it is to be abandoned by people and circumstances, and he knows what it means to be helped to trek across his home country, led through the desert and multiple national borders, until finally reaching safety in the UK. Is it any wonder that Amid does not see himself as the merciful, saving figure of the Good Samaritan?

Instead, he identifies with the victim, beaten up, robbed, and left for dead on the side of the road. Amid's reading of Scripture could only seem surprising from the relative position of privilege that we at St Peter's Church have come to take for granted – academic degrees, overseas work and travel, cultural institutions and so forth – all of which condition and constrain our reading in favour of the Samaritan positioned to help. Inevitably, we rule out the view from the margins. As a Muslim in dialogue in a church with Christians, Amid speaks from a unique, subversive position, underpinning his reading of the Christian Scriptures with a theology of our shared humanity and the welcome of a relentless, border-crossing God.

Conclusion: 'Once you were not a people'

We visited a young woman and her 5-year-old daughter. Having been invited into their home, we sat down to tea and presented the Welcome Box. The girl began to cry. After a while she turned to her mother and whispered something in her ear. When we were about to leave, her mother told us what the little girl had said: 'I am so happy that someone gave me a gift because it means someone likes me. Not everyone hates.'

Through the Welcome Boxes, the befriending ministry of St Peter's Church has been an unexpected education in the legal complexities of asylum. On anecdotal account, it is a difficult, humiliating, disheartening process. People who have spent years in Britain regularly find their applications rejected, their cases playing helplessly against international, political and economic issues over which they have no influence or control. Solving the inherent complications of an asylum seeker's legal status are clearly beyond what we, as Christian companions, can offer. Nevertheless, we argue that God's inclusive welcome of all people, especially those most vulnerable to a social order they had no part in creating, must be a lived reality in the life of the church.

If churches are to formulate practical, ethical responses to asylum seekers and refugees in our communities, a politically percussive theology of welcome and inclusion is imperative. This will require a theology of the Holy Spirit forging a healing and reconciling church – not in spite of but precisely from human particularity and difference. In this chapter, we have sought to offer some biblical, pastoral and theological foundations for this undertaking. We have attempted to extrapolate from the idea of God-in-exile the moral grounds for the welcome of asylum seekers in our midst.

That said, though the ethos of Welcome Boxes is formulated precisely along these lines, it is not politically disingenuous. We recognize that drawing on the biblical, liberating principle that all humanity belongs to God must have implications for present-day discourse on forced migration. As priests and ministers, our response to the anti-migrant rhetoric in the public sphere is the public pursuit of hope. This is a faith driven by our borderless understanding of God, who opens the door to all humanity in the outstretched arms of Jesus on the cross; in sacramental hands holding out bread and wine for communion; in the God who breaks through boundaries of time and place. This theology underpins our ethos of welcoming refugees and asylum seekers. The Church's public identity is never anything other than a foundling in God's world – the Church of whom it is said: 'Once you were not a people, but now you are God's people; once you had not received mercy, but now you have received mercy' (1 Peter 2:10).

References

Brueggemann, W. (2002) *The Land Revised: Place as Gift, Promise, and Challenge in Biblical Faith*. Minneapolis, MN: Fortress Press.

Brueggemann, W. (2010). *Genesis: A Bible Commentary for Teaching and Preaching*. Louisville, KY: Westminster John Knox Press.

Charlton, J.I. (2000) *Nothing About Us Without Us: Disability Oppression and Empowerment*. Berkeley and Los Angeles, CA: University of California Press.

Snyder, S. (2012) *Asylum-Seeking, Migration and The Church*. Farnham: Ashgate.

Travis, A. (2015) 'Migrants, Refugees and Asylum Seekers: What's the Difference?' Accessed on 28/10/18 at www.theguardian.com/world/2015/aug/28/migrants-refugees-and-asylum-seekers-whats-the-difference.

CHAPTER 6

My 'Migration to Migration' in Orthodox Judaism

David Mason

Jewish national history begins in exile: the biblical story of the 'children of Israel' in Egypt. The unfolding story of redemption would make its mark on the future of the Jewish people, but the experience of exile would always be part of our historical consciousness. As a religious Jew, I learned about the directional narrative of Jewish history, from exile to redemption; from diaspora to Israel. But exile can also be of value in itself. So a Jewish history, soaked with forced migrations across the world, can grab onto the flow of history and turn these dislocations into a process of learning about identity. Jewish migration would ensure a modelling of moderation and a cosmopolitan outlook not interested in toppling identity but in preventing its over-entrenchment. In the words of former Chief Rabbi Lord Sacks, our exile and migrations would teach us the 'dignity of difference' (Sacks 2002, p.53).

A double concept of migration and exile is part of every Jewish person's life, but over the last century it has taken its toll on Jewish integrity. After the Holocaust especially, many survivors, or many born in the second generation, were creations of forced migration;

their lives expressed echoes or shadows of Jewish life. It is true that a significant number of survivors of the Holocaust, who had been religiously observant before the war, remained religious after it. But for many, the trauma understandably distanced them from religion and belief.

My mother's parents escaped Germany just before World War II. They met and married in London and settled in Luton, where my grandfather became a family doctor. My father's parents were both born in Bristol; their parents had migrated from Romania, Lithuania, and what today is Ukraine. A melting pot of migration, therefore, greeted my birth in 1973. What is more, my father had accepted work in the early 1970s as a microbiologist in Edinburgh, so my young life was spent in Scotland. Although I was far from a stranger in the local synagogue, and I became involved in local Jewish youth groups, we did not live an observant Jewish life in Edinburgh.

My Scottish upbringing was fundamental to my development. From a young age, I understood the sense of being an underdog, of being part of a vulnerable nation, and the tragedies that result in needing to fight for your national existence. Scottish history was full of these challenges. I still talk of Scotland as a 'homeland', even if I do not yearn to return. Scotland bequeathed me a sense of reflectiveness on identity, political awareness, and an understanding of power and how it plays out between people.

My Scottish identity did not inhibit Jewish expression. I experienced very little anti-Semitism as a child at school and in public. I was allowed time off to celebrate Passover, the Jewish New Year and Yom Kippur. Scottishness and Jewishness could certainly work together; the Edinburgh Jewish writer David Daiches (2001) explains this eloquently. But though my Jewish identity was not suppressed, it was certainly not able to flourish in Scotland in a religious sense. I began to think more deeply about religious identity while at school. When I migrated to London for university, I began to live a more religious lifestyle and to spend time in places of Jewish textual learning, both in London and in Israel.

Religious migration

There is a fascinating concept in the Talmud (the key Jewish text): the *Baal Teshuva*. *Teshuva* ('return') relates to the potential to stop acts of sin, and to return to a state of being before the sin was committed. Sin does not eternally defile. If one does *teshuva*, we believe atonement is readily given. A *Baal Teshuva* is thus someone who carries out *teshuva*: a person who returns. In fact, the Talmud states that 'In the place that a Baal Teshuva stands, a Righteous person cannot stand.' In other words, someone who sins and repents is considered more religiously valuable than someone who has always lived a righteous life.

Today, the *Baal Teshuva* is a label given to someone who has migrated from a less observant to a more observant way of life. As orthodox Judaism is very much defined through law and custom, religiosity is rooted in doing and in action. So the *Baal Teshuva* would change his eating habits to ensure only kosher food is consumed. He or she may pray more regularly with a community and must keep the laws of the Sabbath.

Being *Baal Teshuva* – becoming more religious – is clearly a migration, a movement. The great 12th-century Jewish scholar Maimonides, echoing the Talmud, lists 'exile' as one of the paths a person may take towards *teshuva*, towards return. A person needs to migrate away from his everyday existence, in order to find space to reflect on how he can repair and develop his soul. Today, in an era where the State of Israel is so integral to Jewish identity, it is important to see the therapeutic and character-building impact of exile. This may mean physical relocation to areas where more religious Jews live.

In my case, to be religious in Edinburgh – a town with few Jews – would have been challenging. North London, where I live now, makes religious life much more accessible. But in the migration of religiosity, which many who are traversing this path would call a redemptive one, there is clear potential for exile. Exile can come with significant costs. I have met many people who would fit the label *Baal Teshuva*, for whom the move to religiosity involved exile from family. Parents fear 'losing' their children, and the adult child may express anger at how the parent is not able to accept the newly chosen path. I remember being adamant with myself that my new interest in religiosity would in no way affect the relationship with my family. This was 'my migration', and one I did not want to force on others. This migration of religiosity does not need to be one of movement into a cave of separation and asceticism; rather, it can enrich valued relationships that already exist.

This was an important condition in my own migration to religiosity – that it should happen at my pace, and in a way that did not dislocate me from my surroundings. The first time I went to a *yeshiva* (a place of Jewish learning) in Israel, I studied alongside individuals who had undergone radical changes. For me, these people were just moving too fast. They were not reflecting on what the changes meant for them and their future. They often fell into worshipping one or other of the rabbis who taught there. This experience made me sceptical of outreach and evangelism. There were Jewish organizations who considered their primary focus to be outreach and bringing Jewish people closer to religious observance. Some feared that the numbers of Jews would continue to drop in the diaspora due to intermarriage. Some people thus felt a need to deepen and enrichen Jewish identity – to 'sell' religiosity as something that can exist in the modern world. For others, there was a sense that if 'I' have traversed this path of truth, the only way 'I' can shore it up is to preach it to others and bring them down an identical path.

For me, however, the 'migration' needed to be willed. It needed to be right for the individual and right for the specific time of their life. The individual would also need to find their place in the spectrum of observance. I was pulled to a Jewish ethical statement: *the work is not there for you to complete; but nor are you free to desist from it.* Religion and religious life are not 'all or nothing'. Value can be generated from moving on a religious trajectory of development, however small the steps. The size of the steps should be left fully to the individual making them.

As a rabbi, I have strengthened this attitude through my work as an educator and a pastoral leader. As a communal strategic thinker, I create relationships with local civic and faith communities. I want to model a religious life, but I also want to model a religiosity that values all that people do, rather than a model that only values the end goal. Mine is a religiosity based on human dignity.

Orthodoxy and 'migration to migration'

I spent seven years in Israel learning in *yeshivot* (places of higher Jewish learning), where I received ordination as a rabbi. In 2003, I then took up my first position in Kingston upon Thames, south London, where I spent five great years. As a rabbi, I gave lessons and lectures, ran educational trips and put lots of effort into my synagogue sermons. Quickly, I felt an affinity for working with other faith groups and working within wider society. Considering the plight of *all* people stirred a passion within me. I had heard too many people within the world of the *yeshiva* denigrate the role of the gentile as opposed to the role of the Jew. But I had been electrified by the works of Rabbi Abraham Kook and his religious universalism, which heralded the importance of all in his redemptive vision. I also had been inspired by Rabbi Jonathan Sacks, who explores the Jewish role in this world as interlinked with the fate of many different peoples and identities. Within Jewish texts, I was finding evidence that identity and religious identity did not have to come at the cost of my relationship with the 'other'. Of course, Jewish history comes with a significant dose of the 'other' turning power against the Jewish people; this has clearly bred mistrust. But in the Britain and the Western world of my young life, the Jewish people found a more concrete and trusting place. The State of Israel existed and was accepted (at least in the Western democratic world). It seemed to me that Jewish communities could afford to turn outwards and make society a better place.

I quickly came across dissonance. I wanted to teach and pursue an orthodoxy that was both concerned about learning (e.g., Torah knowledge and Jewish education) while simultaneously concerned about the world outside. In 2004, I was asked by the Office of the Chief Rabbi to represent him on a committee of Jewish organizations involved with the Make Poverty History campaign. Soon I was attending meetings in Downing Street and becoming familiar with non-governmental organizations. I started learning more about international aid, international debt and the United Nations Millennium Development Goals. I then joined the Kingston Interfaith forum, becoming involved in local projects bringing faith leaders together. I befriended leaders at the Kingston mosque and local churches, and we learned about the issues they faced.

Soon, I realized that within the orthodox Jewish world, this stuff was simply not on the menu. It was not considered a necessary part of orthodox rabbinic leadership, and so it did not figure in training or induction programmes for rabbis. This also meant that other Jewish denominations, on the progressive side of Judaism, would be way ahead of orthodoxy when it came to engaging with societal issues. Local progressive communities would be able to set up complex, well-developed programmes such as drop-in centres for asylum seekers.

Yet my organization, the United Synagogue, has come on a journey of migration, which I feel honoured to be part of developing. The recent global migration crisis is a key factor. When the Syrian child Alan Kurdi washed up on the shores of a Greek island, and the pictures of his body went global, many rabbis contacted me with a real sense of human pain. I felt a new trajectory opening within my rabbinic friends – a new direction to consider what is happening outside the orbit of our people and communities.

In late 2015, a number of rabbis accompanied the Chief Rabbi on a trip to northern Greece, where we came face to face with forced migration. We saw thousands of Syrians, Iraqis, Afghanis and others queue up at the Macedonian border. Every 15 minutes, the border would open and another 80 or so refugees would walk off into the distance, hoping to find a new life somewhere in Europe. As rabbis, we sensed the many wanderings of our history, meeting and empathizing with the wandering that we were now viewing. Instead of running from Nazi Germany, we were hearing about running from Islamic State or the Afghan Taliban. Instead of people fleeing Germany in the late 1930s, with black-and-white pictures of their families, we were viewing mobile phone photographs of these refugee families. It was all too familiar.

Due to the leadership of our current Chief Rabbi, Ephraim Mirvis, social responsibility is now considered worthy of reflection and action. The United Synagogue has set up two centres where asylum seekers can receive support. In my synagogue, we became part of a borough-wide winter shelter, housing 12 individuals who were homeless for one night each week. This wonderful project brought together community members, many of whom had not met each other previously in the synagogue. It also revealed the faces of those who are homeless, creating a shared sense of humanity. For several years, I have served on the executive of the Rabbinical Council of the United Synagogue. Recently, I was given the portfolio for interfaith and social action. This is a big step for an orthodox organization, and one that I am immensely proud of.

Migration and utopia

Over the last few centuries, migration for most Jews was a forced undertaking which carried with it the threat of persecution and violence. Then came the State of Israel. Now one can migrate to a place that is called 'home' and join a modern political project of the Jewish people. For many Zionist leaders, the existence of a State would allow the Jewish people to finally take their place on the world stage with honour and dignity. For others, it was just a place of refuge to stem the flow of continuous persecution. But for an increasing number of Jewish thinkers, especially those on the political right, Israel became a messianic project.

I lived in Israel for seven years and received rabbinic ordination there. My wife and I lived in Efrat, a West Bank settlement built in the 1980s; it housed over 10,000 people. I was exposed to nationalist, religious, messianic thought, and I enjoyed reading about the love of the Land of Israel that seeped out of the works of so many religious

Zionist rabbis. Yet something did not fit for me. Messianism related to an end point, a final historic destination. My feeling was that we still had a long way to go. The danger would be real if we mistook our present reality for a messianic one. From that misunderstanding would, and did, spring forth violence and tragedy.

Therein lies for me a critical point, and a difficult one at that. Jewish people are bid to believe in the coming of a messianic era. At the same time, premature belief in messianism for the here-and-now can obscure the view that the world needs attention. This mistaken assumption can be both a religious and a political blunder. There was a feeling in the West that the 'promised land' had been reached; now many Western political commentators are not so sure. History can be understood as one long migration, which will eventually reach a cherished end point. For many religions, that end point is bound up in eschatology (the study of the end of history), with each offering their own narrative as to how history will end.

This difference between the end point and migration is described succinctly by the American writer Michael Walzer. In his book *Exodus and Revolution*, he takes the narrative of the Exodus of the Children of Israel as a frame for political change which overthrows oppression, brings about deliverance and takes a nation forwards. 'Exodus politics', or in my words the politics of the constant migration of history, are opposed to messianic politics. The latter creates a situation where 'politics is absolute, enemies satanic, compromise impossible' (Walzer 1985, p.147). Exodus politics is about the pragmatism of our present situation, bound up with a passion for bringing about a better, freer world:

> We still believe, or many of us do, what the Exodus first taught... about the meaning and possibility of politics and about its proper form: First, that wherever you live, it is probably Egypt. Second, that there is a better place, a world more attractive, a promised land. And third, that the way to the land is through the wilderness. There is no way to get from here to there except by joining together and marching. (Walzer 1985, p.149)

And so I have come to experience 'migration to migration'. That evolution – that migration – has taken me to a place where I understand migration and exile to be core elements of identity. Throwing off a sense of exile and migration comes with serious threats of narcissism, self-obsession and a reduced ability to relate to the 'other'. The centrality of migration, however, allows for self-reflection. It fosters empathy for the migrations of others, helping us to understand the need to ensure that these migrations are smooth, laden with opportunity and, of course, greeted with a welcome smile.

One day, I believe, God will take us all 'home', to a redeemed world. Until then, we are left with the mutual responsibility to make our world a better place, and so ensure that our migration through the 'wilderness' is a tolerable and enriching journey.

References

Daiches, D. (2001) *Two Worlds*. Edinburgh: Canongate.
Sacks, J. (2002) *The Dignity of Difference*. New York, NY: Continuum.
Walzer, M. (1985) *Exodus and Revolution*. New York, NY: Basic Books.

CHAPTER 7

Christian–Muslim Dialogue

Encounters with a Christian Minister

Hassan Rabbani

I began my role as an imam at Annandale Mosque in 2016. The mosque had been established in 1985 to serve the local Muslim community in Edinburgh. When I was appointed, I was informed that my remit would not be limited to the four walls of the mosque. Rather, I was encouraged to promote outreach, to facilitate interfaith and intrafaith initiatives.

Of the various projects I was involved with, by far the most enjoyable were my encounters with Minister Graham McGeoch at Broughton St Mary's Parish Church (Church of Scotland). His interest in interfaith work led him to the front door of Annandale Mosque, where he was offered a glass of guava juice by some mosque uncles who spoke broken English.

In 2017, I was invited to speak at Broughton St Mary's Church on Pentecost. This was a great surprise to me. Unlike Christmas, which has been commercialized to the point where many non-Christians take part in the celebration, I had understood Pentecost to be a strict Christian event commemorating the descent of the Holy Spirit upon the disciples. Although this event has little significance in Islam, I wondered how other Muslims would react to my invitation to speak at a church on this Christian holy day. Thankfully there was no backlash; rather, I received many messages of support and encouragement.

I had never led a congregation at a church for such an important Christian event. I questioned myself: *How would I be received by the congregation? Would they deem it appropriate that an imam is speaking to them on Pentecost? Will my words be effective? Can I stay true to my traditions yet be committed to what I was going to say?* I also felt that some people might have preconceived notions of me, based on their exposure to Islam from the media (Muslims are extremists, misogynist, anti-Semitic, etc.).

The event had been publicized for many weeks. However, a week before Pentecost, Britain witnessed two terrible terrorist attacks in Manchester and London. To my horror, they had been carried out in the name of my religion. Islam, once again, became the media headline. I had planned to speak about the importance of grassroots religious dialogue, but now felt that I had to speak about these events.

A voice in me kept questioning: *Why should I denounce these attacks? These criminals have nothing to do with my faith, and I have nothing to do with them.* When I meet non-Muslims, the response I often hear is, 'You guys are not doing enough.' Alternatively, some of my Muslim brethren argue that we should not have to speak out, as we don't see Christians, Jews and people of other religions speak out when members from their faith carry out terrorist attacks. With frustration and sadness, I began to write the piece that I would share with the church congregation.

On Pentecost Sunday, I arrived at Broughton St Mary's Church in my traditional Al-Azhari garb.[1] Minister Graham welcomed me and took me to the office, where we were joined by Right Reverend Patrick Burke (St Mary's Roman Catholic Cathedral and Vicar General of the Archdiocese of St Andrews and Edinburgh). The church had attracted a

---

1 I graduated in 2010 from Al-Azhar (Cairo, Egypt), one of the world's oldest universities. When I speak in public at a religious institution, I wear the Azhari outfit: a long cloak and a red hat with a thin white scarf wrapped around it. This is to show that as an Azhar graduate, I represent the university's message of moderation.

diverse audience (not all regular churchgoers) of over 100 people. Minister Graham addressed the congregation, stating that had he known this many people would come to listen to the imam, he would invite the imam to lead the service every Sunday. The congregation laughed.

Rising to speak, I was met with spontaneous applause. I mentioned how privileged I felt to attend this special celebration of the Church's foundation. I reflected that people of all faiths seek peace and solace in their religion, and that genuine Muslims are disturbed by those who practise violence in the name of Islam. I emphasized: 'We as Muslims have nothing to do with them, and they have nothing to do with us.'

And I spoke about the importance of religious dialogue in a Muslim-Christian context. I drew on three historical examples (two of which date to the life of Prophet Muhammad) which highlight cooperation, tolerance and pluralism.

Example one: The just Christian king

In 615 CE, a group of Muslim refugees fleeing persecution in Mecca (Saudi Arabia) found refuge under a Christian king in Abyssinia (modern-day Ethiopia). The Prophet Muhammad had instructed, 'If you were to go to Abyssinia it would be better for you, for the king will not tolerate injustice and it is a friendly country.' This is an early example of Prophet Muhammad praising Christian leadership. The group that left for Abyssinia included Prophet Muhammad's daughter Ruqaya and her husband, Usman.

The Meccan chieftains were outraged when they learned of the Muslims' escape. They dispatched their ambassador to Abyssinia to demand the fugitives' return. The Meccan ambassador arrived with expensive gifts for King Negus. He advised the king that the Muslim refugees were criminals and asked that they be repatriated. King Negus, concerned that he might be protecting menaces in his country, summoned the refugees to his court to answer the allegations.

The Muslims responded that they were not criminals but victims of religious persecution. King Negus asked, 'What is this religion wherein you have become separate from your people, though you have not entered my religion nor that of any other of the folk that surround us?'

The Prophet's cousin Ja'far, known for his eloquent speech, stepped forward:

> O King, we were an uncivilised people, worshipping idols, eating corpses. Committing abominations, breaking natural ties, treating guests badly, and our strong devoured our weak. Thus we were until God sent us an apostle whose lineage, truth, trustworthiness, and clemency we know. He summoned us to acknowledge God's unity and to worship him and to renounce the stones and images which we and our fathers formerly worshipped... We confessed his truth and believed in him, and we followed him in what he had brought from God, and we worshipped God alone. (Guillaume 1998, pp.151–152)

Ja'far then recited the following verses from the Quran, which spoke of Mary and Jesus:

> Mention Mary, when she left her family to go to a place in the East. She separated herself from them to stay in an isolated place. We sent the Angel Gabriel to her and he appeared in human form. She said, 'I seek protection of the Kind Lord from you if you fear God.' He said, 'I am a messenger from Your Lord, and I have come to give you a pure son.' She replied, 'How can I have a son when no man has touched me and I am not unchaste?' He told her, that is how it will be; your Lord said, 'This is easy for me, and We shall make him a sign of Our Kindness for people, a command, done!' (Quran 19:16–21)

The Meccan ambassador became alarmed. A shared love for Jesus and Mary had created a bond between the Christians and Muslims, threatening to disrupt the Meccan scheme. The ambassador, who knew that Muslims saw Jesus as a human messenger of God rather than as a divine being, quickly tried to create a rift between the two communities.

King Negus then summoned Ja'far and asked what he thought of Jesus. Ja'far replied that Muslims believed he was a Prophet of God who had been cast into Mary, the blessed virgin. King Negus was not offended by the answer, for he knew that the divine nature of Jesus was an issue that was disputed among Christians, which had led to warfare and fighting. What mattered was deep love and reverence for Jesus.

King Negus allowed the refugees to stay. He ordered the ambassador to return – with his gifts – to Mecca. The king's profound gesture communicated that he regarded Muslims as his brothers and sisters. This encounter has never been forgotten by Muslims.

Example two: Christians and the Mosque of Medina

In 631 CE, Christians were granted permission to pray in the mosque at Medina. The Prophet Muhammad had sent letters to different communities, encouraging them to embrace Islam. For the Christians of Najran (a city in southwest Arabia, about 450 miles south of Medina, near the border of Yemen), the Prophet sent two trusted emissaries, Khaled and Ali, to deliver the letter.

When the Christians of Najran arrived at Medina, Prophet Muhammad allowed them to pray in his mosque. This invitation was not only the first example of Christian–Muslim dialogue, it was also the first time that Christians prayed in a mosque. Although Prophet Muhammad and the Christian leaders were not able to reach common ground on all theological issues, he nonetheless gave them a place to stay near his home, and even ordered Muslims to pitch their tent.

On leaving Medina, the Christian leaders said, 'O, Muhammad, we decided to leave you as you are, and you leave us as we are. But send with us a man who can adjudicate things on our properties, because we accept you.' The Christians left Medina with a written guarantee that Prophet Muhammad would protect their lives, property and freedom to practise Christianity.

The Christians of Najran openly stated they would not accept the Islamic faith, and Prophet Muhammad frankly stated that he could not accept belief in the Trinity. However, they were able to discuss these ideas without putting lives at risk. Finally, they agreed the following treaty:

> The bishops of Najran and their priests and those who followed them and their monks, that for all their churches, services and monastic practices, few or many, they had the protection of God and His messenger. No bishop will be moved from his episcopate, no monk from his monastic state, no priest from his priesthood. There will be no alteration of any right or authority or circumstance, so long as they are loyal and perform their obligations well, they not being burdened by wrong and not doing wrong. (Watt 1956, p.359)

Example three: Omar and the Christians of Jerusalem

In 637 CE, Jerusalem was conquered by the Muslim ruler Omar. Sophronius, the Christian Patriarch of Jerusalem, was only willing to give up Jerusalem if Omar himself came. So Omar set off from Medina on his mule. He was welcomed by Sophronius and given a tour of the city, including the Church of the Holy Sepulchre. When the time came to pray, Sophronius invited Omar to pray in the church. After much insistence, Omar declined. His reason was that if he were to pray there, Muslims might later use that as an excuse to convert the church into a mosque. So Omar prayed outside the church, where the current Mosque of Omar still stands.

For me, the story has two strong moral lessons. First, the graciousness of the Patriarch, who welcomed Omar to pray in the church; his kindness offers helpful lessons for today. I fondly remember reading Friday prayers at a local church in Cambridge. The church had allowed Muslims to pray in their hall, as the mosque was far away and it did not have the space to host us all. While praying in the church, I would reflect on the Patriarch's invitation to Omar. On a related point, it is unfortunate that many mosques do not accommodate prayer spaces for women. I had been informed of one particular incident in the Midlands, where Muslim sisters were not allowed to pray in the mosque. They asked the local church for space; the church welcomed them and allowed them to pray.

The second moral lesson is that Omar was ready to pray, but what prevented him was his concern for the Church. This interesting historical episode led to the famous the Treaty of Umar:

> In the name of God, the Merciful, the Compassionate. This is the assurance of safety which the servant of God, Umar, the Commander of the Faithful, has given to the people of Jerusalem. He has given them an assurance of safety for themselves for their property, their churches, their crosses, the sick and healthy of the city and for all the rituals which belong to their religion. Their churches will not be inhabited by Muslims and will not be destroyed. Neither they, nor the land on which they stand, nor their cross, nor their property will be damaged. They will not be forcibly converted. (Abu-Munshar 2007, p.92)

Reflections

All three examples show the importance of tolerance, formal agreements, and – above all – active interfaith dialogue. I concluded my talk at St Mary's by inviting Minister Graham and his congregation to visit the mosque. When I finished, I walked to the door with Minister Graham and greeted the congregation. The feedback I received was overwhelming.

Two months later, Minister Graham and his congregation visited us at Annandale Mosque during Ramadan, the spiritual month in which Muslims fast. That year, Ramadan was particularly difficult; the fasting lasted around 18 hours due to the long days. Every evening, we hosted around 200 people for the *Iftar* (the meal after sundown to break the fast). World Refugee Day happened to fall in Ramadan that year, so I had organized an event for the date of St Mary's congregation's visit. Minister Graham spoke about the early Christians and how they were refugees. His congregation then shared in a lovely *Iftar* meal.

Iain Stewart, then Executive Director of the Edinburgh Interfaith Association, offered these words:

> We need more of these initiatives and we need more community leaders to follow the lead of Imam Rabbani and the Rev Graham McGeoch of Broughton St Mary's to open their doors and hearts to others... As I observed both leaders stand side by side, I was also watching their wives and their young children (both around one-and-a-half years old) play together. That made me think that if we can come together as a society in the way that these leaders and their children have, there is hope for a brighter future.

I left Edinburgh in October 2017. Coincidentally, Minister Graham also left his post at this time. The locals were extremely disappointed that we were leaving, but they cherished the moments we had spent together. The mosque and the church wanted to carry on this spirit of interfaith dialogue. As always, such initiatives depend on the appetite of the religious leaders.

My personal relationship with Graham, together with the relationship between our congregations, enriched our religious experience, encounters and our understandings of faith, and brought us into a new era of cooperation and respect. Sometimes it is difficult for Muslims and Christians to engage because of our political history. However, it is important that we realize we face many similar challenges.

Minister Graham moved to Brazil to teach. We are still in touch to this day.

References

Abu-Munshar, M. (2007) *Islamic Jerusalem and its Christians*. London: Tauris.
Guillaume, A. (1998) *The Life of Muhammad*. Karachi: Oxford University Press.
Watt, M. (1956) *Muhammad at Medina*. London: Oxford University Press.

CHAPTER 8

Mapping Theology

Katherine Baxter

Maps tell a story.

To see migration geographically – to have a visual picture of movements from one land to the other – suddenly everything is put into context. It's visual language. You can easily say: 'He went from one land to the other.' You can write that. But to draw it is to orientate people.

The figure of Abraham is present behind this entire book. You can read the Bible and think: 'How wonderful that he travelled.' But it's very different to see it. When you visualize how far Abraham travelled, it takes the story to another dimension.

Preaching and painting

I am a Methodist local preacher. A freelance preacher, so to speak. It's a tradition that dates to the beginning of Methodism, in the 18th century. Once a quarter, I preach in Reading and Basingstoke, where my parents live, and sometimes in Cornwall. Primarily, I lead the monthly Taizé service at Wesley's Chapel in London. It was built by John Wesley, the founder of the Methodist movement, and opened in 1778. We still have the original pulpit.

The first time I preached from that pulpit was one of the most terrifying experiences of my life. The pulpit is so high, you walk up a spiral staircase to reach it. But it's an amazing presence up there; you can feel the heritage of the whole place. You get so much energy back from the congregation. And you think: *John Wesley was here.*

Wesley would have liked maps; he certainly would have needed them. He travelled 250,000 miles over the course of his lifetime. A few years ago, I made a map of Wesley's travels. I learned so much in the process of doing it. He exercised every day, on a strange saddle inside his house. He travelled on horseback, and then went by stagecoach when he got older. When you think that he died at the age of 89, and considering the state of the roads back then, it's extraordinary.

Mapping Wesley's journeys shaped my understanding of Christian theology. The research opened doors. When you begin to learn one new thing, you discover more alongside it. By doing the map, I learned about Wesley's theology as well. He left behind his sermons, which he preached over and over again – sermons against slavery, and other incredible topics.

As a preacher myself, I work in pictures first and words second. I was taught by the Revd Dr Leslie Griffiths, the minister of Wesley's Chapel for 21 years. He taught me to preach first from experience, and to have at least three illustrations in my sermon. He taught me to tell stories visually, with words. So, painting with words is what I do in preaching.

There is incredible similarity between illustrating and preaching. It's exactly the same concept. You sketch out a picture. You fill it in. You colour it. Then you put that drawing on the wall for people to find out what they believe. Each person will get something different out of that painting. People always see art differently. I struggle when I see people going around galleries, listening to only one person's point of view. The whole point of art is to see it through your own eyes. You could look at one of my maps and see something – perhaps a little detail – completely differently to me.

All I'm doing with a sermon is illustrating, with words, a painting that I hope will help people. The last thing I ever want to do is to make it a lesson. I know that people can turn off when listening to a sermon. They will remember the first three minutes and the last three minutes. My challenge is this: I want them to hear three minutes here, three minutes there, three minutes there – not necessarily the whole lot. I want people to touch and to be touched by my sermon – even just an element of it, or a colour of it, or a shape. Then preaching becomes mutual.

Maps and community

Recently, I was commissioned by the family of a Holocaust survivor to make a map of her life journey. Her son contacted me out of the blue, from California, and said, 'We want to have a special map of her life.'

At first, I thought: *I don't know – this sounds really hard.* How am I going to explain the story of her journey from her little village in Poland, to Auschwitz, and then from Auschwitz to New York, and then to California? How could I explain that in one picture? How would it work geographically? What projection would I need?

Then I thought of Saul Steinberg, an illustrator from the 1950s. He did an incredible map for *The New Yorker* magazine. It was a one-point perspective of a street in New York, but continuing on, over the Atlantic. I took that idea and thought: *We're going to bring this to where this woman is ending her journey of migration.* So I started the map by looking from Los Angeles beyond. In addition to the little village in Poland, and Auschwitz, I drew the boat coming from Germany after she was liberated from the camp, and then the boat to New York. This was the journey of her life.

Not long after I finished this commission, I was invited to lead a workshop at a conference with the theme, 'Moving Stories'. I brought a poster of this woman's life map, and I showed it to the participants. I asked them to talk to the person sitting next to them – to find out about their life story, their own journey. Then I said, 'I want you to draw a life map of your neighbour's story.' At first, they were frightened. I could see the terror in their eyes. The participants at this workshop were strangers to each other. But they did it. They interviewed the person sitting next to them, learned about their life, and then tried to tell the story in pictures.

The saddest thing I heard during that session was a story shared by many black participants, who came to England from the Caribbean or from Africa, and who tried to go to church here. Many of them were turned away. Their story was of racism and, by talking about it, we were all part of that story on that day.

This exercise brought people together. It created community. Pictures can break down barriers. To draw somebody's life map, you have to find out about them, to find a language. To draw a story of someone's migration – their journey, and yours, both of you coming from different places in the world and being here, together, at that present moment – this is community.

Visual theology

I once preached a sermon, based on one by Martin Luther King, Jr., about having a three-dimensional life. We can go through life in a two-dimensional way, pretending everything is fine. But it's only when we have darkness and shadow that our lives become fuller. I've never liked the idea of loving the suffering Christ on the cross. But darkness – not suffering – is needed to shape people and to make them who they are. It is how we get through the darkness – how we live it – that makes our lives three-dimensional.

All of my pictures are three-dimensional. As soon as I put shadows in – as soon as I do tones and darkness, as soon as I look at the light of a drawing – it becomes something else. The picture comes up and out of the page. It's visual theology.

For this book, I illustrated two maps. When readers look at these maps, I want their theology to come alive.

Abraham's Journeys

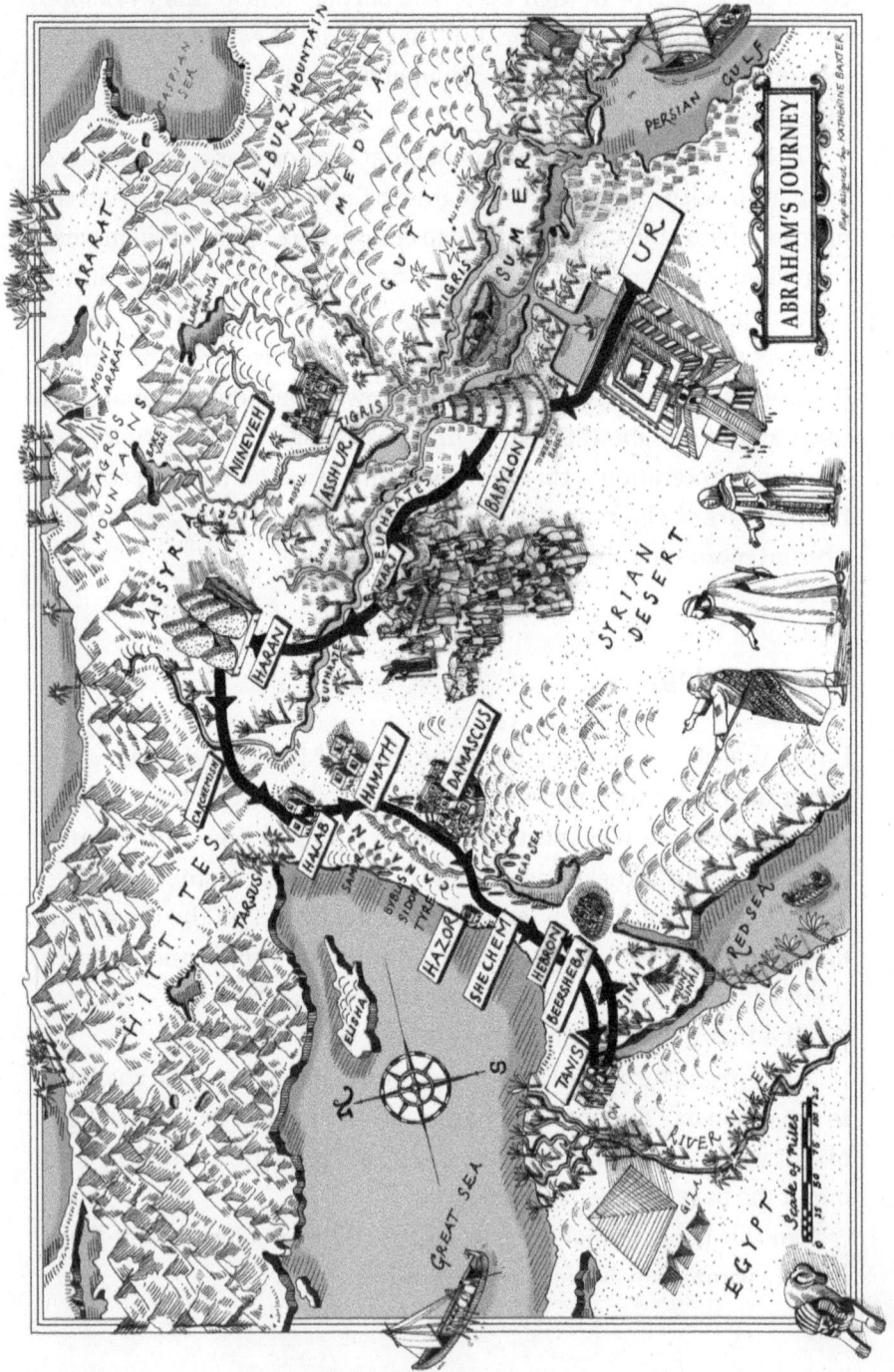

Holy Lands

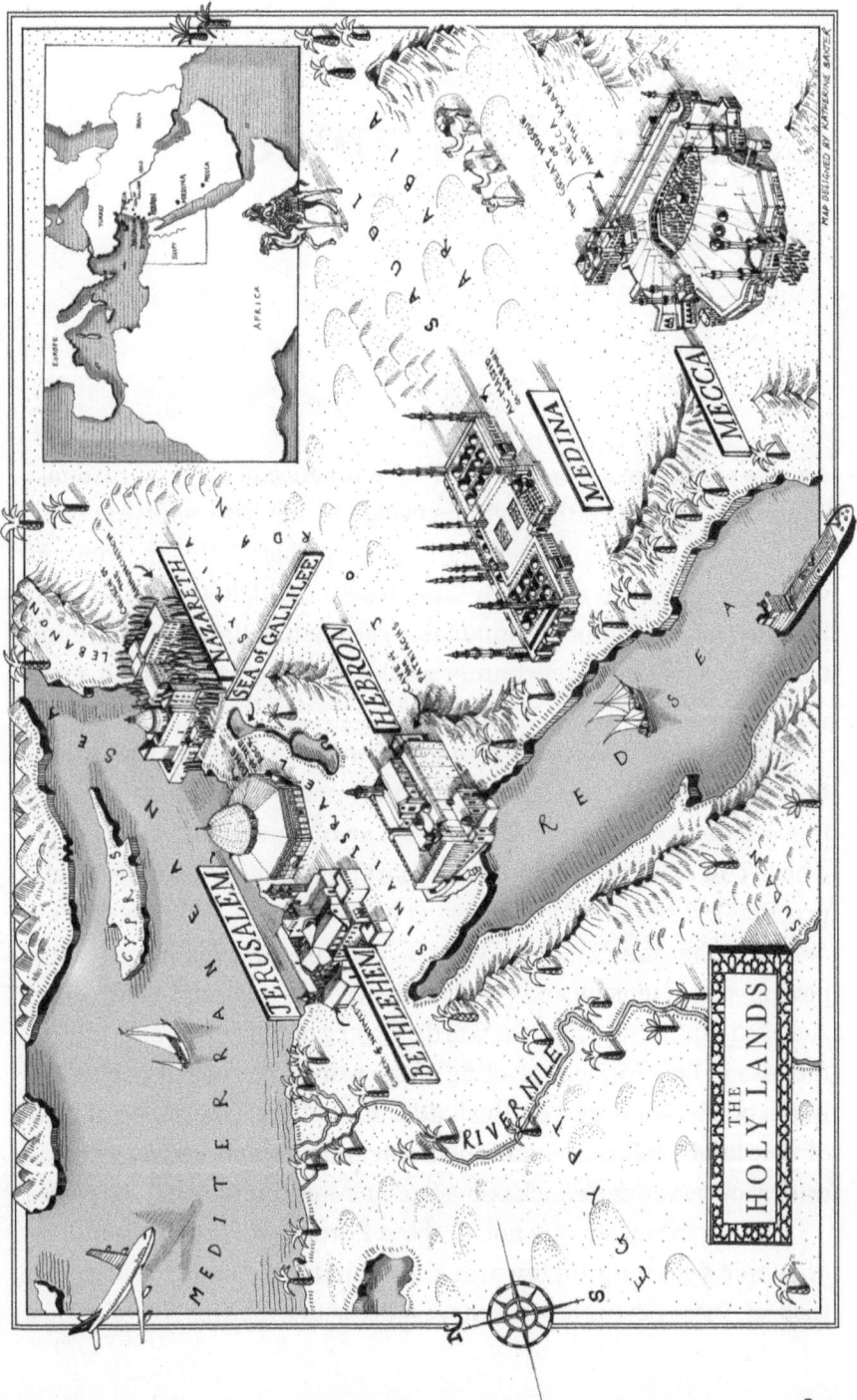

CHAPTER 9

Call and Response

Alison Phipps and Tawona Sitholé

The six poems that follow are part of a practice of call and response which has developed through the collaboration between two poets – one from the global north and one from the global south – meeting and working together in and from Glasgow, Scotland. Both are migrants, but the intersections of languages, race, educational background, tradition, spirituality, encounter and experience have shaped a new practice of collaboration.

Recently, with encouragement from the Arts and Humanities Research Council, they have been experimenting with forms of writing and the spoken word. The project involves working with people who are in exile and seeking sanctuary; it engages Alison in 'poetic practice-led research' and Tawona as playwright and poet-in-residence. Rather than being co-written, each poem holds integrity in a porous-souled tension and conversation, with a back-and-forth across social media, where certain words cluster or resonate, and finding fullness in face-to-face speaking of the words. A range of poems sits in the borderlands and on the battle-lines of the experience of exile, of new lands, migration and the many injuries and losses, joys and critical observations which come from new encounters in new places.

The migration story is not all about Europe, nor the tiny numbers of people who migrate towards the capital-rich lands to the north. Instead, these poems have been working with a multiplicity of stories and angles, of languages and ways of listening, ways of leaning in to hear the echoes of the past, the hopes for futures, the presence of joy and of celebration. Beneath these poems are experiences forged in Ghana, using words in *Shona*, which move to Glasgow and back again. There are words in mother languages, and languages given by journey and companionship; these evoke the work of balancing, when much is unstable in word and thought. Inside the poems is a sensed fear of hospitality, and of the wrenching which comes when land and language are lost.

The poems seek to amplify and fuse these spiritual experiences of language. Even when displaced, there is the possibility of finding a transcendent point which might hold people anew – fragile as this may be, and needing tenderness and care.

Kufemerwa

The breeze
Always on time, even
in
late summer sunshine.

In.
Out.

Each
a bracket in
'the ancient
struggle of
breath against
death'.

Is this why the
Maaori sing back
with a karakia?

Kufemerwa

He calls it.

He
calls.

[...]

Calls
it.

His explanation
as ancient
as the beating
of my heart.

The call, resonating
through the chambers,
the blood paths
of the beat.

The breeze.
Always welcome.
late summer
sunshine.

In.

[...]

Out.

(Alison)

breezily

they spoke of a time

when time spoke
the old song started with

kufemerwa

and all echoed

the cry

of the hunter

of the warrior

of the outcast

of the unheard-of

in the open space

where odd odds meet

where all recognize

the oneness

of feather and fur

skin and hide

tooth and tusk

heart and horn

human and nature

in the open space

where fight fights fit

where all abide by

the oneness

of breath and breeze

they spoke of a time

when

they spoke of a time

the old song started with

kufemerwa

(Tawona)

Gifts are in the feet

You say 'gifts are in the feet.'

It is war time.

So shall I walk away
shall I flee to the hills
cross the seas
ford the rivers in spate?

If I wear out my shoes
will the ache fade?
Will the longing recede?
Will I stand at last
somewhere on the heart's
edge
and sing
again.

of love?

I say gifts are in the tears
I say that salt and water
show what needs
to flow.
I say stay
with the river on your face,
feet on the battle ground
gifts come
from the grieving earth
watered with the
longing in my eyes.

(Alison)

zhira

endeavour is the ringer

of bells of gathering

endeavour too the bringer

of fires of separation

and yet endeavour

must not fear and hide

must not subside

for it is in the feet

that chance is churned

it is by the feet

that path is ground

the battle is on going

the battle is ongoing

people not places

have to do the

turning and returning

the earth only moves

to please the elements

the earth only responds

to the tease of ancients

so legs have to fold

knees have to bend

hearts have to reach

even if misplaced

the idiom

will still be profound

(Tawona)

Seeds of thought – (for the first time)

There was a moment
inside the
wrap of words when
I swore I would never
speak again, for
to do so
would be to
break enchantment

(Alison)

elasticity

the power of hesitation

to prolong the moment

before headfirst hurries

to

fulfil an unkempt emptiness

but to be thoughtfully still

the power of pause

to provide the prospect

of introspect

a message

only as good as it's received

silence as unharmed

uttered as uncharmed

the quiet warrior

shoots from the chest
what the heart can do in a beat
can trouble a whole song.

(Tawona)

CHAPTER 10

Poetry

Yvonne Green

That I May Know You

Let me visit your house
and eat something
of what is on your table
hear you and know
some of your language

Fear those of our
differences which I
am aware of, walk
barefoot, listening
for the steadiness
of breath

Reprinted from The Assay (2010, Sheffield: Smith/Doorstop Books)

We Speak English Now

and gratefully. There's been time to read
and work and break bread together,
to translate ourselves, give ourselves strength
for what comes next. Some of us have disappeared
where we best match. Others remain distinct.
Our minds are peppered with our culture
our children's minds with what they've met.
Can new life be complete without old stories,
are there different ways to live?

Reprinted from The Assay (2010, Sheffield: Smith/Doorstop Books)

Avsonia

You know about coming from a country
that doesn't exist. About the belief
that if you were there it would.

That your grandparents and theirs held on,
afraid to shed blood, being afraid
of the blood they'd seen.

You know about coming from a country
which uses language to change the way you think,
to disenfranchise, or teach you to disenfranchise.

Which takes you into its schools, and gives you
every inch of the world that can be pasted
in a book but leaves your family out of things.

You don't want to be taught what a Jew is,
or what Israel can and can't be,
or what a Moslem is, needs, and how to respect her.

You speak her languages, eat her food, were her neighbour,
know how neighbours behave, and their husbands,
sons, fathers, brothers, uncles, and all their forebears.

Reprinted from Honoured (2010, Sheffield: Smith/Doorstop Books)

Jews

(In memory of Czesław Miłosz)

We're neither poems for you to fetishize
nor emblems of the murdered of the twentieth century,
we don't hold all possibilities in our Talmudic minds
live burdened with the grief you want us to.
We're not the monsters of the Middle East,
the devils of the diaspora, nor do we know
the selves we recognize in one another.
We're in danger in your midst
and where you don't know us,
a barometer of your pasts and futures
that you never consult,
and yet we ourselves live
by the tremble of mercury
which we always ask ourselves to shape,
for which we're quoted against ourselves.
There's no monopoly of suffering
what did the first victims know
whose parents sent them with wobbly legs,
gaped mouths, vacant grins, rage, the evidence
of the trial they were to heart, hands, purse;
yes, look I'm a Jew and I've said purse,
judge me if you want; the first victims
were piped away like Hamlyn's children,
only before the rats and other vermin.

Reprinted from Honoured (2010, Sheffield: Smith/Doorstop Books)

PART 2

Sacred Texts

CHAPTER 11

Scriptural Reasoning

Rachel Godfrey

It's Tuesday evening in a large London mosque. There are approximately 80 people, half from the Scriptural Reasoning community and half from the mosque. We've just finished a session on 'Jesus, Isa and the Jewish Messiah' – not a topic I was particularly keen to run, an instinct borne out by what followed. I had agreed to it at the request of my young, enthusiastic contact from the mosque, who had visions of discovering hidden commonalities between Muslims and Christians. ('They don't realize Jesus is our prophet too!') The session had gone well. All three panellists were scholarly yet engaging, and the small group discussion afterwards went without a hitch.

Then, during the Questions and Comments section, an elderly Muslim lady stands up. 'But didn't the Jews kill Jesus?' A wave of discomfort spreads around the room.

'No, if you look at the involvement of the Romans in the text...' one person replies. 'Jesus himself was Jewish anyway...' says another.

Undeterred, the Muslim lady presses on: 'But it says it *here*, and that's what I was taught.'

A Church of England vicar, one of my regular panellists: 'From a historical perspective, it makes a lot more sense to place responsibility with the Romans. They had the power to crucify those they saw as criminals and a vested interest in punishing the rebellious Jews in Judea at the time, one of whom was Jesus.'

A young, American evangelist: 'And what about "His blood be on us and on our children?" (Matthew 27:25). The Jews said that; it's here in the gospel.'

I respond: 'As a Jew, I reject the idea that anyone can speak on behalf of all other Jews. There is no "The Jews."' I'm struggling to say: *It's not my book and shouldn't be my problem.* As a 21st-century Jew, I can conveniently ignore the difficulties in the text.

A Catholic nun, another regular speaker, joins in the discussion, 'The Church issued *Nostra aetate* in 1965. We don't accept that Jesus's death was the fault of the Jews anymore.'

The young evangelical man retorts, 'That's not my church.'

At this point, I decide to wrap up the session. All sorts of emotions are flying around the room, and I don't want the session to get out of control. As I'm packing up, my contact from the mosque comes up to me: 'Wow. That was a bit mad. Is it always like that?'

'No', I say, 'It's actually never been quite like that before.'

But we do go to places most interfaith dialogue does not. There is more potential for conflict, and sometimes I feel I'm on the verge of pulling people back from the brink. Yet we get to grips with real differences in the way people live now. At its heart, Scriptural Reasoning is conflict resolution mediated through sacred text.

Background

The term 'Scriptural Reasoning' was coined in the 1990s by Peter Ochs (2012), a Judaic Studies professor at the University of Virginia. Its primary influence is the traditional modes of text study that form part of the Jewish, Christian and Muslim faiths. These modes include the sacred texts themselves and also the chains of commentary which have been preserved as part of each religion's textual legacy (for example, the Talmud, Maimonides, Rashi, etc., in Judaism, and the Ahadith in Islam). Another key influence is the study of these religious texts in modern universities, across academic disciplines such as history, philosophy and literature. Finally, we have the influence of Textual

Reasoning, an academic precursor to Scriptural Reasoning. This practice, which dates to the 1980s, involves in-depth text study (in groups of 6–30 people) of just one faith's holy writings.

Since then, Scriptural Reasoning has developed beyond the confines of the university. A key principle is the acceptance that multiple readings of a text can simultaneously be true for different people. The three largest Abrahamic faiths all have traditions of text study, but these are by their nature subjective and assume the student's acceptance of dogma and religious practice; they exist within that faith's outlook and are not available to those outside that tradition. In contrast, the academic study of religion is open to people of all backgrounds, but it has often taken the approach of contrasting 'comparative religions' with Christianity. More recently, it has adopted a secular, liberal world view where the scholar analyzes sacred text for its veracity or examines faith communities through the lens of sociology. Biblical criticism is a widespread example of this approach.

The format of Scriptural Reasoning is simple: choose a theme; find a representative speaker from each faith (usually, although not always, the Abrahamic faiths) to present a relevant excerpt from their scriptural tradition; and discuss perspectives in small, mixed-faith groups. The ground rules are also straightforward: no proselytizing; don't speak on behalf of your entire faith community; be honest but show respect and sensitivity; and understand that these texts are special to the attending participants. The results are often complex and nuanced, centred around the readers rather than around an analysis of the text's origins. The process brings out multiple perspectives. These can be understood as 'true' in their own way and accepted as such by the multi-faith community engaged in Scriptural Reasoning.

Since the Enlightenment, the common approach towards interfaith dialogue has been to suppress and gloss over religious differences – to focus instead on commonality, or to reach a joint understanding of religious texts which elides differences of belief that underpin the different readers' perspectives. Although it is true that many stories and beliefs are shared by people of the Abrahamic faiths, important differences persist in both key details and the meanings attributed to those narratives.

The focus in Scriptural Reasoning is on *interpretive hospitality* (Ochs and Johnston 2009, p.5). There are few opportunities in modern society where you can look closely at religious texts from another religion, in the presence of members of that religious community, and where you can ask questions and share your perspective without expectation that you will join their faith. Many interfaith projects suffer from a tendency to make participants feel as if they must find the 'right thing to say' in order to show appropriate respect, and for members of the faith under discussion to present their views as canonical. Neither approach is helpful.

Scriptural Reasoning is not without its critics. Theologian Adrian Thatcher (2008, pp.193–194) believes that Scriptural Reasoning can encourage participants to elide differences in the approach their respective traditions take to textual interpretation. Gustafson (2004, pp.37–43) criticizes it from the perspective of 'Modernist Reasoning' – the idea that texts should be examined for their veracity in an objective manner. Certain Muslim and Jewish groups feel that Scriptural Reasoning brings participants into the danger zone of considering heretical ideas about their faith's own texts. However, in 2017, London Central Mosque issued a *fatwa* (a ruling on a point of Islamic law), allowing Scriptural Reasoning with certain stipulations.[1] For example, Muslims should share an equal role in the leadership of the Scriptural Reasoning group; the Quran should be presented in Arabic even if translations are present; and material that includes Quranic verses should not be left on the floor but disposed of appropriately. (These last two concerns are also shared by observant Jews).

As for Christian theological criticisms, as a Scriptural Reasoning coordinator I have not found it to be the case that differences are glossed over, *provided the atmosphere is such that disagreement is welcomed and seen as a sign of strength.* Once participants understand

---

1   The full text is available in English at scripturalreasoning.org.uk/fatwa_ english.pdf.

that they are not being asked to come to an agreement or that it would be more polite to do so, they are very happy to disagree in a convivial manner. This resonates with the Jewish practice of *chevruta* (paired text study), in which challenge and debate are encouraged as a means of creating generative, textually grounded interpretive discussions of classical Jewish texts (Kent 2010). Although I agree somewhat with Gustafson's criticism, described above, I believe the solution is to practise Scriptural Reasoning alongside other, diverse methods of engagement and interpretation.

Holding a session

Marylebone Scriptural Reasoning is based in Central West London and our participants primarily come from the various places of worship that we use as venues. Their composition is influenced by the organization's location in a large, cosmopolitan city with substantial numbers of Muslim and Jewish residents. One of the difficulties inherent in organizing interfaith activities is creating a balance between the numbers of attendees of each faith. In a British context, it is inevitably easier to find Christian participants (particularly from the Church of England) than any other religious background. We make a concerted effort to engage a variety of Jewish and Muslim communities. Some Muslims and Orthodox Jews are uncomfortable with the way Scriptural Reasoning demands acceptance of a spectrum of religious opinions, so at times this balance can be difficult to achieve.

In 2013, Marylebone Scriptural Reasoning was established as part of the Interfaith and Social Action department at West London Synagogue, one of the country's oldest synagogues and the flagship synagogue of the Reform Movement in the UK. The synagogue was founded in 1840 by members of both the Ashkenazi (Eastern European) and Sephardi (Spanish and Portuguese) Jewish communities when they moved from the East End to West London. One of the synagogue's distinctive features is its liturgical and architectural influences from

English Christianity. For example, services involve a choir and organ, members sit in pews, 'wardens' wear top hats and rabbis wear clerical robes – something not found elsewhere in Judaism. This stems from the desire of the founding generation to blend into the upper-class English society of the time.

Integration into wider society remains a core value of West London Synagogue. Today, the synagogue devotes considerable funding and resources to social action and interfaith projects, including a success-ful winter night shelter and a drop-in service for asylum seekers. An annual *Iftar* (the meal eaten by Muslims after sunset during Ramadan) is held on the same night as the *Tikkun Leil Shavuot* celebration (a tradition for the Jewish festival of *Shavuot*, which involves all-night learning). Marylebone Scriptural Reasoning is part of this vibrant set of programmes.[2]

The themes of the Scriptural Reasoning sessions range from con-ventional interfaith dialogue standbys (forgiveness, sin, compassion) to those closely tied to religious law (food laws, tattooing, clothing and modesty), to those related to current festivals (sacrifice around Eid al-Adha, atonement just before Yom Kippur), to the occasional off-the-wall choice (masculinity, morally challenging texts). Sometimes certain themes work well for two of the faiths and are less relevant for the third, such as the session on 'Jesus, Isa and the Jewish Messiah', or food laws, which are less relevant to Christianity.

Much is lost in translation. For example, the English word 'modes-ty' is closely related to the concept of avoiding excess, as is the Hebrew term *Tzniut*, related to *Tzena* ('austerity'). The Islamic word for mod-esty, *Haya'*, primarily means 'shyness'. Another example: Hebrew has three words for sin, *Chet*, *Avon* and *Pesha*. *Chet* is unintentional, *Avon* is deliberate and done for the benefit of the sinner, and *Pesha* is done specifically to anger God. *Chet* comes from the verb *Hechti'* which means 'to miss the mark'. Only *Avon* really covers the same ground as the English term. When I organized a Scriptural Reasoning session on

---

2   For further information: www.jewishgen.org/jcr-uk/london/wls.

this topic, I had to title it 'Sin' because our group's common language is English. In doing so, we lost much of the linguistic subtlety in the original texts.

The speakers, usually a mixture of faith leaders and learned community members, select a short excerpt from their religious text which relates to the theme. They read it aloud in translation, reciting it as is customary in worship. They then speak briefly on the personal meaning the text has for them and how they wish to tie it to the session's theme. The texts are compiled in a pack, and each participant receives a copy, both in the original languages and in a suitable translation. This is more ideologically laden than it might sound. Translations into English can differ radically from each other, and religious use of the texts often differentiates between the plain meaning – in Judaism the *Pshat*, and in Islam the *I'bara*, at least according to the Caliph Ja'far al-Sadiq (Corbin 2001, p.5) – and various other forms of interpretation which are more allegorical, comparative or mystical. Historical ways of reading and understanding the text by faith communities are often reliant on these less accessible forms of interpretation.

After the panellists have finished speaking, they join the audience to form small, mixed-faith groups and discuss the texts together. Again, guidelines apply: no proselytizing; be honest but phrase your views respectfully; do not speak for all members of your faith. The last guideline is trickier than it seems. When you have a mixture of scholars, faith leaders and ordinary believers, there is a tendency to look to the former for authoritative positions on text interpretation. In fact, although the scholars will usually have a broader textual knowledge which can be useful for discussion, the opinion of each participant in Scriptural Reasoning is equally valid. This is a cornerstone of the practice. Through this process, the small groups generate many questions and new angles through which to view the texts.

To close the session, each group can nominate a spokesperson to summarize its discussion, and to direct a couple of brief questions to the panel. Most questions will either be ironed out during the group discussion by those more familiar with that scripture, or simply have no straightforward answer. However, there are sometimes queries which can be answered by the speakers, drawing on their background knowledge in a way that enhances the study sessions.

Sometimes we hold the Muslim evening prayer (*Isha*) and the early evening prayer (*Maghrib*) before the session or during the break. Including time and space for prayer makes it easier for Muslims to attend. We have also organized *Ma'ariv*, the Jewish evening prayer.

Scripture and migration

London is home to many diasporas and migrant communities, and this diversity is reflected in our Scriptural Reasoning participants. Although approximately two-thirds of the Christians who regularly attend our sessions are from a white British background (mostly from the Church of England, Quaker or Methodist communities), there are significant numbers of black Christians too, mostly Afro-Caribbean and often from Gospel or Seventh Day Adventist churches. There is a different tenor to these branches of Christianity: they are more aspirational, more emotional and have a sense of urgency that the world is not what it could and should be.

Our Muslim attendees come from a variety of backgrounds. Mosques are often more ethnically diverse than churches or synagogues, due to the larger number of worshippers. Many of our Muslim participants come from London Central Mosque in Regent's Park, a large Saudi-run mosque with a main prayer hall for 5000 people. The mosque was established in 1944, following an exchange of land in London and Cairo, for a mosque and an Anglican cathedral, respectively. Other participants come from East London Mosque in Whitechapel, established to serve the religious needs of the local Bangladeshi community and still very much a community hub. We are also involved with the Al-Manaar Centre in Ladbroke Grove, which played a pivotal role in providing support to survivors of the fatal Grenfell Tower fire in June 2017.

Jewish attendees usually have a refugee background, although most are not first-generation immigrants. At Scriptural Reasoning events, it is interesting to see the interplay between Jewish participants and members of the other faiths. Initially, Jews often appear 'white', and there is an expectation that they will fit well with white Christians (see Cannon 2014; Hershkovitz 2019). However, the way Judaism is structured shares much more with Islam than with Christianity. Once participants discover this, they find far more common ground than expected. The global Jewish community is similar to a large extended family, an idea also present in Islam with its *Umma*, although the greater number of Muslims and the huge ethnic diversity of Muslim communities of London make this concept difficult to realize fully at times.

Since becoming the Coordinator of Marylebone Scriptural Reasoning in 2014, I have come to appreciate its power and elegance as a vehicle for exploring one's own religious texts, learning about those of other religions, and forming close bonds with members of other faiths. I sincerely hope that our community continues to grow and develop, and that Scriptural Reasoning is adopted widely in schools, universities, prisons, grassroots community organizations and places of worship. It has an incredible amount to offer.

Scriptural Reasoning is a form of migration. Everybody who participates is on a journey of discovery through the process of grappling with sacred texts. Faith communities are often close-knit groups with their own norms and values, which provides a necessary source of support but can also encourage insularity and conformity. Taking inspiration from these faiths, bringing that inspiration into the open, and exposing them to the critical gaze of people from outside the community is sometimes uncomfortable. Yet this journey can lead to profound growth and bring fresh insight into scriptural texts.

References

Cannon, B. (2014) 'Jews, white privilege and the fight against racism in America.' *Haaretz*. Accessed on 30/11/18 at www.haaretz.com/jewish/jews-white-privilege-and-racism-in-u-s-1.5340307.

Corbin, H. (2001) *The History of Islamic Philosophy.* London: Routledge.

Gustafson, J.F. (2004) *An Examined Faith: The Grace of Self-Doubt.* Minneapolis, MN: Fortress Press.

Hershkovitz, H. (2019) 'Ashkenazi Jews are not white.' *Temple Beth Shalom.* Accessed on 30/11/18 at www.tbshamden.com.

Kent, O. (2010) 'A theory of Havruta learning.' *Journal of Jewish Education,* 76, 3, 215–245.

Ochs, P. (2012) 'An introduction to Scriptural Reasoning: From practice to theory.' *Journal of Renmin University of China,* 26, 5, 16–22.

Ochs, P. and Johnson, W.S. (2009) 'Introduction' In P. Ochs, P. and W.S. Johnson (eds) *Crisis, Call, and Leadership in the Abrahamic Traditions* (pp.1–11). New York, NY: Palgrave Macmillan.

Thatcher, A. (2008) *The Savage Text: The Use and Abuse of the Bible.* Oxford: Wiley-Blackwell.

CHAPTER 12

Translation and Re-Centring 'Ā'isha in the Hadith Canon

Sofia Rehman

Excavating the voice of 'Ā'isha bint Abu Bakr

When we think of forgotten voices, we imagine people lost to history. Seldom do we consider that the pursuit of discovering these voices will lead us to personalities well known to us, hidden in plain sight. My current research is a partial translation and critical study of a 14th-century classical Islamic text, *al-Ijāba li-Īrādi mā Istadraktahu 'Ā'isha 'Ala al-Ṣaḥābah – The Corrective: 'Ā'isha's Rectification of the Companions*. It was penned by the Muslim scholar Imām Badr al-Dīn al-Zarkashī (d.794/1392), and it has led me to exactly such a discovery: the voice of a prominent female in Muslim history: 'Ā'isha, hidden in plain sight.

The text comprises traditions in which 'Ā'isha bint Abu Bakr, wife of the Prophet Muhammad, corrects, refutes and corroborates narrations ascribed to the Prophet by primarily male companions. My research considers the value, significance and challenges this text presents for the existing hadith[1] canon. By considering the voice of 'Ā'isha, the highest female authority in the history of Sunni Islam, it explores opening the canon in order to re-centre female voices. Her voice echoes into related Islamic sciences such as Qur'anic exegesis,[2] Islamic law and legal theory, which would indubitably have an impact on Muslim daily practice.

When I began researching methodologies for the translation of Islamic texts, I found a great body of material dealing with the topic of translating the Qur'an, but very little on translation methodologies which focus on the hadith. This is despite the hadith's sacred status in Islam as a foundational basis for Muslim belief and praxis, second only to the Qur'an. The hadith are a core resource for Muslims seeking guidance on how to live faithfully, but they are distinguished from the Qur'an for not being the verbatim words of God, for requiring investigation into their authenticity, and for their unique and distinct trajectory and formation in Islamic history. As such, there are different considerations when translating hadith.

Al-Ijāba itself is interesting – not least because in manuscript form, it was almost entirely lost, despite the stature of its author and the preservation of many of his other works. In 1939, Sa'eed al-Afghani published a critical edition of the text, having found a copy in Damascus, Syria. In 1999, Dr M.B. Arül worked on another manuscript he discovered in Istanbul. In the critical edition he published, Arül (2004) described how the text was neglected and almost lost; only two manuscripts are known to have survived since al-Zarkashī first penned it six centuries ago, neither of which was catalogued. Arul stumbled

---

1   Hadith are narrative accounts of the speech and actions of the Prophet Muhammad. They have been transmitted from one generation of Muslims to the next in usually unbroken chains of narrators who are considered reliable by a scholarly standard. They have been examined against set criteria to determine their authenticity, and recorded in a number of compilations. The most venerated is the canonical six, or *Ṣaḥāḥ Sittah*, deemed widely in Sunni Islam to be the most authoritative statements of Prophetic tradition.

2   *Tafsīr* in Arabic, that branch of Islamic sciences concerned with interpreting the Qur'an.

across the manuscript in an obscure Istanbul library by pure chance. Despite producing two critical editions, neither publication inspired further scholarship in Western academia or in traditional Muslim research. My inclination is that this is due to the nature of the text: it is about 'Ā'isha refuting male companions whose opinions have, in the long run, been preferred over hers as the most authoritative statements on Prophetic practice.

The text has genuine potential to be radical, thus warranting a translation and wider audience. It contributes something new to the study of Islam within academia, allowing for critical examination of sacred texts without an overly sceptical position. For Muslims, it also provides another way of imagining Islam. By establishing the scholarly dissent and the validity of that dissent by 'Ā'isha, a new reading of the history of Islamic scholarship can be considered. This opens new ways of conceiving the future of Islam – one in which there is a female voice at the very core of the production of knowledge; a future in which the female voice, in the process of interpreting Islam, is normalized.

If 'Ā'isha's voice can be obscured, how many other female voices have not reached us?

Descending the Ivory Tower: Taking research into the community

Despite dedicating over a decade to the study of Islam through traditional centres of study and teachers, and being thoroughly enriched by them, it was only when I returned to academia as a Master's student that I gained access to the wealth of scholarship written by contemporary Muslim women. Never before had I found the daily struggles, questions, and lived experiences of Muslim women centred in readings of the Qur'an or Islamic legal theory like I was now finding in the works of amina wadud, Kecia Ali, Asma Barlas, Aziza al-Hibri and many others. It was exhilarating to find myself in the literature, to have my questions legitimized, to find my way of living considered the norm, rather than the exception to the standard of male life.

In the first year of my doctoral research, I was thrilled to be award-ed funding to run a series of workshops in Bradford, working with the Muslim Women's Council. We held three workshops, each dedicated to the life of a female member of the Prophet Muhammad's family. It was a great success. Approximately 60 Muslim women attended each workshop, from 10-year-old youngsters to grandmothers.

In the session dedicated to 'Ā'isha, I gave a brief introduction to her life, the book *al-Ijāba* and its author. Then I presented three well-known hadiths that I was confident most of the participants would be familiar with. All three are problematic in that they can be (and often have been) misconstrued as misogynistic. I divided the participants into groups and asked each to consider the following:

- How familiar were they with the hadith?
- How would they interpret it?
- How might they have applied it in their life?
- How, in their experience, have these hadith been framed?
- How they would reconcile them, given their potentially prob-lematic content?

The first statement was attributed to the Prophet: 'Bad luck is found in three things: your abode, your mount (i.e., your transport) and your women.' This is a widely circulated hadith that has been classified as 'sound' – that is, authentic – and recorded in the canonical hadith collections.

The responses were fascinating. The women attempted to rec-oncile what was ostensibly a misogynistic statement with what they knew of the equitable and generous manner in which the Prophet dealt with his female followers. After the participants discussed how best to make sense of the statement, I introduced 'Ā'isha's version of the same hadith, which provided the context we needed to understand it. Her statement has also been classified as sound, but unfortunately it was not recorded in the canon. In 'Ā'isha's version, we learn that the male companion (Abu Huraira, who reported the original hadith) had not heard the Prophet's statement in its entirety. He thus provided an incomplete report. The complete statement was: 'There *had been people who would say* that bad luck is found in these three things, and that not only were they incorrect in that belief but cursed for holding it.' Excluding the voice of ʿĀ'isha therefore leaves us with a very different reading, with potentially damaging results.

In the workshop, I asserted the importance of contextualizing hadith statements and the value of historicizing them – that is, understanding them within their historical circumstances and place. We repeated the exercise with two more hadith, and it was delightful to see the gradual change in the women's attitudes. There was an unmistakable shift from hesitance to engagement, to intrigue and excitement. Clichéd as it may sound, there was a palpable feeling of empowerment in the room.

I imagine there might be readers who may see this as a feminist success: women empowering women, through the example of historical women. However, had I used the word 'feminism', the workshop participants may have completely disengaged. 'Feminism' can be an antagonizing concept within the Muslim community. This is understandable when you consider feminism's historical entanglements with colonial projects, imperialism and neo-liberal 'white feminism', which dominates contemporary mainstream feminism. At best, 'white feminism' remains silent on Muslim women's experiences, and at worst it has been complicit in the particular experiences of misogyny that Muslim women face.

This sort of ambivalence is not unique to Muslim women. For marginalized women – be they women of colour, disabled women, or so on – many mainstream feminist spaces remain hostile. This is why 'intersectional feminism'[3] is important, yet I chose not to steer the conversation in this direction. It was more important to focus on

---

3   Intersectionality describes the various systems of oppression (racism, sexism, ableism, etc.) that may converge or *intersect* in the experience of an individual. Intersectional feminism strives to recognize the multi-faceted ways in which women experience systems of discrimination and oppression, rather than awarding one dominant group monopoly in ways which often undermine marginalized women. (See Cho, Crenshaw and McCall 2013.)

what we, as Muslim women, were invested in: the Islamic tradition. My objective is not creating feminist affinities, but the formation of an empowered Muslim practice through excavating and mining our religious traditional heritage for the gender-just readings and understanding it offers. If a feminist consciousness is formed in the process, then that's a prodigious – and possibly even an inevitable – outcome. But it's not the primary goal.

I am grateful for the opportunity those workshops provided to the community and to myself. I received enthusiastic feedback; people asked for more. Since then I have set up an Islam and Feminism Critical Reading Group at the University of Leeds, in partnership with the Iqbal Centre. This group is open to both the community and academics, in order to bridge the gap between the two. But the excitement is not for Muslim women alone. The Muslim men around me are also excited about my work. In the current climate of institutionalized and mainstreamed Islamophobia, Muslim men and women seek to gain from any work that strengthens Muslim identity and that speaks to their concerns. While my work primarily focuses on the female voice and on stripping away patriarchal interpretations of the hadith literature, it also liberates Muslim men from the constraints of socially constructed gender roles.

New directions in migration

Twelve years after first receiving revelation, the Prophet Muhammad and the nascent community of believers embarked on a momentous exodus from Makkah to Medina, following years of persecution by the Makkan leadership. 'Ā'isha's father was the Prophet's companion during this migration. Her older sister is reported to have brought them provisions while they waited on the outskirts of Makkah to throw off the Quraysh, the people who were trying to hunt down the Prophet. This migration was so pivotal in the history of early Islam that in the year 638 – 17 years after this journey took place – the Islamic Calendar was inaugurated. It began retrospectively from the year in which the Prophet migrated to Medinah.

The verb 'to migrate' in Arabic is *hājarah*. In its various forms, it is mentioned in the Qur'an more than 20 times, usually flanked by the phrases 'those who believe' and 'to strive in God's path'. For example, in verse 20 of Chapter al-Tawbah of the Qur'an, God states:

الَّذِينَ آمَنُواْ وَهَاجَرُواْ وَجَاهَدُواْ فِي سَبِيلِ اللّهِ بِأَمْوَالِهِمْ وَأَنفُسِهِمْ أَعْظَمُ دَرَجَةً عِندَ اللّهِ وَأُوْلَئِكَ هُمُ الْفَائِزُونَ

Those who believe, migrate, and strive in the way of God with their wealth and selves, have the highest rank with God, they are the victors.

Ibn al-Qayyim, the famous 14th-century scholar, wrote a treatise called *al-Risālat al-Tabūkiyyah*, in which he discusses the migration of the heart. This is another definition of migration: the migration of the heart to God and his messenger, Muhammad; the movement of the heart, from worldly distractions and false promises to the delight to be found in turning to its Creator. It is about abandoning the self-serving nature of the ego, to ascend to the heart's service in love to the Divine. In this treatise, Ibn al-Qayyim expounds the ways in which the heart migrates to God by turning its hopes away from Creation and towards the Creator instead. This idea was important for my own research, because physical migration for the sake of God, by the believer, is only as useful as the heart's migration towards God.

Though the Prophet migrated primarily due to persecution, migration is not always possible, nor even desirable. Even the Prophet and the first community of believers remained in their hometown of Makkah for 12 years after revelation began. They sought to bring about change in their society and remained committed in their spiritual development. If Muslims are compelled to migrate every time they are persecuted, how will society be held to account for its bigotry? Why should Muslims remain in a perpetual state of dislocation, bearing the burden of the intolerance of others? And what good is physical migration if the heart, which is the home of the spirit, has not made its own, internal migration towards God?

My work aids Muslims, as individuals and as a community, in their spiritual migration towards God. Part of that is to turn away from patriarchal interpretations, which are ungodly and intervene in the understanding of the spirit of Islam. Any system that puts intermediaries between God and an individual, or that creates hierarchies based on anything other than good deeds (the merit of which is only known to God), is one that has strayed from the message of the Qur'an. My work seeks to reclaim Islam from patriarchal interpretations, and to aid Muslims seeking to submit fully, from the heart, to God alone.

Translation: The migration of words

The act of translation is much like the act of migration. There are words that easily transfer from one language to another, just as human beings migrate from one place to another. And there are words that simply cannot be translated; they force entry into a new linguistic domain, a new language, and take up their own position. In my research, I have run into words I cannot translate into English. I must retain them in their original Arabic and try to give my best explanation. Sometimes a single word requires an entire explanatory sentence or paragraph. The untranslatable words are much like those parts of ourselves that are at odds with the new places we inhabit. We carry them wherever we go.

One of the words which I have not translated is *muḥrim*. The word might be rendered as 'pilgrim' in English, but this does not encapsulate the full meaning of the Arabic. *Muḥrim* is about a specific spiritual, as well as physical, state. It is not enough that one has simply started on a religious journey. There are certain conditions that must be met according to Islamic jurisprudence, and there is a certain geographical and spiritual point at which one becomes a *muḥrim*. To remain faithful to the full implications of the word, I retained its Arabic form in my translation, and I included an explanatory note to deliver *muḥrim* to an English-speaking audience. Yet there is no safeguarding from distortions in pronunciation.

Some foreign words have become adopted into the translated language. A regular source of amusement for my friends and me is 'naan bread', which is as good as saying 'bread-bread', or 'Chai tea': 'tea-tea'. In English, it has become common to use these words, *naan* and *chai*, because these are the things that have survived migration and found an approval that has merited them recognition, even though in the process they have been comically distorted. Language replicates the experience of the transposed human in many ways.

Translation and migration – there are many parallels. One is about our physical movement, and the other is the movement of our language, our thought and our expression. What is language except the expression of the human being? When translations are done with distance and commitment to objectivity, keeping space between the translator and the text, it takes something away from the translation. Rather than enriching the translation, it deprives it. When I first took up the translation of *al-Ijāba*, I was committed to being an 'invisible' translator, to being as literal as possible. But the idea of 'invisibility' in translation is a flawed notion. When engaging with a text, the translator makes a series of subjective decisions. To deny these decisions is to be wilfully ignorant of their influence.

To remove or deny human expression in the translation process degrades the results. Likewise, with migration; when the human element is removed, such that the movement of some people from one place to another is dehumanized, the consequences are callous and, too often, colossal.

Conclusion

The Prophet is reported to have said: 'Be in this world as a traveller', for that is our reality. As time displaces us from generation to generation, we are met by new challenges. Just as the traveller would do well to set down their luggage to dispose of what is no longer useful and to acquire that which is more helpful for the new leg of their journey, so the faith community that finds itself in new contexts must reassess the religious provisions with which it is travelling. It must see which provisions continue to support our purpose on earth; to graciously let go of those that no longer serve us; and to explore new provisions that the eternal Word of God, and the guidance of the Prophet and his companions, can produce. New articulations of Islam, derived from sacred texts and guided by Qur'anic principles of justice and unity, need not be looked on with suspicion, but embraced with the knowledge that new times and places are yet to be traversed, and that the faith of Islam can travel those miles in a manner that is positive and purposeful.

The Muslim is instructed by God in the Qur'an, '...And take a provision (with you) for the journey, and the best provision is *taqwa*' (Chapter 2:197). *Taqwa* is to have God-consciousness in all that one does. It is to submit to the knowledge that as humans attempting to understand the wisdom, intentions, stories, and instructions of the Eternal, Living, One God, our interpretations will always be limited. As scholarly and rigorous as they may be, their limited nature means they will periodically need revisiting, with renewed commitment to re-interpreting. The process of re-reading sacred texts, in order to arrive at new conclusions and interpretations, is not betrayal of the tradition, but loyalty to it and, moreover, to God. It is a necessary stop in the journey of the wayfarer, migrating with their whole heart towards God.

References

Arül, M.B. (ed.) (2004) al-Ijāba li-Īrādi mā Istadrakathu 'Ā'isha 'ala al Ṣahāba.
Cho, S., Crenshaw, W. and McCall, L. (2013) 'Towards a field of intersectionality studies: Theory, application and praxis.' *Signs: Journal of Woman in Culture and Society*, 38(4) 785–810.

CHAPTER 13

Difference without Domination

Listening for Religious Attunement in Times of Polarization

Michael Nausner

I begin by reflecting on a conversation between two world citizens – the conductor Daniel Barenboim and the literary critic Edward W. Said. Barenboim and Said are unlikely partners: Said comes from a Christian Palestinian tradition and Barenboim from a Jewish Israeli background. But music unites them, and in 1999 they together founded the West–Eastern Divan Orchestra, made up of musicians from both Arab and Israeli territories. Through music, the orchestra has become a symbol for peaceful co-existence across difference. It also serves as a model for peaceful *religious* co-existence among the three largest Abrahamic faiths. Like a prism, this conversation between Barenboim and Said throws light on the relation between faith and migration, helping us to re-imagine it. I focus not so much on *what* representatives from the different faith traditions believe, but rather *how* they sing their songs (so to speak) and *how* they relate to the migratory identity of their own faith traditions.

Identity without singularity, difference without domination, participation without exclusion

Three aspects are significant to this conversation about migration and faith. First, a notion of identity as fluid. Second, the need to promote difference and at the same time to reject domination. Third, music as an experiential medium in which participation without exclusion becomes possible.

First, the question of *identity*. The conversation between Barenboim and Said begins with the provoking question: *Where do they feel at home?* Barenboim is happiest when he 'can be at peace with the idea of fluidity' (Barenboim and Said 2004, p.4). In a similar vein, Said reflects on identity as 'a set of currents, flowing currents, rather than a fixed place or a stable set of objects' (*ibid.*, p.5). As a Christian theologian, having myself lived in half a dozen countries, serving as minister, professor and researcher in various cultural contexts, this dynamic understanding of identity makes sense. Many people feel that migration threatens their identity, and that therefore 'the other' needs to be rejected. To perform music well, Said reflects, 'one has to accept the idea that one is putting one's own identity to the side in order to explore the "other"' (*ibid.*, p.12). Barenboim affirms this understanding: every human being needs to first achieve his/her own identity, 'then have the courage to let that identity go in order to find the way back. I think this is what music is about' (*ibid.*, p.47). I believe this applies to any real human encounter, but also to the act of reading and interpreting – not least interpreting Holy Scripture. The challenge is to become sensitive to the complexities of one's own identity, in order to imagine common belonging across difference.

Second, the question of *difference*. Said reflects that 'the basic human mission today' is to preserve 'difference without, at the same time, sinking into the desire to dominate' (*ibid.*, p.154). To me, this could also be applied to respectful and attentive interreligious relations. The issue is not only to tolerate, but to preserve differences to enrich each other, instead of competing with or eclipsing each other.[1] From a musical perspective, the practice of polyphony aids our understanding. Polyphony, meaning 'many sounds', depends on difference in melody, rhythm and expression for a full and beautiful sound to emerge. What would music sound like if there was not the continuous play between differences, if there wasn't an intentional but attentive insistence on one's own tonal identity? Domination would destroy the beauty of the polyphony, and so would homogeneity.

Third, the question of *participation*. The West–Eastern Divan Orchestra is an exercise of unlikely participation, shaped by the passing experience of music. While playing, the Palestinian musicians overcome their preconceptions about Israelis as oppressors, and the Israeli musicians unlearn their prejudice about Palestinians as terrorists. They just partake in the joy of music-making. But this participation is fleeting and fragile, because sound as such is passing and necessarily ends, becomes silence again (*ibid.*, p.29). In a similar way, the practice of Christian faith is always transient and only momentarily transformative. But its resistance to exclusive and divisive forces points toward an imagined way of co-existence. Its goal is to embody a way of participation that breaks through the constructed divisions of race, ethnicity, class – and religion, for that matter. Christian faith performs freedom in fragmentary ways, every time it is lived out: in communal singing, in social action and in its foundational liturgy. The celebration of the Eucharist has profound ethical and political implications (Nausner 2012), embodying a communal practice that cuts through social, economic and religious categories (cf. Luke 13:29).

---

1   In February 2019, Pope Francis signed a document together with Grand Imam Ahmed el-Tayeb, affirming religious difference as God given: 'The pluralism and the diversity of religions, colour, sex, race and language are willed by God in His wisdom, through which He created human beings. This divine wisdom is the source from which the right to freedom of belief and the freedom to be different derives.' *Human Fraternity for World Peace and Living Together*. Accessed on 07/02/19 at www.vaticannews.va/en/pope/news/2019-02/pope-francis-uae-declaration-with-al-azhar-grand-imam.html.

The Abrahamic faiths and migration

Music, of course, can be used in manipulative and destructive ways. The 5th-century Christian theologian Augustine cautioned his readers not to underestimate the damaging role that music can play in believers' lives. Today, we know of such damaging use of music in the context of propaganda for authoritarian regimes. So, I am *not* suggesting here a reconciling, let alone a redeeming, function of music. Equally, justified critique could be voiced against the metaphor of the orchestra as an institution for the socially, culturally and economically privileged,[2] and as a venue of hierarchical power relations. The critique against the bourgeois character of a classical orchestra is valid, which is why I do not want to privilege the classical orchestra over other forms of musical performance. Rather, I use it as an example of an intricate, mutual process of listening and communication.

The orchestra metaphor highlights the dynamic relation among different voices and tunes and the necessarily diverse interactions among people of faith. What is required is both difference and mutual listening; that is, identity and interaction with 'the other'. When Barenboim defines music as 'listening to the other', the same can be said for the life of faith. The media is full of polarizing depictions of Jews, Christians and Muslims. Discussions of whether they worship the same God never come to an end. It is especially under such heated conditions that a re-imagination of the interrelation of and interdependence between the Abrahamic faiths is called for. There is no mature religious identity without a genuine willingness to listen to the 'religiously other'.

Migration is 'a constant theme in the Abrahamic traditions. The biblical narrative is one of people on the move' (World Council of Churches 2018; see also Padilla and Phan 2014; Admirand 2014). In the three largest Abrahamic faith traditions, migration works as 'a trope of

---

2   I am grateful for a critical conversation about this issue with my colleagues Cheryl Kirk-Duggan, Jong Chun Park and Joerg Rieger at the Oxford Institute of Methodist Theological Studies in August 2018.

salvation' (Irvin 2014, pp.7–25). Exodus and exile are key contexts for Israel's deliverance (*ibid.*, p.11), and pilgrimage constitutes the backbone of much Christian and Muslim practice of faith (*ibid.*, pp.12–17). In the Hebrew Scriptures, God is depicted as a God who accompanies God's people into exile (Admirand 2014, p.677). In Islam, *hijra*, 'the notion of going into exile for the sake of God', is associated with the story of Hagar. Her fate is a precursor for the more central *hijra* in the Muslim tradition, when Mohammed fled from Mecca to Medina in 622 CE (*ibid.*, p.681). The three Abrahamic faiths are thus rooted in stories of migration as key sites for divine presence and guidance. Hospitality towards the stranger, therefore, must belong to the core ethical challenges within all three faith traditions. Remembering the migratory context of sacred texts is of special importance in times of contested public discourse on migration (*ibid.*, p.684).

Siblings can choose how to relate

In times of increasingly polarized discourse, discovering how much our Holy Scriptures focus on migration can be the first step towards developing a constructive and reconciliatory approach. Believers can always choose how to relate. As a Christian theologian, I reflect on the English Rabbi Jonathan Sacks and the German-Iranian Muslim scholar Navid Kermani. Amid polarizing and populist discourses on the assumed hostility of religions, they both talk about interreligious affairs in a constructive and reconciling tone.

In his book *Not in God's Name: Confronting Religious Violence*, Jonathan Sacks (2015) contests the increasingly common view that religion is the root cause of violence. Instead, he recommends understanding the relation between the three Abrahamic religions as a relation between siblings – and, of course, as sibling rivalry. Sacks suggests that sibling rivalry is part of the Jewish–Christian–Muslim narrative tradition, and that we need to focus on it if we want to understand and heal the hate that leads to violence in the name of

God (*ibid.*, p.92). He offers an intriguing reading of Genesis, showing that the classic rivalries between Isaac and Ismael, between Jacob and Esau, and between Joseph and his brothers need not be read in purely antagonistic terms. (This is how the Christian tradition tends to read these stories.)

Instead, Sacks focuses on the complexities that emerge on closer reading, which make it impossible to understand them as narratives about right and wrong, good and bad, inside and outside. He presents the story of Isaac and Ismael as a story of reconciliation, in which God has not forsaken Ismael (*ibid.*, p.111), and Ismael and Isaac show up together at the funeral of Abraham (*ibid.*, p.118). In my own Christian tradition, this encounter is rarely (if ever) noted, let alone interpreted, as a story of reconciliation. I realize that there still is much to discover in the Hebrew Scriptures that can inspire a more attentive attitude toward people from other faiths. In all the key stories, Sacks detects God's inclusive love as the last word; that Jacob is chosen does not mean that Esau is forsaken (*ibid.*, p.142), and in the story of Joseph and his brothers, God does not prove God's love by hating others (*ibid.*, p.173). Through non-exclusive reading, the stories of sibling rivalry in Genesis show that we all have a space in God's universe of justice and love (*ibid.*, p.218).

From a Christian perspective, I conclude that it is important to see believers from the other Abrahamic faiths not as competitors, but as siblings waiting to be reconciled. The tools can be found in our common narrative traditions. This is in tune with an ecumenical Christian spirit professing God's universal love. God loves the world – not a specific community of faith – and never ceases to engage with it (Lutheran World Federation 2017). Therefore, the Church never is called to dominate the public space (*ibid.*, pp.20, 23, 36) but rather to share it with people of other faiths and convictions (*ibid.*, p.22). We need an understanding of Christian community in order to create a 'participatory public space' that fosters dialogue and cooperation (*ibid.*, p.25), 'deepens mutual understanding' and 'constitutes a strong public witness' (*ibid.*, p.29).

Listening to the 'religious other' to deepen identity

The Muslim writer Navid Kermani is a soul friend of his Jewish colleague Jonathan Sacks. In 2015, Kermani received the Peace Prize of the German Book Trade for his creative, profound writings about the possibilities of peaceful co-existence between religions. In his acceptance speech, he described a Christian monastery in Syria with a mission to love Muslims. Inspired by the monastery's leader, Father Jacques Mourad, Kermani offers a simple, twofold rule for encounter between Muslims and Christians. The first rule: defend the representatives from other faiths against misrepresentation. The second rule: if you love your faith community, criticize it. Kermani adds, 'Father Jacques defended the community he does not belong to and criticized his own... The love of one's own – one's own culture, one's own country and also one's own person – manifests itself in self-criticism' (Kermani 2015a, pp.3–4). This is a profoundly non-polarizing view of interreligious relations.

With that, I return to the orchestra, or the choir, as a metaphor for the polyphony of religious tunes and voices. The encounter between believers from different faith traditions is, after all, as much about the *way* of encounter and its aesthetics as it is about an exchange of *beliefs*. The musical metaphor can open our imagination to more peaceful and attentive engagements with people from other faiths. One could summarize Navid Kermani's two simple rules as a 'double listening process': first, an attentive outward listening to the 'tune' of the other religion; and then a critical inward listening to the 'tune' of one's own religion.

In all three Abrahamic religions, music plays an important role for transmitting the message. Both the Torah and the Qur'an are supposed to be sung in order to become a living word in the ears and hearts of the believers. In Christianity, music has a similarly important function for communicating the Gospel – not only into the heads but into the hearts of believers.

Kermani has reflected extensively on the aesthetic dimension of the Muslim mission. It is a common prejudice that Islam was spread by means of violence. Kermani's research, however, shows that poetic and musical beauty played a key role in early Muslim conversion narratives. Often it was the beauty of the recited and sung Qur'an verses that overwhelmed people and led them to convert (Kermani 2014, pp.25–26). The Qur'an cannot be understood in depth only by reading it. It must be heard, which is why not only the call to prayer but also the texts of the Qur'an are sung rather than read. Here, religious insight takes the form of an experience of acoustic beauty (Kermani 2015b). The decisive point in Islam is what one could call the audible 'inverbation' – a poetic transformation into recited or sung words (Kermani 2014, p.36). Angelika Neuwirth, professor of Arab studies, emphasizes, 'The sung recitation of the Qur'an is like the resonance of the voice of God' (2012, p.11, my translation). Indeed, I personally know the feeling of being touched by the citation of the Qur'an, especially when it is not read but cited by heart – an art that has become rare in Christianity. Knowing texts by heart, and singing them, deepens the experience of spiritual transformation. I am challenged here to rethink the role of music in my own faith tradition.

Kermani is aware of the problematic side of aesthetics; some Muslims believe the beauty of Arabic makes it susceptible to ideological misuse (Kermani 2014, p.38), as with Islamist populists (*ibid.*, p.40). Kermani distances himself from fundamentalist ways of reading holy texts which ignore the plurality of interpretations. Instead, he commits himself to a way of reading that preserves 'the Qur'an's poetic quality and its poetically structured language'. The Qur'an, Kermani maintains, 'ceases to be poetic once it becomes unambiguous' (*ibid.*, p.42, my translation). Its beauty is intimately connected to the plurality of its meanings. And if that is so, there can be no monopoly of interpretation.

A similar belief can be affirmed from a Protestant Christian perspective: no person nor institution can claim to have access to the final, authoritative interpretation of the Bible. Only together – at times inspired by encounters with Jews and Muslims – can we understand the deeper significance of Scripture.

Listening to each other's tunes

There are at least two lessons I take away for my understanding of my own Christian faith. First, it is important to remain attentive to the ambivalence and shadow sides of my own faith tradition, and to rethink them critically. Second, when listening to the beauty of other tunes, I am challenged to refocus on the beauty and the poetic quality of my own holy texts. The emphasis on beauty, not least audible beauty, inspires me to rethink how the truth of faith in my own Christian tradition is communicated in poetic and musical ways: in the Psalms, in the Proverbs, in the Song of Songs, in Ecclesiastes, and also in many passages of the New Testament.

A religious truth that is expressed in amazement, in ecstasy – in a finely balanced rhythm and in music – is ill-fitted to be used in competition against another truth. It starts to speak as vibrations in the lives of people. This is why the boundaries between religions cannot be understood as strict lines of division. There is an existential connection between believers from different religions who have a sense for the aesthetic, the musical quality of faith. If the claim to truth in the Christian tradition ultimately is inseparable from the lived witness of Christians (i.e., its ethical dimension), imagining the relations between Abrahamic religions as a community of music – of communal vibration – may be helpful. Despite its limitations, this approach can inspire peaceful co-existence between religions without abandoning their uniqueness – to live 'difference without domination', as Edward Said proposed in his conversation with Daniel Barenboim.

Making music or singing in a choir can be understood as an exercise of difference without domination, and it can be a metaphor for concrete, constructive encounters between people from different faith traditions. To be touched by the beautiful recitation of the Qur'an does not mean that I, as a Christian, have to learn the art of Qur'anic recitation. But it inspires me to re-evaluate the significance of music and singing in my own faith tradition. It inspires me to trust the vibrancy of the biblical message and to practise with new joy and expectation the singing of Psalms. It inspires me not least to recognize anew that the Bible is not simply a book with texts, but a living tradition that needs to become a living tune, over and over again.

I want to understand the interrelation between the Abrahamic religions as similar to the polyphony of a choir, of the West–Eastern Divan Orchestra. This is about more than tolerance; it is an attentive, mutual listening process. Each voice in a choir or orchestra contributes its particular sound, simultaneously listening to the other voices. Attention to other religious voices helps us to widen our horizon and to deepen our understanding of our own religious identity. This means that I am dependent on Jewish and Muslim voices for the deepening of my Christian identity, and vice versa. Only together can these voices make the choir of religions come alive and contribute to each other's maturing. To understand the life of different faith communities as voices in the same choir opens an understanding of belonging without separation, and an affirmation of difference without domination.

References and suggested reading

Admirand, P. (2014) 'The ethics of displacement and migration in the Abrahamic faiths: Enlightening believers and aiding public policy.' *Journal of Ethnic and Migration Studies*, 40, 4, 671–687.

Barenboim, D. and Said, E.W. (2004) In A. Guzelimian (ed.) *Parallels and Paradoxes. Explorations in Music and Society*. New York, NY: Vintage Books.

Irvin, D.T. (2014) 'Theology, Migration, and the Homecoming.' In E. Padilla and P.C. Phan (eds) *Theology of Migration in the Abrahamic Religions*. New York, NY: Palgrave Macmillan.

Kermani, N. (2014) *Zwischen Koran und Kafka. West-östliche Erkundungen*. Munich: Beck C.H.

Kermani, N. (2015a) 'Beyond the Borders – Jacques Mourad and Love in Syria.' Accessed on 09/21/2018 at www.friedenspreis-des-deutschen-buchhandels.de/445651.

Kermani, N. (2015b) *God is Beautiful. The Aesthetic Experience of the Quran*. Cambridge: Polity Press.

Lutheran World Federation (2017) *The Church in the Public Space*. Geneva: Lutheran World Federation.

Nausner, M. (2012) 'Gebrochenheit und Erneuerung der Schöpfung. Das Abendmahl als theologische Basis sozialer Gerechtigkeit.' *Ökumenische Rundschau*, 61, 4, 440–456.

Nausner, M. (2017) 'Changing identities, changing narratives. Can theology contribute to a new cultural imagination of migration?' *Interdisciplinary Journal for Religion and Transformation in Contemporary Society*, 3, 226–251.

Neuwirth, A. (2012) 'Ist der Koran vom Himmel gefallen?' *Welt und Umwelt der Bibel*, 1, 11–17.

Padilla, E. and Phan, P.C. (eds) (2014) *Theology of Migration in the Abrahamic Religions*. New York, NY: Palgrave Macmillan.

Sacks, J. (2015) *Not in God's Name: Confronting Religious Violence*. New York, NY: Schocken Books.

World Council of Churches (2018) 'Message from the conference "Xenophobia, Racism and Populist Nationalism in the Context of Global Migration".' Rome. Accessed on 09/21/2018 at www.oikoumene.org/en/resources/documents/message-from-the-conference-xenophobia-racism-and-populist-nationalism-in-the-context-of-global-migration-19-september-2018.

CHAPTER 14

Wandering Jews

Mobilizing Exile to Create Communities and Change

Robyn Ashworth-Steen

If a person makes himself humble like this wilderness, which is open to all and upon which everyone treads, the Torah will be given to them as a gift.

(Bavli Eruvin 54a)

A beginning

Wearing my *kippah* (Jewish head covering) embodies my (ironical-ly) deeply rooted identity as a Jew who is, on many levels, in exile.[1] Particularly as a woman and a rabbi, when wearing my *kippah*, I am noticeably a member of many minorities: Jewish, female and progres-sive. Without my *kippah*, my Jewish identity is hidden (Lawton 2018). I can blend in as I am white, educated and British and, thus, privileged. Without the *kippah*, I ostensibly become one of the majority. As a

---

1   A *kippah* is also known as a *yarmulke* or skull-cap. In Orthodox Jewish denominations, only men wear *kippot* (plural), but in progressive denominations both men and women are able to wear them. The reasons for wearing *kippot* are extensive: as a connection to God; as a reminder of the Jewish covenant and religious obligations (however understood by the wearer); as an identity marker; as an act of solidarity; because it is a long-held tradition within Jewish communities and it is 'just what we do'.

result, I do not need to worry about anti-Semitism or discrimination, from outside my Jewish community or inside it. I need not disclose to anyone that I am a rabbi or justify my path. I am comfortable and 'at home' while, at the same time, hiding key parts of my identities. With this choice, I am in exile from myself and my people.

Every time I wear my *kippah*, I am wrenched from my 'home', my safety. While my primary reasons for wearing my *kippah* are to be in connection with divinity, to embrace my heritage and to remind myself of my duties as a Jew, the very act of wearing a *kippah* brings with it so much more. I can no longer hide my Jewish identity. I am 'out', and I become a target, for good or for bad. Like a *hijab*-wearing Muslim, my *kippah* is seen as a marker of identity and allegiance and, for many, is understood to be a public statement rather than a private choice.

As Jews, the space which we inhabit, demonstrated through the *kippah*, is liminal and marginal. As former refugees, and like modern refugees and migrants, we exist in the spaces between. We wear a *kippah* and are visibly 'other', or we put the *kippah* away and are a hidden 'other'. Both states are uncomfortable, as we juggle our multiple identities as a minority group and part of the privileged elite. To quote Edward Said (1985, p.8), we are wanderers, 'going from place to place to gather materials, but remaining essentially *between homes*'.

Conditions of exile

We are, as a people, *unheimlich* – 'not belonging to the home' (Freud 1919, p.2). Wandering is fundamental to Jewish identity, but this identity is not exclusive to the Jewish people. It is deeply part of what it means to be human. Yet as with other migrant communities and individuals, these feelings of being un-settled – of living in uncertain times and being, in essence, 'not at home' – is more keenly felt. This is due to the many threads which construct this exilic condition for Jews.

First, Jews have: 'dwelt on the boundaries of various civilizations, religions, and national cultures... lived on the margins or in the nooks and crannies of their respective nations. [Been] in society and yet not in it, of it and yet not of it' (Deutscher 2017, p.27). This Jewish border-crossing identity spans our timeline, beginning with Abraham, arguably the first Jew. With his wife Sarah and family, he set out from their homeland, and we follow their journeys. At *Bereshit/ Genesis* 14:13 we hear Abraham described as ירבעה (*ha-ivri*), which can be translated as 'the border crosser' or 'the one who stands at the other side'.[2] We are border crossers. We have wandered and become wanderers. We no longer have a home or know what our home is.

Second, our sacred stories present overarching themes of exile which weave their way through the stories we tell of ourselves. Our Torah tells the immense story of our liberation from Egypt and slavery and our journey towards the Promised Land. Note: our journey *towards*. The five books of Moses do not record our arrival; instead, we stand on the brink of entry, of redemption. We read these books on a loop every year and, as a result, perpetually live in exile, never arriving. Indeed, our story begins in *Gan Eden* (the Garden of Eden), and we are quickly banished and placed in exile. We never return but are left longing for that particular paradise. We pray for redemption and the messianic age. There is a reaching *towards* in our prayers and, with it, an assumption that we may never arrive. We read texts written by those in exile such as the Babylonian rabbis. We study *kabbalistic* theologies of the broken vessels and our duty to rescue the shards of divine sparks lodged in us and all around us. We are always seeking, never at home, unsure what home is and whether return is possible.

Third, we are in exile from God. Or maybe God is in exile. Through our Judaism, we seek to connect, to cleave to God: *devekut*. This is the ongoing spiritual practice of the Jew. The prophet Jeremiah writes: 'You will seek me and find me when you seek me with all your heart' (29:13). We want to experience the divine, yet we cannot even pronounce God's name. We have lost the original pronunciation. All we

---

2   The Torah consists of five books: Genesis, Exodus, Leviticus, Numbers and Deuteronomy. The books' Hebrew names (*Bereshit, Shemot, Vayikra, Bemidbar* and *Devarim*) take a key word from the opening verses of the book. As Hebrew is a sacred language and the Torah tells stories by my ancestors, I choose to use the Hebrew names in referencing texts. The word 'Torah' can also be used more generally to refer to Jewish teaching.

are left with are the consonants *YHVH* (called the 'tetragrammaton'). Scholars have tried to re-create God's name, which was uttered by the High Priest in the Holy of Holies in the Temple once a year at Yom Kippur and is now lost. As Jews, we worry about mispronouncing God's name or saying the holy name by mistake, and so we leave it as a mystery. To this end, we place the word *Adonai* (meaning 'Lord') over the tetragrammaton – the four letters which, without the vowels, remain unpronounceable. In this way, we are a people of words, but we are speechless. How can we be intimate with divinity if we cannot use a direct name? We have many names for God, perhaps in hope that the variety and quantity will make up for the lacuna. One such word is *Ha-Makom*, meaning 'the place', 'space' or 'dwelling place'. With this name, we align divinity with space. We are looking for a home, for God, a Godly home.

Fourth, through our historical and spiritual exile and our own particular journeys, we are individually and personally in exile. Adrienne Rich, the great feminist poet, wrote of the 'starved Jew' in herself, which urged her to seek a 'path to that Jewishness still unsatisfied, still trying to define its true homeland, still untamed and un-suburbanized, still wandering in the wilderness' (Rich 1986, p.202). Rich considered the identities of being a woman and a Jew as sharing important characteristics, and thus helps describe the exilic condition:

> We exist everywhere under laws we did not make; speaking a multitude of languages, excluded by law and custom from certain spaces, functions, resources associated with power; often accused of wielding too much power, of wielding dark and devious powers. (Rich 1986, p.203)

The choice before us

As Jews, we have a choice about how we utilize this exilic condition. We can put the *kippah* out of sight, hiding our particularity and heritage as the outsider, and embrace our privilege at the expense of others and ourselves. We can, having been the victims of the violent, genocidal oppression during the *Shoah* (Holocaust) and beyond, remain within the cycle of oppression and use our woundedness to wound others. We can be passive and complacent to the hate around us. We can build the fences higher and live in our own world, divorced from reality, and pretend that we are at 'home'.

Or we can don the *kippah* and choose to embrace and inhabit our *unheimlich* ('not-at-home-ness') nature, to stand on the margins of society to critique injustice – which we have ourselves experienced. We can, as outsiders intentionally wearing our *kippot*, stand with others who are marginalized, hidden and oppressed. Instead of hiding and being passive we can rebel, subvert and act. We can use our experiences to cultivate empathy and openness through meaningful dialogue. We can decide that the wilderness is a gift, that redemption and liberation can be found in our wandering. Perhaps we can realize that the Promised Land *is* this uncertain, liminal space which we inhabit.

Being aware of this shadow side to our *unheimlich* nature should save us from becoming complacent or dangerous. We must realize the power involved in being wanderers. With our freedom, on the margins, comes great responsibility. Crucially the Boyarin brothers state that the Jewish diaspora must be understood and considered as 'the most precise or concentrated diasporic experience' (J. Boyarin 2002, p.10). And through its context and history, we must view the Jewish diaspora alongside other diasporic communities:

> For if a lost Jerusalem imagined through a lost Cordoba imagined through a lost Suriname is diaspora to the third power, so is a stolen Africa sung as a lost Zion in Jamaican rhythms on the sidewalks of Eastern Parkway. To say as much as that is, we hope, to catch a lucid glimpse of how creative the powers of diaspora could be. (Boyarin and Boyarin 2002, p.lx)

Hannah Arendt, the controversial political theorist who stood on the edge of her people, also sought to teach that the Jews' condition is connected to everyone's condition. She drew out the dangers inherent in the Jews' 'worldlessness'. We were, following emancipation, asleep to the world around us. Arendt argued that rather than becoming dreamers divorced from reality or social climbers, we should become 'conscious pariahs' who use our marginality to become political, involved in our world. '(T)he emancipated Jew must awake to an awareness of his position and, conscious of it, become a rebel against it – the champion of an oppressed people' (Arendt, 1944, p.108). Retreat into the world of fantasy is no longer possible: 'the pariah must become political' (Feldman 2007, p.lvi).

Returning to our symbolic and real *kippah*, we understand that once we put it on, we ally ourselves with others – with our *hijab*-wearing Muslim sisters, with the visible minorities and many others who do not have the luxury of hiding one of their key identities (Lawton 2018). We must not hide behind our label of wanderers or arrogantly embrace our status as the 'chosen people' while losing sight of the fact that we are all created *b'tzelem Elohim* (in the image of God) (*Bereshit* 1:27). Our destination and methodology in our fight to embrace our marginality must be in solidarity with others, and to be working towards liberation and justice for all.

Our relationship to the Torah and its darkness

We always have a choice before us: 'even in the darkest of times, the question of one's response and responsibility can and must be raised. There is the possibility to initiate, to begin, to act' (Bernstein 1996, p.38).

This principle is best illustrated with the Torah scroll itself. In some ways, it acts as a blank canvas. It has no vowels and no punctuation; it is deeply and widely open to interpretation. This is at once terrifying and liberating. We are gifted a choice in how we enter into relationship with our most sacred of texts. We can be fearful and construct firm answers and fixed modes of interpretation, or we can embrace the confusion and be open to many questions, answers and suggestions. We can, as it says in *Tosefta Sotah*, 'make a heart of many rooms' (7:12).

With the doors that are opened with our understanding of our Torah as a blank canvas, as a progressive Jew I must also recognize that Jews and our ancient family, the Israelites, have erred. And that the Torah itself often falls from its ideals of justice and compassion (Mandolfo 2007, p.9). In our marginality and as victims of violence and oppression, we have also done wrong. I believe it is crucial that rather than our *unheimlich* nature leading us to embrace the label of the 'chosen people', thus distancing ourselves from others and creating false divisions of 'them' and 'us', we instead understand that in our vulnerability, we are capable of lashing out. We can use the Torah as a mirror to show us that we are capable of bad and of good, and that we are all 'other' in some way.

Our texts contain violence, calls to genocide, misogyny, homophobia, racism, hate, abuse of power, colonialism. In this naming, there is great power. While we repeat the commandment that we are to love the stranger as we love ourselves, as we were once strangers in the land of Egypt (*Devarim* 10:19, for example), we know that those strangers were understood to be those who we knew and lived with us. For the strangers in other lands, we were commanded to face them with extreme violence and force. We must face the darkness in our texts which demonize other wanderers. We read the Hebrew word *ger* for 'stranger' and are aware of the root of that word, *gur*, meaning to 'disrupt' or 'change'. We can see that fear of the 'other' leads to darkness.

The (im)possibility of return

The Boyarin brothers, Adrienne Rich, Hannah Arendt, our Torah, and the 'other' call us to enact our *unheimlich* nature for good, which requires and creates *teshuvah*: 'returning'.[3] We return to God, to

---

3   *Teshuvah* ('returning') is a concept most noticeable in the liturgy and customs surrounding Yom Kippur (our main day of fasting), where we seek to return to ourselves, each other and God through repentance, prayer and good deeds in order to find personal and collective redemption.

ourselves, to our people and to the world. If we have wandered *from*, what are we returning *to*? What is our destination? Is return possible? For many refugees and migrants, to return home is impossible. Their home, and their connection to that home, has irrevocably shifted. If a physical return is impossible, are there other forms of return that hold promise and thus offer the potential for healing and liberation?

Ursula Le Guin, the exceptional science fiction writer, wrote in *The Dispossessed* a line which was taught to me and many others by Rabbi Sheila Shulman (z"l)[4]: 'you can go home again ... so long as you understand that home is a place where you have never been' (Le Guin 1974, p.48). This quotation offers a guide and warning for our quest. Le Guin and Rabbi Shulman teach us that it is crucial to remember that we are not returning to *Gan Eden* or to a nostalgic, glorious past, nor looking towards a physical space or messiah or god-like figure that will solve our exilic condition. Instead, we are commanded to live in the wilderness and to see it as a gift. There is no arrival. Our challenge, politically and spiritually, is to embrace this uncertain, liminal condition and to use our uncertainty for good instead of turning our insecurity into fear. Our challenge is to embrace this uncertainty and mystery as divine.

Conclusion/Beginning

To enable *teshuvah* (return), it is key that we build *textu*red communities that face the darkness in our texts and, therefore, in ourselves. We must work in critical, reflective dialogue with our texts and with each other. We must inform our rootlessness, to ensure that it is positive and creative rather than destructive. The sacred texts are an anchor to our Judaism. By grounding ourselves in text, we will be connected, through our wanders and sojourns, to our complex and plentiful words, our dialogue and our textual heritage and, ultimately, to God.

---

4   *Zichrono livracha* (May her memory be for a blessing) is a term of honour and remembrance.

As Jews, this sacred work must be done in community. Communities have the power to effect great change. In fact, inhabiting our exilic condition should naturally turn us to each other:

> My hope is that the movement we are building can further the conscious work of turning Otherness into a keen lens of empathy, that we can bring into being a politics based on concrete, heartfelt understanding of what it means to be Other. (Rich 1986, p.203)

Our wandering nature means that instead of withdrawing and distancing, our only chance of redemption is to hold tight to our texts and to our communities. Indeed, the Israelites, when in the wilderness, found strategies such as a relationship with God, covenant, community, texts and a temporary, portable space: the *mishkan* (understood to be the dwelling place of God). Using the symbol of the *mishkan*, which was constructed during the Israelites' period in the wilderness, we realize that there is no 'home'. We construct our homes (and narratives), and there is opportunity, in every moment, to understand and utilize our exilic condition. We try not to become obsessed with buildings and territories. Instead, we attempt to be open and willing to de-construct and re-construct our spaces and homes, to welcome others. Today's *mishkan* evolves and travels with us and offers us a chance at peace and completeness.

We inhabit our Jewish condition of exile and cultivate empathy for others. We weave our Jewish texts with our lives and our relationships and create an intricate web that is strong enough to hold us in the wilderness. And we take action, so that other groups and individuals who migrate and wander can find liberation. Crucially, there are tools at our disposal for our individual and communal sojourn in the wilderness, to enable us to accept our reality, and to construct and re-construct our portable, ever-evolving *mishkan*.

First, as Jewish readers in community, how we read can affect how we are in our world. Through a reading strategy that is grounded in dialogue and struggle, which uses rabbinic learning methods showcasing constructive conflicts, we can create redemptive reading strategies. The rabbinic interpretative model of PaRDeS is particularly suitable, as it uses four lenses to approach the text: *peshat* (surface reading), *remez* (hints), *derash* (comparative *midrashic* reading[5]) and *sod* (secrets). This model enables the reader to appreciate the multi-dimensional nature of the text (and our reality) with its numerous meanings. A critical approach to text mirrors how we read and understand the world around us. Doing so through dialogue enables us to deepen our understanding, hear the experiences of others, and challenge our thoughts and unconscious biases.

Second, I believe any teaching around the Torah and activism should focus on the creative and destructive power of language. It is crucial to study texts in their modern contexts, such as contemporary genocides, hate crimes and online abuse. It makes us critical readers who are aware of how we speak to others. This will hopefully enable difficult dialogues, outside our own echo chambers, to take place. Systems such as Nonviolent Communication provide a model of how we can change our narratives and effect change (Rosenberg, 2015).

Third, it is essential that we hear stories of people who have been oppressed and marginalized and whose voices have, historically, been forgotten, censored or hidden – our modern-day wanderers. Studying alongside and hearing from the oppressed is indispensable in the quest for meaningful and effective activism. Hearing these stories engenders empathy in others, allows for deep encounters, and invests one in the other. Alliances are thus formed and ready to activate. Stories also enable us to understand our role as individuals within the collective. Instead of the collective being privileged over the individual, the dignity and worth of each individual can be celebrated. We could express this as the principle of *b'tzelem Elohim*, being created in the image of God, which confers an inherent divine worth on each person.

My hope is that a new reality can be realized within Jewish communities, one where a nuanced, sophisticated textual reading is woven

---

5   A form of Jewish biblical, creative interpretation of Jewish texts. In a strict sense, the word *midrashim* (plural) refers to particular works of Rabbinic Judaism. In a looser sense, *midrash* refers to a creative retelling and playing with Jewish text.

with Jewish social justice activism, all predicated on our awareness of our fragile and potent nature as wanderers.

References and suggested reading

Arendt, H. (1944) 'The Jew as pariah: A hidden tradition.' *Jewish Social Studies*, 6, 2, 99–122.

Bernstein, R.J. (1996) 'The Conscious Pariah as Rebel and Independent Thinker.' In R.J. Bernstein, *Hannah Arendt and the Jewish Question*. Cambridge, MA: Polity Press.

Boyarin, J. (2002) 'Introduction: Powers of Diaspora.' In J. Boyarin and D. Boyarin *Powers of Diaspora: Two Essays on the Relevance of Jewish Culture*. Minneapolis, MN: University of Minnesota Press.

Boyarin, J. and Boyarin, D. (2002) *Powers of Diaspora: Two Essays on the Relevance of Jewish Culture*. Minneapolis, MN: University of Minnesota Press.

Deutscher, I. (2017) *The Non-Jewish Jew and Other Essays*. London: Verso.

Feldman, R.H. (2007) 'The Jew as Pariah: The Case of Hannah Arendt (1906–1975).' In J. Kohn and R.H. Feldman (eds) *The Jewish Writings: Hannah Arendt*. New York, NY: Schocken Books.

Freud, S. (1919) *The Uncanny*. Cambridge, MA: Massachusetts Institute of Technology. Accessed on 07/11/18 at web.mit.edu/allanmc/www/freud1.pdf.

Lawton, C. (4 February 2018) *The 10 Commandments – Less a Few. The 7 Noachide Laws*. Lecture. Manchester: Limmud.

Le Guin, U. (1974) *The Dispossessed*. London: Orion Books.

Mandolfo, C.R. (2007) *Daughter Zion Talks Back to the Prophets: A Dialogic Theology of the Book of Lamentations*. Atlanta, GA: Society of Biblical Literature.

Rich, A. (1986) 'If Not with Others, How? (1985).' In *Blood, Bread and Poetry: Selected Prose 1979–1985*. London: Virago Press Limited.

Rosenberg, M.B. (2015) *Nonviolent Communication: A Language of Life* (third edition). Encinitas, CA: Puddle Dancer Press.

Said, E. (1985) *Beginnings: Intention and Method*. New York, NY: Columbia University Press.

CHAPTER 15

Welcoming Refugees

The Canaanite Woman and Breaking Down Borders

Sheila Curran

Around the world, an unprecedented 65.6 million people have been forced to leave their homes (United Nations High Commissioner for Refugees 2018). Among them are nearly 22.5 million refugees; over half are under the age of 18. As they seek safety, all are crossing borders, bringing changes to the religious landscape. These changes are often met with hostility – even within our Christian churches, congregations and communities. As Christians, we profess to believe that we are called 'to love God and to love our neighbour'.

I grew up in the Irish county of Donegal, which borders Northern Ireland. Consequently, I have a heightened awareness that borders are social and political constructs that create division and cultivate fear. I am also a Sister of Mercy, an international congregation founded in Ireland in 1831 to respond to the needs of the poor. Our charism (the characteristic vision of a religious congregation) is constantly evolving. Today, it urges us to respond to what Pope Francis (2015) calls 'the cry of the poor and the cry of the earth'. I joined in 1981. For ten years, I worked in Lima, Peru, living in a shantytown on the south side of the city. In the evenings, I helped with the parish pastoral programme for women and young people. This background gave me a deeper understanding of the challenges experienced by people who cross different kinds of borders.

My present ministry, responding to the plight of displaced peoples, is based on practical theology: 'the attempt to relate theology, church and the world together' (Messer 1989, p.155). Jesus is the ultimate practical theologian: 'deeply versed in the Hebrew Scriptures and traditions. He focused on praxis and responding to the common situations of life that he faced' (*ibid.*). As Carmen Nanko-Fernández (2010, p.xviii) explains: 'The practice of Christian faith, the accompaniment that constitutes pastoral ministry, and the critical reflections that arise from within are inextricably intertwined. This occurs within the context of our daily living.'

Practical theology is the primacy of lived experience over doctrine, committed to critical reflection in ministry.

Refugees, asylum seekers and migrants present challenges to Christian communities. In the book of Leviticus, we read: 'You shall treat the stranger who sojourns with you as the native among you, and you shall love him [her] as yourself, for you were strangers in the land of Egypt: I am the Lord your God' (Leviticus 19:34).[1]

Irish people, throughout history, have been strangers in other lands. While we are largely welcoming of migrants and refugees today, shortcomings in policy can lead to negative attitudes toward 'the other'. In some ways, it is easier to welcome a stranger, hoping they will only stay for a short time, than it is to embrace them indefinitely and to recognize their contribution to creating a diverse community. As a Christian, I believe there should be no borders to helping those in need.

Feminist liberation perspectives

To reflect on the cultural challenges related to the movement of people, I analyze the story of the Canaanite woman – the prophetess for the 'other'. In my re-reading of this text, I combine a practical theological method with a feminist, liberationist, theological perspective. I seek to rescue the Canaanite woman from anonymity and to acknowledge

---

1   All Scripture quotations are taken from New Revised Standard Version of the Bible.

her role in enabling Jesus to move out of the comfort zone of his own culture.

The feminist liberation approach interprets text in the interest of women, asking what it means to engage in a reading of Scripture for liberation. The theologian Elizabeth Schüssler Fiorenza (2001) developed seven steps for this method:

1. Begin with women's experience.
2. Identify the interpreter's social location.
3. Ask 'Who says?'
4. Evaluate: What does the text do?
5. Unleash creative imagination.
6. Remember and reconstruct.
7. Take action for transforming change.

The starting point is the everyday lived experiences of women, particularly the ways in which they are oppressed. The method brings these experiences into dialogue with Scripture, tradition and philosophy (Gebara 1986, p.132). This is a methodology whereby writers acknowledge the context and place from which they are writing. For example, I am a white, middle-class, Irish, Catholic woman, who is also a Sister of Mercy. There can be a dangerous tendency to see women as a homogenized group, just as people struggle to see migrants and refugees as individuals coming from different places, cultures and identities. Context matters.

Feminist biblical interpretation attempts to create an egalitarian reading, bringing awareness that most of the Bible was written by men, for men, to serve men's interests. This interpretation goes beyond the traditional historical-critical method. When women began to engage with the field of biblical studies, they asked new questions of the text: Where were the women? What are their experiences? Where are their voices? Feminist biblical methodology starts from daily life and the lived experiences of the believers. It is then illuminated by God's word and fosters new action.

From a feminist perspective, the story of the Canaanite woman reveals a prophetic woman. She challenges Jesus, enabling him to eradicate preconceived borders and expanding his idea of God. Re-reading this text, using the methodology outlined above, in turn expands our understanding of Scripture, towards a vision of liberation for all.

The Canaanite woman: A borderland story

> *Jesus left that place and went away to the district of Tyre and Sidon. Just then a Canaanite woman from that region came out and started shouting, 'Have mercy on me, Lord, Son of David; my daughter is tormented by a demon.' But he did not answer her at all. And his disciples came and urged him, saying, 'Send her away, for she keeps shouting after us.' He answered, 'I was sent only to the lost sheep of the house of Israel.' But she came and knelt before him, saying, 'Lord, help me.' He answered, 'It is not fair to take the children's food and throw it to the dogs.' She said, 'Yes, Lord, yet even the dogs eat the crumbs that fall from their masters' table.' Then Jesus answered her, 'Woman, great is your faith! Let it be done for you as you wish.' And her daughter was healed instantly. (Matthew 15:21–28)*

This is a borderland story, which takes place between two towns in the upper Galilee. In the Bible, we hear of tension between the Canaanites and the Israelites; they saw each other as enemies. As Jesus and the Canaanite women meet, it is not clear who is in whose territory. This context sets the story up for something new to emerge.

In this story, the woman is marginalized because of her gender and her race; the label 'Canaanite' emphasizes her distance from Jesus (Wainwright 1994, p.651). She represents the 'outsider' and 'other', crossing cultural boundaries to seek healing for her daughter. For the Canaanite woman, the land itself becomes the border she crosses. In her desperation, she challenges Jesus to work a miracle for a gentile. She is proactive, not silent, and she makes an imperative plea: 'Have mercy on me.'

The shock of this story of boundary encounter is that Jesus does not respond to the woman's cry for mercy. In fact, the narrator tells us that Jesus ignores her, followed by rejection by the disciples: 'Send her away'; 'I was only sent to the lost sheep of the house of Israel.' Jesus was human and like many of us today, he was conditioned and limited by cultural context. Was his message only for the Jews? Did he come to restore only Israel, or did he come to respond to all?

Jesus: Fully human, culturally biased

The Canaanite woman chooses not to play the victim. We can imagine her courage, her commitment, her guts and her wit. She refuses to accept the construction of 'insider' and 'outsider'. She persists by kneeling before Jesus, proposing that she and her daughter share bread with him and the disciples – 'like the dogs that eat the crumbs that fall from their masters' table'. She then speaks directly to Jesus again, 'Lord, help me.' Jesus responds, 'It is not fair to take the children's food and throw it to the dogs.' His words could be interpreted as a racial slur or even hate speech.

The Canaanite woman has done all in her power to save her daughter. Her courageous, persistent engagement with Jesus challenges him to move back to the margins, where he now recognizes that what she desires is 'of God'. Jesus can now respond positively to her request. The Canaanite woman is the only person in the Gospels who argues with Jesus and wins, who gets him to change his mind. Jesus finally listens to her. He praises the woman's faith. Her daughter is healed.

The Canaanite woman's respectful, insistent response, in both word and gesture, triggers a profound change in how Jesus understands the scope of his mission. He begins to remember who and what he is. He may be the Son of Man – fully human, culturally biased – but he is also the Son of God. The Canaanite woman, with her inner strength and courageous sharpness, transpires for Jesus the universality of God's love and healing. Jesus opens himself to the challenge; he changes his mind. He listens to the Spirit awakening his humanity to God's inclusive and egalitarian dream. Jesus's own mission is now enlarged. Mercy has no limits. Borders and boundaries have been crossed. God will always be new in the cry of those most in need! Tradition, the Word of God, holiness, justice and right will always need to be negotiated in the face of human need. The Gospel is for everyone.

A conversion moment

So, what can we take away from this story? Today, migrants and refugees, like the Canaanite woman, are asking us to enlarge our mission. They are calling to us to help them cross borders and to respond with mercy and compassion. They are pleading with us to provide safe and legal access to all who seek protection. Just as Jesus was invited by the Canaanite woman to move beyond the borders of his own cultural experience, we too are asked to move out of our comfort zone of privilege. The Canaanite woman's story shows how even the best of humanity – Jesus himself – can become tangled in systems of oppression, in a culture of supremacy.

What is important is what happens in the moments after we realize our limitations: in the way we respond, when confronted with the narratives of the stranger, the 'outsider'. Through our actions and responses, we reveal who we truly are and want to be. Do we ignore or deny those who are excluded? Do we mock them? Do we brush refugees aside as dogs, monkeys, uncivilized, underdeveloped, or whatever labels our cultures teach us?

In this transformative encounter, Jesus moves from ethnocentrism toward a more intercultural sensitivity. It is a conversion movement – one that is always mediated by the stranger in our lives. We need the 'other' to challenge our ways and broaden our horizons. As a counter-cultural movement, it will surely be awkward, uncomfortable and frustrating. It will also be precious. Whether we find ourselves as 'insiders' in a position of power, or whether we are 'outsiders', we are called to conversion.

The Canaanite woman's story is challenging. We would prefer to think of Jesus as perfect – unbiased and free from prejudice. As we see from this text, however, Jesus had to face his ethnocentrism in order to align himself with God's inclusive plan for humanity. It took a face-to-face encounter with the Canaanite woman for Jesus to turn away from the forms of exclusion that were normative in his own culture. Like us, Jesus was challenged to move counter-culturally, in order to bear witness to God's kingdom. This is the good news! His response to the Canaanite woman encourages us to confront ourselves with honesty. His willingness to let her question and broaden his vision challenges our own ethnocentrism. This is a call to conversion.

Conclusion

Ireland has fallen short of its commitment to take in 4000 refugees. In the larger picture, this is a small number; Ireland can and should do more. The call to discipleship is for everyone who thirsts, searches, questions and is prepared to enter into dialogue with God. It is the prophetic voice that we hear but are afraid to follow. It is costly; it means leaving behind all that causes us to erect borders (race, status, gender, fear) so that we can bear witness to the reign of God, which offers life in abundance for all humankind. True boundary crossing expands our image of God.

The current crisis is an opportunity for Christians to realize our prophetic commitment. As they risk travelling to a new country, migrants and refugees cross multiple boundaries, be they geograph-ical, cultural, societal or religious. The perspective of the 'other' broad-ens our vision, challenging us to confront our own cultural lenses, systems, stereotypes and patriarchal prejudices. Border crossing is not only the task of the newcomer, the migrant or the refugee. It also demands risk-taking by those in the host country. Like Jesus, we are asked to change our perspective, to rethink our theology. Only when we dare to move to the margins, towards the stranger, can we truly discover who we are and what we are called to be as disciples of Jesus in mission.

The story of the Canaanite woman encourages us to seek the one-to-one encounter, to enter into dialogue with those who cross borders, to take risks and to allow for complexities to emerge. Barriers of geography, race and gender must be crossed. Today, the 1951 United Nations Refugee Convention is under threat. We need to ensure that it is strengthened and embraced. Fear can prevent us from taking risks. However, as Christians crossing cultural barriers and breaking down borders, this is what we are called to do.

Lives depend on it.

References

Gebara, I. (1986) 'Women Doing Theology in Latin America.' In V. Fabella and M.A. Oduyoye (eds) *With Passion and Compassion: Third World Women Doing Theology* (pp.126–134). Maryknoll, NY: Orbis Books.

Messer, D.E. (1989) *Contemporary Images of Christian Ministry*. Nashville, TN: Abingdon Press.

Nanko-Fernández, C. (2010) *Theologizing En Espanglish: Context, Community and Ministry*. Maryknoll, NY: Orbis Books.

Pope Francis (2015). Encyclical letter Laudato si' of the Holy Father Francis.

Schüssler Fiorenza, E. (2001) *Wisdom Ways: Introducing Feminist Biblical Interpretation*. Maryknoll, NY: Orbis Books.

United Nations High Commissioner for Refugees (2018) Figures at a Glance. Accessed on 12/05/18 at www.unhcr.org/en-ie/figures-at-a-glance.html.

Wainwright, M.E. (1994) 'The Gospel of Matthew.' In E. Schüssler Fiorenza (ed.) *Searching the Scriptures: A Feminist Commentary* (pp.635–677). London: SCM Press.

CHAPTER 16

Prophetic Narratives of Migration and Resilience

Sayed Razawi

In a well-known Muslim tradition, the Prophet Muhammad instructed desert dwellers to 'seek knowledge, even if takes you to China' (Rayshahrī 1385 AH, vol. 8, p.26). At that time, China had no links to Islam. The Prophet was alluding to perennial wisdom, which illuminates the mind and speaks to the heart. It is a form of awakening, of emancipation from uncertainty and pain. The tradition continues: 'It is divine knowledge of the self, and in it lies the divine knowledge of the Creator' (Al Sadiq 2004, p.5). 'Migrating' from that which is routine allows us to explore unknown depths, awakening the very universe inside us which houses the secrets of creation. Within Islamic mysticism, there are whole chapters on 'migrating', from the shackles of suffering to the bliss that unity with the divine brings. In the words of the Muslim Sage Imam Ali (d.661)[1]: 'Your sickness is from you, yet you do not see it. Your remedy is within you, yet you do not perceive it. You presume you are a small body; yet encapsulated within you is the entire universe' (Majlisi 1406 AH, vol. 2, p.81).

---

1   Imam Ali was the cousin and son-in-law of the Prophet Muhammad. He is recognized as the rightful and immediate successor to the Prophet by Shia Muslims, who took his name as their own. Sunni Muslims also recognize Imam Ali, but as the fourth of the four rightly guided Caliphs. The Sunni–Shia schism began on the point of succession to the Prophet Muhammad.

In this chapter, we look at an Islamic perspective on migration. May our discourse allow us to explore sacred text together.

Theology of resilience

Judaism, Christianity and Islam claim descent from the sons of Abraham, either Ishmael or Isaac. The faiths uphold the core principle of monotheism, or belief in one God. Islam refers to Jews and Christians as 'People of the Book' and so upholds teaching from the Biblical Prophets. There is a survival instinct in Judaism, Christianity and Islam – a shared theology of resilience inspired through centuries of biblical and Quranic parables. Adam, Noah, Abraham, Moses, Jesus and Muhammad nurture through their lives and examples this very theology of resilience. They created great nations out of oppression, destruction and death. They faced heartbreak, tears and loss. In the end, however, they never lost hope. They were resilient and, through infliction, came to understand patience in the divine will. It was through suffering that a deep connection with God was established. Through resilience, not only did their knowledge of the nature of God increase, but their faith also deepened.

So they turned to migration. They uprooted their families and sometimes whole nations in search of the promise of God, moving from the familiar to the unfamiliar. Quranically speaking, Adam moved for most of his life; Noah restarted life afresh after the divine flood; Abraham migrated; Moses went in search of the Promised Land; and Jesus did not restrict himself to one locality. And the Prophet Muhammad moved from Makkah (Mecca) to Madina. Within ten years of this move, Islam not only grew but flourished. Some of the most profound stories, in each of these faiths, epitomize hope while facing tribulation. They emphasize deeper comprehension of the divine. The wisdom in these stories speaks to the hearts of all adherents: the stories of Moses and the Jewish nation's emancipation from the Pharaoh; compassion through suffering, as witnessed in the life of Jesus; and mercy in the face of death and oppression as reflected in the life of Muhammad. They had faith and were faithful.

Throughout history, believers in the biblical message have migrated with God. The conviction is deeply rooted in the Quranic belief that God is closer to you than your jugular vein (Quran 50:16). There was timeless wisdom in the Prophet's wish for his followers to travel. Migration enabled Islam to strengthen its foundations in its formative years, by absorbing the best of the civilizations that had preceded it. Through migration, cultural identities formed as they came into contact with host cultures. Faith thus manifested in various forms, like light as it passes through a prism, revealing different shades and colours. Having experienced these shades of diverse light, one should never forget the origin and universal principles deeply rooted in revelation which Muslims hold dear.

Sacred text: The Quran

When exploring revelation, Muslims look toward two main sources: the Quran and the Prophetic traditions. The Quran (perhaps contrary to popular understanding) is not a book of history, law, science or philosophy. It may contain these disciplines, but the Quran describes itself in this threefold manner: guidance, mercy, and either glad tidings to those who live a moral and virtuous life, or a warning against evil actions. To refute another misconception, the Quran is not a book of *Sharia* (the collective body of literature from which Islamic law derives[2]). From approximately 6300 verses, only 400 deal with principles through which *Sharia* could be extracted. These principles need to be interpreted through a complex process, so merely reading the Quran to learn the law is impossible.

The Quran has approximately a dozen verses addressing migration. Nearly all these verses are in the context of oppression and

---

2   Although *Sharia* is commonly translated as 'Islamic law', it is rather the 'Islamic way to behave'. It is a guide to religious practices, as well as principles of interaction. It means 'a clear pathway' and can be compared to *Halakha* in Judaism.

persecution. On the one hand, there is an obligation to save one's life; and on the other, to flee from places where you cannot worship freely. These two conditions become the main principles for migration. God indicates that migration is not easy: 'Yet surely your Lord, with respect to those who immigrate after they are persecuted, then they struggle hard and are patient, most surely your Lord after that is Forgiving, Merciful' (Chapter of the Bee, verse 110).

God commands the believer to strive, not to be a burden on society nor to give up on aspirations and dreams, but instead to be patient and to know that divine mercy will follow. In the Chapter of Women, verse 100, God goes further: 'And whosoever migrated in Allah's way, he will find in the earth many a place of refuge and abundant resources...' Here, God again encourages the believer to migrate within the context of oppression or the inability to practise faith freely. God comforts those who may be apprehensive. He assures them that refuge and abundant resources await.

The stories of Abraham and Ishmael are common among the Abrahamic faiths. Both men were effectively exiled from what they called home, although for very different reasons. When asked why he was migrating, Abraham replied, 'I am migrating to a place where I can be free to worship God. He shall guide me. And may he grant me righteous children' (Quran, 37:99–100). Abraham proceeded to move with his family and followers from Babylon to the Levant. His faith challenged the status quo: Nimrod,[3] the ruler of Mesopotamia, had made it difficult for Abraham and his followers to worship. As a persecuted community, they had no choice but to migrate. The Quran concludes that for the sake of their eagerness to migrate, God not only saved Abraham and his followers, but also blessed them and the land they journeyed to. This blessing would later be felt by all of mankind (Quran 21:71).

Fast-forward a generation. Abraham was faced with another dilemma. Within a year of conceiving his son Ishmael with Hagar, the handmaid, he expected another child with his wife Sarah. His son

---

3   Nimrod was a biblical figure, who is also described in the Quran as the great-grandson of the Prophet Noah, and Abraham's arch enemy.

Isaac was born, but joy turned to bitterness. Sarah was troubled by the presence of Hagar and Ishmael. She insisted that Abraham send them away. So Hagar and Ishmael fled to the desert. In the Hebrew Bible, God assures both Abraham and Hagar that this trauma has a divine purpose: 'As for Ishmael, I have heard you. I have blessed him and make him fruitful and exceedingly numerous. He shall be the father of twelve princes, and I will make him a great nation' (Genesis 17:20).

Similarly, in Islamic traditions:

Abraham asked his Lord: 'Where shall I take them?'

God replied: 'To my sanctuary, to the first place I created on earth – to Bakkah.'

Arriving in Bakkah (which later became Makkah, or Mecca – the most sacred site for Muslims), Abraham prayed:

Lord, I leave my family in this valley which is bereft of pasture, near your sacred house, not for worldly gain, but according to your command so that they may establish the prayer; so make people's hearts incline towards them and provide them with sustenance so that they may be thankful. (Quran, 14:37)

Hagar implored: 'Why do you leave us in a place where we have neither friend nor water nor pasture?' (Kulayni 1384 AH, vol. 4, p.201)

Abraham, with tears in his eyes, replied: 'The one who ordered me to leave you in this place will take care of you.'

Angel Gabriel concurred: 'Abraham has left you in the care of the one who will suffice you.' (*ibid.*)

With conviction in the will of God and with pain in his heart, Abraham left Hagar and Ishmael in the deserts of Bakkah. Abraham submitted to God. In return, God not only saved Ishmael but nurtured him and – through him – a great nation.

In time, from the Children of Ishmael came a tribe known as the Banu Hashim, who became the custodians of the *Kaaba*. According to Islamic history, the *Kaaba* had been built by Abraham and Ishmael as the house of monotheism, where none other than the One God was to be worshipped. It was this very tribe that the Prophet Muhammad belonged to. Following in the footsteps of his ancestor Abraham, he too migrated from his hometown to escape oppression. With his followers, the Prophet migrated from Makkah to Madina. This was the humble beginning of a religion that would become a vast civilization. It was through migration and hardship that Muslims came to find peace in the Divine Plan. This was their theology of resilience.

Sacred text: Prophetic traditions

Prophetic traditions are the actions, speech and everyday interactions of the Prophet Muhammad. Their purposes are twofold: 1) to decode the intricate messages that God has codified in the Quran, and 2) to learn how to live in a holistic manner, with balance between the physical world and the spiritual self. The Prophet, after all, teaches us how to read the Quran.

In prophetic traditions, Muslims are advised to travel. The Prophet emphasized the need to travel for spiritual and physical wellbeing (Muttaqi Hindi 1387 AH). On a practical level, it was also financially profitable. There are, of course, downsides to travelling. One prophetic tradition describes the 'tribulations' of travelling, namely disturbances in food, water and sleep (Rayshahrī 1385 AH, vol. 5, p.309). While travelling may be considered a positive endeavour, it is not without anxiety (Majlisi 1406 AH, p.222). An important prophetic tradition illuminates the Quranic ethos of migration: 'A Muslim is someone who spares people from the harm of his tongue and a migrant is someone who migrates from what God has forbidden' (Bukhari 1412 AH, Book 1, Hadith 211). The underlying theme of this tradition is the need to preserve one's character and to practise faith freely. This is the primary reason for migration, as seen in the life of the Prophet Mohammed.

The Prophet's 23-year mission had two parts. He spent 13 years living as a minority in Makkah (Mecca). Here, the Prophet gained prominence through social and charitable works. He taught us that hearts – not laws – change mentalities. As minorities, whether feeling oppressed or secure, religious responsibilities such as *sadaqa* (charity), *khidmah* (selfless service) and *rahmah* (mercy unto others) will aid in removing mistrust and developing a sense of togetherness.

The latter ten years of the Prophet's mission were spent in Madina, among Christians and Jews. If service, patience and charity are the Meccan way, the Madani way is dialogue. When the Prophet migrated to Madina, he ensured that those migrating with him were accommodated and that those hosting were respected. As he became leader of the majority, he instructed that charity, service to others and compassion should continue; and he also encouraged dialogue. The Prophet made it a covenantal responsibility on Muslims to safeguard their neighbours. This meant a moral obligation as opposed to just a legal duty.

Today in Britain, I advocate the prophetic methodology of charity, dialogue and service. I emphasize the importance of teaching children the value of serving others – even more so in a climate deemed polarizing to Muslims. It is dangerous for any community to become insular due to feeling oppressed. It is not easy to interact with people considered foreign to our way of life, but dialogue is the only way to bring down those walls that we, in our insular communities, create. Through dialogue, we come to understand that 'the other' is not as foreign as we perceived them to be. In fact, 'the other' is just as human – and perhaps just as British – as we are.

Islam as a migrating religion

Traditionally, seven cultures – Slavic, Maghrebi, Arabic, Turkic, Persian, Subcontinental and Malay – made up what came to be known as the Islamic civilization. Islamic art, music, literature and philosophies varied from place to place, yet with such diversity also came essential unity. At the core was faith. In the words of Imam Ali, Islam can be summarized as *one's duty to God* and *one's duty to humanity*. It is a journey, a migration. The first part represents a vertical movement to the divine (and, perhaps, to enlightenment). The second part represents a horizontal motion – a quest to refine the moral virtues required to be a good human being.

Islam spread as an abstract faith. As Muslims migrated, they manifested their Islam through the lens of local culture. Arab culture, which was once found between Benghazi and the river Euphrates, has on its border the relics of a great Persian civilization. Today, an Arab and a Persian may have different cultures, but they share a common faith. Muslims in West Africa, Eastern Europe or those of Turkic origin are unique in their cultures and ways of life, but with distinct manifestations of Islamic culture. This is a product of centuries of migration. Within two generations, Muslims living in Europe – particularly Britain – should develop a distinct European or British Islamic cultural identity. If allowed to evolve organically, we will experience evolution as a product of migration and integration. Just as Persian Muslims may feel Persian and Muslim, seeing no contradiction, British Muslims may feel both British and very much Muslim.

However, Islamophobia could halt further evolution. When a community feels under attack, its natural inclination is to become insular, rigid and defensive. A consequence of Islamophobia is that communities, if polarized, become defensive to any form of negativity. Tightly knit communities become a form of comfort and support in difficult times, but may lead to a generation of young adults feeling victimized and oppressed. The ability to integrate has historically been a quality that Muslims, living as a minority, were very good at doing.

History teaches us that Muslims are resilient. The essential principles taught by Islam contribute to wider society through compassion, love and kindness, but most of all through empathy. From the life of the Prophet Muhammad, we learn charity, social welfare, coming to the aid of those who are less fortunate, and dialogue as a way bridging

hearts. The prophetic principle is that regardless of worldly acknowl-
edgement, the work of God must continue.

Conclusion

A common theology of resilience can be found among the Abrahamic
faiths – a thread that aligns the histories of the Jewish, Christian and
Muslim peoples. When hope was lost and destruction was the natural
conclusion, faith in God nurtured profound resilience in the hearts
of the faithful. They came to understand God's divine nature in a way
that strengthened them. It was when these nations were tested that
they truly came to know God. Migration teaches us to connect with
God, when faced with uncertainty of the future.

As the word of God was delivered in a particular time and context,
it is important to take core principles from these sacred texts and to
contextualize them. Re-reading sacred texts within the context of our
own time is not a foreign exercise just for theologians and jurists. The
contextualization of sacred texts will become increasingly important
in a rapidly changing world, with its evolving challenges and increased
polarization of faith-based communities.

When the Prophet Muhammad was asked which was the best type
of migration, he replied that it was to migrate away from that which
attracts you to commit evil deeds (Muttaqi Hindi 1397 AH, Hadith
3935). When read in light of the Quran and the prophetic traditions,
the Prophet's vision was to appreciate multiplicity, diversity and the
freedom to practise faith throughout God's earth – to be a solution and
not a problem. That the Abrahamic faiths are a product of migration
should be enough to instil (in Muslims, at the very least) a sense of
moral obligation to others. We were once 'the other', too.

A Bedouin once came to the Prophet and grabbed the reigns of his
horse. He then asked: 'O messenger of God, teach me something to
go to heaven with!'

The Prophet replied: 'As you would have people do to you, do upon them; and what you dislike to be done to you, do not to them' (Kulayni 1384 AH, vol. 2, p.125).

Islam was meant to be a religion of compassion and mercy to others, so that we could all flourish together. This is our narrative of migration and resilience.

References

Al Sadiq, Imam Jafar. (2004) *Lantern of the Path* (third edition). London: Zahra Publications.

Bukhari, M.I. (1412 AH) *Sahih Bukhari: The Book of Miscellany* (fourth edition). Beirut: Dar Ibn Kathir.

Kulayni. M.Y. (1384 AH) *Kitab al Kafi*. Qom: Eram Publications.

Majlisi. M.B. (1412 AH) *Bihar al Anwar li Darar Akhbar al Aimmah al Adhhar (Bihar al Anwar)*. Beirut: Dar al Ihya al Taraath.

Majlisi, M.T. (1406 AH) *Rawdhatul Muttaqin Fi Sharh Man La Yahdhuruhu al-Faqih* (second edition). Qom: Kushanpour Islamic Cultural Institute.

Muttaqi Hindi (1397 AH) *Kanz al Umaal fi Sunan al Aqwal wa al Afaal (Kanz al Umaal)* (first edition). Beirut: Al Taraath al Islami Publications.

Rayshahrī, M.M. (1385 AH) *Mizan al-Hikmah*. Qom: Knowledge and Cultural Institute, Dar al Hadith.

CHAPTER 17

What is a Refuge for Migrant Women?

Testimony, Witness-Bearing and 'The Rape of Tamar'

Alison Phipps

My home has been offered as a place of refuge for over 15 years, especially housing migrants seeking sanctuary. Those coming to stay have mostly been women, across all ages and generations. Many are pregnant, always a long way from those they love or those who brought them violence. The precarity which comes with migration – the loss of roots, of easily trusted persons; the claustrophobia in family settings around protective relationships – are especially acute for migrant women. They are a group for whom sexual violence is commonplace, and a group who find it especially difficult to articulate. This is for multiple reasons. The shame which is associated with sexual violence is heightened in many migrant women; the language with which to speak of assault may be entirely lacking; families may or (more likely) may not have equipped women with safeguarding resources: safe people to confide in, routes to safety or credibility.

Sometimes over the years of living together – and knowing many migrant women who have found themselves in danger, sometimes in the heat of crisis – with the safety of a warm home, a bed and a quiet place, I have witnessed the intimacy of hosting. The tears come, and the story – and the touch between women who know and care and hear – opens out, and the terrible knowing that is sexual violence is shared, for the first time. Such violence accompanies the story of migration and exile, but also the story of stasis and community, of the siege that is needing to settle and dwell in a place, when flight would be preferable.

Although not directly a story of migration at the outset, by its conclusion the biblical story of Tamar becomes one of exile. We don't know what became of her after she was thrown out on the streets and tore her garments. In the intimate moments of sharing, migrant women who have found themselves exiled, outcast, without the care of family close by, can read the tale of Tamar against their own experiences. The story helps reveal the hidden structures of silence, as we read against the grain of texts which have been controlled, written and edited by men.

In the story of the rape of Tamar (2 Samuel 13), we hear of a girl (the narrator calls her 'beautiful') who has a brother, Absalom, and a half-brother, Amnon. King David is a common parent to all three. Amnon is obsessed with Tamar and moans to his friend that he can't have her. His friend plots with him to trick her into bed. She refuses, and he rapes her. She is the one shamed, thrown out and sworn to silence. The story becomes known to the king, but he does not act. Instead, he and Tamar's brother Absalom brood and plot vengeance on the rapist. Amnon is later killed by Absalom; Absalom is sent into exile; and King David longs to be reunited with his son. The Tamar story echoes an early biblical story of the rape of Dinah. The violation was followed by revenge killings of all the men in a city, sowing hatred and enmity between families for generations.

Feminist readings of biblical texts, as part of the movements of liberation theology, have pioneered a way of interpretation that is suspicious of claims to truth (Trible 1978; Tamez 1989; Schüssler Fiorenza 1988). They offer resources for hope, opening a space for reading through the imagination, for contextual Bible study, for according dignity to women. Other theologians have come to such texts as examples of stories of the failure to overcome violence and the consequences following such acts (Dietrich and Mayordomo 2005). In particular, The Tamar Campaign in South Africa,[1] an initiative of

---

1   www.fecclaha.org.

the Fellowship of Christian Councils in the Great Lakes and Horn of Africa, seeks to bring ways of reading and understanding which start from where people are rooted and what people know of their lives and violations. It uses the Tamar story to inspire a struggle for liberation and justice for all affected by gender-based violence in the churches of the region.

A careful posing of contextual questions resonates with the situation of gender-based violence today:

- Tamar was sexually assaulted, not by a stranger, but by someone she knew.
- The violation took place not in a desolate remote place at the hands of a stranger, but by a member of her own family, in his home.
- Tamar was exploited through her most vulnerable traits: her kindness, her culturally-instilled obedience, and her upbringing to take care of others.
- Tamar said 'No' and her 'No' was not respected.
- When Tamar sought help, she was told to be quiet.

(Cooper-White 2007, p.27)

Fulata Mbano-Moyo, trained by the Tamar Campaign, developed contextual Bible study notes for the International Ecumenical Peace Convocation. These notes aim to draw together stories and responses from many different contexts and to use the text 'to break the conspiracy or chain of silence that often exists around issues of sexual violence in a community' (Mbano-Moyo, 2011).

The experience of engaging with Tamar's story, in international ecumenical contexts, has drawn me into practical, pastoral reflection with women who themselves have suffered sexual abuse and rape. I seek to understand what feminist or resistant readings would look like as prophetic, liturgical acts of repentance. I want to think through practical theological understandings of this text. I use creative writing to develop fictional scenarios which are woven from experiences of encounters with survivors of rape and sexual abuse.

This work follows in the spirit of West and colleagues' (2004) contextual readings practices, developed at the Ujamaa Centre at the University of KwaZulu-Natal. Here, the Tamar Campaign began by taking a theme with the power to generate thinking and action (Freire 1970), in the case of the Tamar story, from the reality of women who have experienced violence. This inspiring work has helped shaped educational encounters with texts that have been skipped over, and which critique gender-based violence. It has helped to reveal the abuse of the female throughout history, and enabled tale-telling as a retelling *in memoriam* (Trible 1984, p.3). It has nurtured a context where women have felt able to 'name their worlds' (Freire 1970) and tell their histories; a context for trauma healing and work towards transformation.

However, in reading these texts in the context of my own ongoing listening to abused and raped women – readings which take these women into a place of unproblematic heroine status, or which redeem Tamar easily 'for the sisterhood' – there remains a profound problem. Discussions of rape and justice revolve around the requirement to 'speak out', 'find words', 'go public'. Tamar is presented to us as a model: virtuous, a public activist and a speaker. She immediately, and in anguish, 'names her world' and is hung out to dry. She engages directly in the kinds of dramas of resistance drawn out from Old Testament narratives by Brueggemann (2000), where there is a public expression of pain which brings about a dramatic breach and a changed direction. But for Tamar there is no transformational change. This is the repeated experience of sexual abuse victims and is palpably present in the raw moments of intimacy with a trusted sister or friend.

I have found myself grappling repeatedly with the aspect of speaking out and naming – of articulate articulation, especially when this is to be done in accents which are not trusted as testimony, or in languages not admitted to the courts, which privilege English. The now commonplace championing of people who 'speak out' comes with a certain expectation of articulacy and of education. It has been a feature of feminist practical theology, charting a path from what Graham (1999) terms 'terrible silence' to 'transforming hope'.

The polished narrative of Tamar's story, and the sophisticated analysis of language and discourse undertaken to elaborate the themes of the text (Smith 1990), reveals something of the control and artistry of the narrator. But such control and artistry come over time and are not necessarily present in the survivor, nor can we demand that they be present. And even where there is agency and resilience, such artistry and coherence rarely accompanies those who (as in my own experiences of encounter) are strangers in a land.

Public speaking can be difficult for a range of reasons. Articulate, activist speech, highlighting the deep wounding and vulnerability in the context of rape, takes place all too often in societal and institutional contexts where ambivalence (at best) and ostracism (all too often) are likely to follow. Justice, if done at all, is done painfully (Kennedy 2005). The sophistication of argument and tonal balance required by public and activist discourse all too often equate with education and class position. There can be many good reasons for maintaining silence – sometimes as an act of resistance; sometimes because it is judged better, for now, between sisters or friends or trusted others.

In the narratives from the Tamar Campaign, we find the repeated, rich theme of difficulty of speaking in public, of 'being like Tamar':

> The Tamar Campaign has given me the strength to face my worst devil, for I was abused by my biological father. *I have been quiet about this for 25 years*, but now I have decided to have counselling with the minister.

> Umfundisi [minister], *what does it help if I say what I feel* and what I experience? You get in your car and go back to your manse [church home], but I stay here behind and starve to death and you are nowhere to be found.' (West *et al.* 2004, p.41; my emphasis)

This woman was starkly stating that in contexts such as this, for people like herself, there was still not enough safety to tell their stories. Indeed, telling her story would mean being cast out from her family and the community resources, resulting in starvation.

Ragged 'first tellings' of rape are not usually found in empirical 'research contexts', but are pastoral, and marked by immediate concerns that do not fit with the luxuries of time for reflection or scholarship. This is not to say that research cannot also have therapeutic, pastoral or restorative qualities. Indeed, I have argued elsewhere that research should strive for ways of proceeding and design which are restorative and do not privilege the already privileged (Phipps 2019). I have become increasingly convinced, however, that to speak out may not be the best route for every individual – that there may be a time for speaking and a time for keeping silent, within alternative social economies of grief and anger. There is wisdom in silence. Through my work with asylum seekers, I have seen that the constant demand by officials and support workers for the retelling of difficult narratives of persecution keeps alive an aspect of trauma and spreads it among a community of listeners, creating conditions of secondary trauma and contagious helplessness that are ultimately disempowering (Weingarten 2003).

As a way of exploring this space between raw telling and the difficulties of 'speaking out', I have followed the creative trajectories opened out by the practices of the Tamar Campaign, to consider the weight and difficulty of 'going public'. Instead of offering yet another propositional argument about the importance and difficulty of public speaking in the context of rape (this has already been done by exemplary legal theorists and feminist scholars of criminology), I use an approach to reading known as 'rhetorical criticism'. This approach attends to the text itself and its resonances for readers, and retelling, through creative writing. I do so in order to work within the narratives which form rape myths and the social constructions of what Kathryn Ryan (2011, p.774) terms 'sexual scripts' that affect sexual beliefs and behaviours.

Ryan's work is important for practical theology, as it intervenes in the myth creation process. It views critically the myths of eloquent virtue and their unproblematic imposition on survivors of rape. It also recuperates silence, as used and owned by others, especially as understood in postcolonial contexts. Minh-ha (1989, p.83) maintains that 'silence as a refusal to partake in the story does sometimes provide us with a means to gain a hearing'. Importantly, she does not see speech and silence as set against each other. I am not attempting to set up an argument for silence, or for speaking, but to explore the spaces where stories are in the process of being born, and of the felt experiences which are present in the attempts to speak, go public, or to utter the first cries.

Many contextual, pastoral Bible study and transformational approaches to education rely on the format of the small-group discussion and on circle processing, whereby dialogue and attention to the speaker are not subject to cross-examination or debate. Facilitators enable dialogue and listening, so allow equal sharing, not dominant voices. These are wonderful methodologies, but they privilege verbal processing and create a social context where verbal dexterity is presumed. In Fiji, gatherings traditionally are accompanied by a weaver – someone listening and weaving together the strands, quite literally, into a cloth. *Textare*, in Latin – from which we take our words for 'text' as well as 'textile' – means 'to weave'. Recently, in participating in discussions of gender justice, I have seen practices of 'silence' emerge around knitting and tapestry. Those women who feel too raw to share in the groups have concentrated instead on different makings. They have spoken, knowingly, to one another, of the fabrics they are creating – not of those torn.

What I offer below is a practical theological reading in the tradition of exposing the abuse, and of tale-telling *in memoriam*. I fuse this with language-destroying experiences and raw emotion in the face of demands to 'go public' to the authorities with a story of what was transacted in speech between rape survivor and rapist.

> Warning: What follows contains strong language and may
> trigger deep emotions.

She'd been raped before. This wasn't the first time. How else could she possibly have had a voice, and a reasonable sounding one at that? You may say that it's only after reading a text that we can begin to evaluate our moral role within the text. Only then will the moral become visible, and only in dialogue with others and with their stories.

The first time

Standing in the kitchen, he has eaten very little of the food she has prepared. 'I want to put my hand up your skirt, between your thighs', he says suddenly. Memory is vague, not vivid, sense is torn. 'I want you', he says coming to her, zip open, flesh out, against her now, hard. 'No!' Was it spoken? There was barely a sound. Inside, the voices are screaming. She thinks she will vomit. She cannot speak as the bile fills her mouth. She is as stiff as he is, frozen, paralyzed, taut. He plays her like a drum. Her tongue, heavy, immovable, sticky with the metallic taste of blood. Her reason deafened by the sound of it pounding round and round and round her body.

Did she really say?

Do not do this, my brother

Do not do violence to me (do not hurt me)

Because this is not good behaviour in this country

Don't do something disgraceful

And where would I go with my disgrace?

And you, you would be one of the most scorned of Israel.

I've a better idea – speak to the king

He won't refuse you what you want.

Did she appeal to custom, law, reason, carefully weighing the consequences, bargaining with a better solution, giving a neatly linear argument?

Like f*** she did. Reasonable, articulate, in the face of such physical fear and for the first time. Like f*** she did. And if she did then I want none of it. It is a greater betrayal than his towards our 'her' here. That men could tell this story, read this story, this way, for thousands of years, believing, believing that she could speak in words of the sweetest reason in the midst of all that. F*** it! She didn't, not if it was the first time.

She felt nothing but shame at her silence.

I should have said:

Do not do this, my brother

Do not do violence to me (do not hurt me)

Because this is not good behaviour in this country

Don't do something disgraceful

And where would I go with my disgrace?

And you, you would be one of the most scorned of Israel.

I've a better idea – speak to the king

He won't refuse you what you want.

But I am not as good as she is. So I didn't say these words.

She would tell herself again and again and again and again. I should have shouted 'No!' – pushed him again, kneed his groin ('non-violence; self-defence; be a good girl...violence is wrong...a good girl') Breathe. Deeply. I am not a coward too, surely not.

The second time it happened – for of course she still encountered him – he was powerful and had some control over her future and they would have to sit together and this time, when he reached for her, she was quieter and reasonable. The body and blood were still screaming the same dread mix of fear and now, perhaps, perhaps... though God help her that this may be so. Her practised words were steady, learned and performed according to the narratives and readers' 'reasonable' demands. The second time, she knew what the world of moral violence needed her to say to have any chance of compassion and a fair hearing from history. No wonder he – Amnon – hated her, she was not as satisfying as he'd hoped. There was no tearing this time, no cry at the pain, no blood of his producing. And her knowing speech, practised from the first time, produced now in perfectly delivered, crafted lines:

Oh no you don't, my brother in Christ

For this is a greater injustice than the first

one you did to me

If you now chase me away.

The deed itself is always confused with a body repulsed and arching in unstoppable, undeniable, reflexes of terrified spasm, which appear to say 'yes' as the blood screams silently 'No, No, No – struggle – F***, no.'

'Oh no you don't' The power of rhetoric, the voice learned from the warnings of mothers, the contradictions of fathers, brothers 'No, no you don't!' spoken in the power and confidence of a lived, practised post-rape morality. The violence that teaches 'No'.

How dare she! Correction: how dare they! How dare she be a moral example for the first rape if this is a second. How dare they tell this story as if it is the first and leave to self-condemnation all those running terrified, but free of the clutches, with hair flying and tears streaming, sore, sore, sore and bleeding and alone, so very alone...up the stairs, past the dismayed surprise of the family, into her room... 'Leave me alone, just leave me alone. I hate you all.' They didn't know, Absalom didn't know for sure...he just learned from the first time how to act the second (perhaps he had been the first. We do not know). 'He is your brother, don't take it to heart.' Don't you dare, any of you, don't you dare tell me/us/her – for we are as one in this – that we must behave this way when you rape us; that you will only believe and celebrate and tell this, this as the moral behaviour in the first (or any other) knowing moment of rape. Don't you dare. Don't you dare suggest that when she comes to me, when she came to me, after he had grabbed her, and she could not speak the words, any words, for sobbing, that I should ask her if she has said sweet reasonable words, Tamar's words. Don't even think about it.

If you want to know what becomes of a woman and her silence the first time, then look at Dinah. Dinah knows.

She vanishes from her story. She had no words. There are never any words in this, the first grief.

David hears the story of the rape of Tamar and is furious but does nothing. Is anger not action? Jacob wraps himself in a cloak of silence until the end. Is this passivity or strategy, you ask? Is passivity not a strategy? And what of silence? But these questions come too soon.

The fusion in the account between the rape survivor, myself as author of this chapter, and the parallels with Tamar's story are becoming hard to follow. This is what happens when triggered by memories (ancient and less so) of sexual assault – not least when these occur in the absence of any obvious protections or places to go, other than the arms of a friend, for solace.

So, a different story, and a continuation of the first...

Six months ago now, not so long ago really, I am holding her in my arms as she sobs. We are back in the first story at that point when she came to me after he'd grabbed her, if you recall. It's only after a long time, after she'd run up to her room (in tears, again) following a fraught phone call, that I followed her, with a cup of sweet tea. 'Do you want me to go away? Do you want to be on your own?' Wordlessly shaking with grief she shakes her head and I hold her. In her something has died. Eventually the grief is spent and she is still – silent – still.

'I couldn't say, "No, stop it". He grabbed me. I can't bear the shame. I can't bear the shame. And they know. They will talk, because they know. He just grabbed me. I had – my body had a life of its own. I just went numb.' For how else other than with a body that has a life of its own and with a body which is numb could she live with the judgement of those who tell us to be like Tamar.

> *F*** you, narrator, and your male courts and your insistence that we speak in your f***ing perfect, rational, prose. F*** your judgement which refuses to allow our silence. Dinah's silence. F*** you and your timescale in Law. 'You must report this within 24 hours. You can only expect the organization to act if you speak to your employer while still in their pay.' F*** your legal economies and your insistence that she speak, even, now, oh so graciously allowed – to a policewoman. F*** you all for your immoral refusal of our silence; for your demand that we go public.*

'What are you going to do?' I hate myself the moment I ask the question. Immediately there is a demand for action when it is way too soon for anything. Gentler, apologetically, with as much love, 'What do you want?' The tears come again. Big, silent, quiet, unstoppable. No sobbing. It cannot be said. How can it be said?

'He shouldn't have done this. I did it all wrong. I should have said those words, Tamar's words. How can this be made good? But...he just grabbed me...' and the tears roll on like a river to the sea.

Later, over food – for this too restores – we are steadier. The private chamber of a woman's grief and her sister is moving, slowly, into conversation. The taboo-desires and questions known in the silence, now only carefully, hesitantly, taken out and turned over. The trust, it seems, must always be a fragile storied thing. The question lingers. 'What shall we do?' 'Do you want me to speak to his boss?' A long pause. 'It may be easier for me to speak for you.' The sad shake of a confused head. The head placed on folded arms on the table. Long, slow looks, a sip of wine. The nervous, fingering of a full glass. The look of such heart-breaking shame. The look of open desire. The look, the words: 'I'll be stronger next time.'

Time passes and I ponder these things. There is silence.

'I don't know if I did the right thing doing nothing. I didn't know what to do.' Her words are my words. 'I should have been more directive. I should have had a clearer sense of what to do...' but there is no clarity, no reason, no ways of being so moral in speech and deed when there is the volatile chaos of grief and violence and the great, great tearing danger of the social order entirely at war. Her rape, Tamar's rape, Dinah's rape, fade from the story, for after it and in the necessary silence of its holding is the space for quiet memorial. Only later, much, much later come the stories. And the passivity and lack of action? David, Jacob? Me? Is this ambivalence? Not entirely, though the ambivalence is there of course, for readers wanting action, wanting clarity, wanting public-speaking heroines, wanting redemptive order to be restored at any cost. Would a judgement have helped earlier? This is not your story, says Jesus to Peter. This is not the story. This is a story of forced migration, forced exile.

So Tamar dwelt and was desolate.

Hindsight is a terrible thing.

Dinah knows.

My friends, this was not the first time.

References

Brueggemann, W. (2000) *Texts that Linger, Words that Explode: Listening to Prophetic Voices*. Minneapolis, MN: Fortress Press.

Cooper-White, P. (2007) 'The Rape of Tamar, the Crime of Ammon.' In F. Nyabera and T. Montgomery (eds) *Contextual Bible Study Manual on Gender-based Violence*. Nairobi: Fellowship of Christian Churches in the Great Lakes and Horn of Africa.

Dietrich, W. and Mayordomo, M. (2005) *Gewalt und Gewaltüberwindung in der Bibel*. Zürich: Theologischer Verlag Zürich.

Freire, P. (1970) *Pedagogy of the Oppressed*. London: Penguin.

Graham, E. (1999) 'From "Terrible Silence" to "Transforming Hope": The impact of feminist theory on practical theology.' *International Journal of Practical Theology*, 3, 2, 185–212.

Kennedy, H. (2005) *Eve was Framed: Women and British Justice*. London: Vintage.

Mbano-Moyo, F. (2011) 'The Rape of Tamar.' World Council of Churches. Accessed on 30/05/19 at www.overcomingviolence.org/en/resources-dov/wcc-resources/documents/bible-studies/iepc-bible-studies/peace-in-the-community-the-rape-of-tamar.html.

Minh-ha, T. (1989) *Women, Native, Other: Writing, Postcoloniality and Feminism*. London: John Wiley & Sons.

Phipps, A. (2019) *Decolonising Multilingualism: Struggles to Decreate*. Bristol: Multilingual Matters.

Ryan, K. (2011) 'The relationship between rape myths and sexual scripts: The social construction of rape.' *Sex Roles*, 65, 11, 774–782.

Schüssler Fiorenza, E. (1988) 'The ethics of biblical interpretation: Decentering biblical scholarship.' *Journal of Biblical Literature*, 107, 1, 3–17.

Smith, J. (1990) 'The discourse structure of the Rape of Tamar (2 Samuel 13:1–22).' *Vox Evangelica*, 20: 21–42.

Tamez, E. (1989) *Through Her Eyes: Women's Theology from Latin America*. New York, NY: Orbis Books.

Trible, P. (1978) *God and the Rhetoric of Sexuality*. Philadelphia, PA: Fortress Press.

Trible, P. (1984) *Texts of Terror: Literary-Feminist Readings of Biblical Narratives*. Philadelphia, PA: Fortress Press.

Weingarten, K. (2003) *Common Shock: Witnessing Violence Every Day – How We Are Harmed, How We Can Heal*. London: Penguin.

West, G., Zondi-Mabizela, P., Maluleke, M., Khumalo, H., Matsepe, P.S., and Naidoo, M. (2004) 'Rape in the House of David: The biblical story of Tamar as resource for transformation.' *Agenda*, 61, 36–41.

CHAPTER 18

Taking the Talmud for a Walk

Jacqueline Nicholls

I use my art to explore traditional Jewish ideas in untraditional ways. My drawings are my handwriting. It's an act of transcription, and every transcription is also an act of translation and deviation and interpretation of the original. You can't help but put your own handwriting into it, taking ownership, putting your personality in the text.

I am fascinated by traditional Jewish scribal art and all its accoutrements. Each scribe makes their own ink, from their own recipe. You make your own, handcrafted quills. Then there's the parchment, and how it's treated and prepared. When people think of parchment, they tend to think about historical re-enactment. But I come from a background where parchment is very much living. Parchment is perceived as belonging to the male world. In the Jewish tradition, there is huge controversy about whether or not a woman can be a scribe.

I come from a traditional, Orthodox Jewish background in London, where text is paramount. The Talmud, a multi-volume text, is a transcription of a rabbinic oral tradition, containing many voices, topics and tangents. These texts, and the discussions within them, form Rabbinic Judaism; they are the foundation for the way Orthodox Jews live today. You have a sense of holiness around these texts and books. If a book is dropped on the floor, it is lovingly picked up, kissed and comforted.

Only recently have women been able to learn the same holy texts as men – at the same level and the same depth of learning. Growing up, nobody told me that I was not allowed to study these texts. But I certainly was never encouraged. In my late teens, I began to study the Talmud. I remember the first time I opened the pages and looked at these texts. It was thrilling.

One of my ongoing projects, since August 2012, is to learn one page of the Talmud every day. There is a ritualized learning, started in 1923 by Rabbi Meir Shapiro, where every day, people study the same page of the Talmud. His vision was that Jews all over the world would be able to have a global conversation. You could have a Jew living in Poland, who gets on a boat and, a couple months later, gets off in New York. They could go into their synagogue and join the conversation, because everyone is, literally, on the same page. Today, this is happening on social media. It's an ongoing, global conversation.

It takes seven and a half years to go through the whole Talmud. Every day, I study a page, and then I do a drawing in response to my learning.

It's fascinating and disturbing to do this, because I'm seeing what is really written in this collection of books that is held so precious to Rabbinic Judaism. I'm seeing how women are discussed; there is no agency. Female characters may appear in the text, but these texts have not been written or edited by women. It feels subversive for a woman to be learning the Talmud. When I read these texts, I am very aware that I am female, that I cannot step away from my woman's body.

I use different drawing mediums for different sections of the Talmud, giving each part its own identity. At the time of writing, I am working on the section called *Chulin*. The text does not anticipate me as a reader; it needs to enter into my space. So I will transcribe it, put it into my page, take ownership. The page is full of my handwriting, in Hebrew. Then I disturb it, and I see what comes from that. When I put water on the page, the ink smudges and breaks up.

I draw sequentially, every day a new page. It feels as if I'm running a marathon, but I'm not sure where I'm going. I'm not the same as the person who started this project. The drawing has taken me to a different place. I knew it would be challenging; I knew there were pockets of problematic and tricky texts. But I had not anticipated how much it would impact me emotionally. To reflect, I need to have a pen in my hand or a pencil and paper. I need to use my art to understand, because this is how I process. This is how I can track where I've been, and where I've come from. I allow the text to speak to me, and then I speak back to the text. I don't want to just read it passively.

Disrupting the page

I really love learning the Talmud. I really hate learning the Talmud. I say both with exactly the same expression in my voice, because they are both equally true. There is constant tension. Do I stay? Or do I go? Do I shut the book? Or do I keep the page open? If I keep the page open, I don't want to be too reverential, but I don't want to be too dismissive.

It's a very delicate balance, how to keep the page open.

Walking the Talmud

Migration is the act of becoming Other, of becoming different. How compassionately and ethically we respond is a test of our own morality and humanity.

Within the Jewish text that I'm working with, women are very much Othered. It's not something that is particular to Jewish Orthodoxy; it's in the world around us. Women are not the default citizen. So while I would never claim to truly understand the immigrant experience, I do have experience of being Othered. I have experience of trying to find a way of being present in a space that does not expect you. Like the Talmud.

My background in Jewish Orthodoxy has made me sensitive to when I am Othered as a woman. There are huge politics around being a woman, moving and walking in the public space, especially when you are on your own. You have to be mindful of criteria that make you view your body defensively. When women feel vulnerable, we tend to shrink into ourselves. We try to make ourselves invisible. As a woman, I am aware of the barriers that may deter my movement. How do you fight against that?

In her book *Wanderlust*, Rebecca Solnit (2001) describes how our human brains only started to grow larger once we started walking, freeing the upper limbs to make tools and to make marks. The act of walking (and using tools) increased our brain capacity – not the other way around. Drawing, mark-making and walking allow us to be fully embodied in space and time.

These drawings, from my daily Talmud series, are inspired by pages *Shabbat 33* and *Shabbat 34*. They describe a story of Shimon bar Yochai, of mystical knowledge and walking.

Shabbat 33 and Shabbat 34

Shabbat 33

The hero of the story, Shimon bar Yochai, is on the run from the Roman authorities with his son. He stops in a cave, which is his refuge but also becomes his prison. For 12 years, he and his son survive by being buried up to the neck in sand. When you're stuck in sand, you are stuck with only one point of view.

When Shimon bar Yochai comes out of the cave, he finds that the world is more complex. He starts destroying the world.

God says to him, 'What are you doing? Get back in the cave.'

When he comes out of the cave a second time, he sees the world but he no longer destroys it. He meets a man who is carrying two branches. He asks, 'What are these two branches for?'

The man replies, 'It's Friday, twilight time. It's to honour the Sabbath.'

Shimon bar Yochai says, 'Why do you need two?'

The man carrying the branches responds, 'The text says to *honour* the Sabbath, and to *remember* the Sabbath. So, you need both.'

This is key to my understanding of this text. You need both points. You need complexity. When we walk, we don't have a fixed viewpoint. Our eyes are going everywhere. We know that there is no single image that defines an object.

As Shimon bar Yochai walks around, he is now able to shift perspectives. He no longer sees the world from one point of view. He has walked, and he emerges at twilight – a time when day and night mix together.

When Shimon bar Yochai comes out of the cave, his body is covered in sores and boils from the sand. A town takes him in and treats his body. Shimon bar Yochai is grateful for their healing. He wants to help them.

The townspeople say, 'There is a field where we cannot walk, and the priests cannot walk, because some bodies are buried there. It's impure.'

Shimon bar Yochai proceeds to walk that field. He notices the complexity in the ground. He sees that field not as one space, but as a complex network of different spaces. As he walks, he marks the graves – making his mark as he walks. So he uses his knowledge, wisdom and experience to open the field for access to all.

From this story, I have taken the idea of looking at the world through different points of view, through engaging with the ground in a physical way. Shimon bar Yochai's engagement is intimate. He was first buried in the ground, up to his neck. He then walks the ground and feels it with his feet. Walking is a way of defining space, of opening it up, of understanding the complexities.

Shabbat 34

In the second part of the story, on the next page of the Talmud, there is discussion about the time the Jewish Sabbath begins.

The Sabbath comes in at sunset, but what about twilight – is that the Sabbath, too? Are there certain activities that, although it's not yet the Sabbath, you should stop doing? This page of the Talmud asks: How long does the time of twilight last?

There are various answers to the question. One is about noticing different colours in the sky. Another answer is that *twilight is the time it takes to walk a certain distance.*

I find it stunning that on the same page of the Talmud, you have a story about *walking to define space*, and now you have a discussion about *walking to define time.* An activity that we do with our entire body defines our world, and our markers in the world.

So, I think of migration as less political and more as the spiritual practice of walking the world. I immediately jump to the line in the Book of Job, where God asks Satan what he's been up to. Satan says, 'Oh, I've just been walking up and down the world.' Walking is an act of knowledge – of learning the space that you are in, of seeing it in a complex way through multiple viewpoints. This is a powerful, vulnerable realization.

Travelling

The story of Shimon bar Yochai and his son, on the run from Roman authorities and entering the cave, is well known. But the second part – about what he does when he comes out of the cave and repairs the town's relationship with their field – is less familiar. When I have learned it in the past, or when I have heard somebody quote it, the story tends to stop earlier. Only when I was learning the Talmud, through the discipline of reading and drawing, did I learn the story with this ending about defining twilight through walking.

Structurally, this second part does not belong to the story of Shimon bar Yochai; it discusses a different law. But it just happens to be on the same page of the Talmud. Because of the way the Talmud is laid out and printed, these two stories are now together.

This is the experience of learning the Talmud: There is a path of travel. And the Talmud travels to a place that you don't quite expect.

Reference

Solnit, R. (2001) *Wanderlust: A History of Walking*. London: Verso.

CHAPTER 19

The Language of Shame

Aviva Dautch

I am writing this as debate is raging across traditional and social media about what constitutes anti-Semitism, especially in relation to articulating views about Israel. Both sides are hardening into seemingly immutable polemical stances, with no will to bridge the divide. Out of all the poems I've written, the one that has caused me the most heartache is the most explicitly political, exploring my own views on Israel, a country whose existence is central to my identity and that of my community. We love it as a post-Holocaust safe haven for Jews, even as we are critical of the current government's right-wing, reactionary approach and its terrible treatment of the Palestinian people.

It is a *ghazal* with the refrain 'Hebrew', written after Agha Shahid Ali, a Kashmiri-American poet. Ali was responsible for popularizing the ghazal (a medieval form that was the sonnet of the Arab world) in 20th-century Anglo-American poetry. Ali's ghazal, with its refrain 'Arabic', was the first he wrote. He continued to create his own, and to translate others from Persian, Urdu and Hindi. He published a collection of what he called *Real Ghazals in English* (2000) – contemporary American poems using versions of the ghazal's couplets and repetition, although in his introduction he berated how few employed traditional rhyme and metre. In later years, Ali rewrote his 'Arabic' ghazal into a strictly metrical, rhymed poem. I far prefer the impulsivity and roughness of his original version.

My first reading of Ali's ghazal was viscerally shocking. Couplets which referred to the massacre of Palestinian Arabs in the village of Deir Yassin by Israeli paramilitary groups during the 1948 War of Independence, and called to both the great Palestinian poet, Mahmoud Darwish, and the national poet of Israel, Yehuda Amichai, positioned it at the crux of the 20th-century Israeli–Palestinian conflict. He described a diasporic identity that was simultaneously based on land, language and the handing down of traditional forms of art. My need to respond to him was overwhelming, yet at first my poem felt like appropriation. I struggled with the writing, until I figured out why the ghazal as a form resonated so strongly with me: its rhymes and refrains were a central prop of the Hebrew liturgical poetry that I had grown up reciting as part of my Jewish prayers. The medieval Andalucian Hebrew poets, such as Solomon Ibn Gabirol, Judah Ha'Levi and Ibn Ezra, used the ghazal and related forms as tools for dialogue with the Arabic poets they lived alongside, as well as a way to debate theological concepts with their fellow Jews.

The nature of the ghazal – non-linear, with each couplet its own thought – allowed for a philosophical equivocation that many of Ibn Gabirol's Jewish contemporaries found heretical, but which I find permission-giving. The ghazal is a way to articulate the complexities of the shame felt when identity is bound up in a damaged home, and homeland, and the beginning of finding a language that can communicate across walls and borders. The process of writing my ghazal is described in my poem 'Moorish Home', about a moment when I returned to Spain, the birthplace of those early ghazal writers, alongside my friend and mentor Mimi Khalvati, an Iranian-born poet who brought Ali's work, and the modern ghazal, to my attention and revived it as a form in contemporary British literature.

Ghazal

after Agha Shahid Ali

Beloved, I fear the language of shame is Hebrew.
Once loss was all, now loss is hard to frame in Hebrew.

Yours is the well from which my sorrow springs,
your water, but the earth that steals the rain is Hebrew.

With you I have railed at the shuttered sky
and wept, yet know that tears are not the same in Hebrew.

In the wilderness Jews yearned for a home –
the home that we built, the home that we maim, is Hebrew.

Uprooting olive trees, scarring the soil,
we fight, crush foes like fruit, apportion blame in Hebrew.

Each body-bomb blown up and rocket fired
inscribes my anger when the land aflame is Hebrew.

Like the smear of dust on skin, grief mars me.
We brush off dust but who can brush off pain in Hebrew?

Don't protest we're not our brothers' keepers:
the tale that poets wear the mark of Cain is Hebrew!

Witness our songs – I am yours Beloved
and you are mine – witness Solomon's claim in Hebrew.

To resist complicity, 'not in my name!' –
how? when the root of my soul, of my name, is Hebrew.

Reprinted from Primers Volume Three (2018, Rugby: Nine Arches Press)

Moorish Home

for Mimi Khalvati

In our hanging house, one wall sheer to the dry riverbank,
rooms staggering across split levels, the hours are sticky

with fever and all I see of you is a passing shadow climbing
the stairs opposite my open door. We spend our days apart

but in the evenings we walk and distribute our greetings, Hola,
Buenos Noches, to the people in the street, or exchange

Farsi for Hebrew: *Laila Tov*, we say to each other, *Shabékheyr*.
Last night we talked of Córdoba, alliance of Muslim and Jew,

and you pulled me back for a moment – *this is how it was, this!* –
when we strolled past a woman cooking barbeque on the steps

of the village square, a man (her man?) humming a cante jondo
to his father. You were wearing my gipsy shawl and I,

slipping back to the Golden Age, began to compose a gacela
as Lorca called them. How easily it built in my sleep, couplets

folding into themselves like accordion scales, rising from
    kitchen
to living room to the vine-shaded terrace where you lay

on the rattan chair, smoking, always smoking, and in my sleep
we became Al-Ghazali and Halevi, dreaming of this: a new
    Jerusalem.

Note: *Buenos Noches* (Spanish), *Laila Tov* (Hebrew) and *Shabékheyr*
(Farsi) all mean 'Good Night'. *Gacela* is Spanish for 'ghazal'. The
medieval Spanish Jewish poet, Judah Halevi, was greatly influenced
by the Persian Sufi philosopher, Ibn Muhammad Al-Tusi Al-Ghazali.
Al-Ghazali's name translates as 'The Ghazal Writer', Halevi's as 'The
Priest'.

Published in The North, Issue 50 (2013)

Suggested reading

Ali, A.S. (ed.) (2000) *Ravishing DisUnities: Real Ghazals in English.* Middletown, CT: Wesleyan Poetry.

CHAPTER 20

Poetry

Pádraig Ó Tuama

Things to Bring

vi   Nothing of what you've come to know as yourself

i   Just as much as you can carry

xi   Things to sell

xii your self

xiv Photographs, of course, photographs. no frames

viiiAll the reasons you left

ix   Money. Stored in little packets.

xvii Something with a blade.

ii   More than you can bear to remember.

iii The reasons they gave you to justify the fighting

iv   ~~everything you cannot leave behind~~

v   That book with that inscription.

vii Something small and beautiful. Something that can be hidden

x   Shoes that you can walk in – ones nobody will notice.

xx   The closest things.

xiii The memory of that small hand in your hand.

xv And the smell of her soft skin.

xvi Something to make you presentable. A facecloth a shawl a
       future

xix That moment just before it all went. boom.

xxi Nothing.

Aftermath

This is me now
reduced to this —
holding a photo of you
against my chest
as a substitute for
all that took you away.
I held it to my face yesterday
hoping it would carry your scent:
arrowroot and fennel.

Yes yes yes.
There was conflict, yes.
And we moved from there to
here, yes.
And we did not have a map.
And we did not
know the language
of our own survival.
And I didn't know where
~~you~~ your remains were.
And we did not know how
to reach each other.
Because underneath us
the ground moved.
In fact, it blew up.
Yes yes yes.
This is what happens when wars happen.
People fall apart. Yes.

Earth shifts, Places Open Up.
The centre is now the edge.
Yes. Y

Did I   tell you
I survived?

Well.   Mostly.
    And   then there's this.
              My me   m o r y.

Collect for the Living and the Dead

If I keep my head low
it is not because I'm bowing,
but because I don't want to see

You, maker and breaker of worlds and boundaries.
Look at me now,
shrouded in all the dust that war makes.

You ask me if I have anything to say.
I notice that blood cakes my eyes shut
and the ringing in my ears hasn't stopped.

Back there, was a story I knew, a story whose truth I doubted
and was devoted to. Now here, is a border within a border;
a form turning within a form; a policy, burning on itself.

And anyway, there is no ink
and I cannot even read the script
never mind the language.

If I could do anything, I'd lick the pages clean
from all the stories we've told about you, about us.
I'd start with a mountain, a valley, a place between two rivers

and Men, and Women, and Telephones and Provisions;
and a Writing in the Sky calling this place our home;
and a name that would protect us; and mourn.

In the name of everything and nothing,
I would shout, and everything would echo back
Yes.

Orpah writes to
  her beloved sister,
  Ruth

I hear they've named books after you.
Now women named Naomi will dream of naming
daughters like Ruth.

And painters will capture our departure
and lovers will sing those words of yours to each other.
Where you go.

I did not go.
I wonder if I'd followed whether I'd have found
a home. You were always keen to go.

What songs for those of us who stayed?
I picked up the old economy, I made a life of it,
the way everybody at the hem of hunger does it.

In time, there was food, and a man, and some children,
and glory for my widowed head. In time, there was a god who
gathered scattered stories.

I made you up. I sit here, writing stories
of you whose life I cannot see.
So I write:

Where you go, I will go. Your people, my people.
All those other gods, my gods too.
May fire fall on me if I forsake all that your memory gave me.

PART 3

Diaspora

CHAPTER 21

Keeping Faith in the Diaspora

The story of Tumelo's Three Congregations

Harvey Kwiyani

Faith in diaspora

This essay is a semi-fictional narrative of an African pastor who leads a church in Birmingham. In a long journey of ministry, the church morphs from a Zimbabwean congregation to an international one and later gives birth to a second-generation British-African congregation. As a theologian and researcher, I draw on a series of interviews conducted in December 2017 and January 2018; excerpts are woven throughout this chapter. The chapter concludes by discussing how an African understanding of personhood in *ubuntu* philosophy offers a useful theological framework for a world in which the migrant and the host engage each other in mutual hospitality.

Born and raised in Zimbabwe, Pastor Tumelo found his way to South Africa in the early 1990s, when Zimbabwe's economy started to lose its footing. While in South Africa, Tumelo joined an African-initiated Pentecostal denomination and, having quickly risen in the leadership ranks, was made director of the mission strategy in southern Africa. When need arose for a missionary in Europe, there was no hesitation that Tumelo was the man for the job. The denominational leaders had become concerned that their members were backsliding when they came to Europe, so Tumelo migrated to Birmingham in 1998. He assumed that since there are many Zimbabweans in Britain, it would be easy to galvanize them into a mission movement that could 'set Europe ablaze for Christ'.

He has been on this journey for more than 20 years.

Migration and diaspora Christianity

Migration tends to intensify religious convictions, causing people to think more about God's sustaining power as they move from one part of the world to another – often on treacherous roads and seas, only to end up unwelcome in a new land. Indeed, for the members of Tumelo's congregation, religion played a major role. Prayers, fasting and night vigils for a smooth transition were a normal part of the process. Some people had their passports anointed with oil before their visa interviews. Others sent the passports to their 'man of God' to be prophesied over. Even those who were not Christian might consult their *ng'anga* (herbalist) to intercede on their behalf for safe travel and assure them of entry. Indeed, religion is so ingrained in the African life that many African people would not know how to survive if it was taken away.

For Tumelo's members, religion had become more important in the diaspora than it was in Zimbabwe – only God could have made it possible for them to settle in Britain. The effect of secularism on Western culture is unattractive to many Africans, who usually explain their migration as a religious event. Many struggle when they cannot practice *their* Christianity in the way they knew it back home. Tumelo's members missed their African worship so much, they created their own Zimbabwean congregation in the city centre. It provided not only space to worship, but also the social capital they needed to survive in Britain. The cultural differences – and the ensuing culture shock – required them to count on fellow Zimbabweans to help them maintain a sense of cultural bearing. Most of them did not feel that other local churches met their spiritual needs the way their African denomination did. While their bodies were in Britain, their hearts and spirits continued to long for worship as it was in Zimbabwe. Unlike the Israelites who refused when taunted to sing the Lord's song in a strange land, and who sat weeping by the rivers of Babylon during their diaspora (Psalm 137:1–4), the Zimbabweans wanted to sing the Lord's song from Zimbabwe in a strange land. The miraculous God that had served them in Zimbabwe was with them in Britain, ready to answer their prayers and deserving the same praise. So they asked their denomination in Africa to send them a pastor.

Congregation one: First-generation migrant church

It did not take long for Tumelo to realize that the training and experience he had gained in Africa would be of limited use in Europe. Previously, he had exercised an all-family ministry, with thriving youth and young adult involvement. In Britain, his own children were not interested in religion. His congregation had failed to connect with other nationalities apart from Zimbabweans, and not even with South Africans (who preferred another one of their denomination's congregations on the other side of town, much to Tumelo's dismay). It was even harder for them to imagine reaching out to their Western neighbours. Tumelo's vision to evangelize Europeans seemed impossible.

Overall, religiously-inclined, first-generation migrants tend to stay committed to their religion. They attend church, Bible studies, prayer vigils and other events. They pay tithes and they hope that their children will inherit their religious zeal (to which effect they bring them to church and involve them – usually in the music ministry). However, being immigrants, they find that adjusting to life in Britain demands more of their time and energy; their availability for religious events tends to suffer. Those who prioritize church events usually have little time for other cross-cultural, social activities.

This pattern is common in other black-majority churches. Nevertheless, many people maintain their religious commitment in the face of busy schedules and work shifts. In a research interview, a Ghanaian pastor leading a church in Wolverhampton observed:

My membership is mostly new migrants. I have four 'congregations' that never meet in one place. Each Sunday, I preach to people who were not in church the previous week, and they are not coming the following week because of work shifts.

Overall, while first-generation migrants have a strong devotion to their religion, circumstances affect how they express it in the diaspora. When they find a good church, they stay. According to one Jamaican pastor in London: 'If you want your church to grow and be steady, you need to find African Christians, especially those who have settled in the UK for a while.'

However, many migrant churches find themselves frozen in time. Tumelo's members behaved as they did in Zimbabwe in the 1990s. Entire church services duplicated those their members had known in Africa: everything from the singing to the dancing, preaching, offering-collection and dressing. A Zimbabwean mother visiting her daughter in Birmingham was shocked to observe how the church behaved: 'It feels like we are in Harare in the 1990s.'

This freezing in the diaspora happens for two reasons. First, most migrant churches operate in a bubble in which only those who are familiar can be trusted – especially for leadership. When they are not at work or at school, migrants tend to connect only with people from their own countries. Most first-generation migrant churches are built around national identity. Tumelo's church was Zimbabwean. South African members of the same denomination, living in the same city, attended another congregation made up of mostly South Africans. These nationalistic bubbles make it difficult for migrants to gather in multi-national contexts. Their members are usually too busy in their own churches, where activities are spread throughout the week. Thus, they have no time and energy left to engage Christians from other denominations or countries.

Second, all ecclesiology (the theology of churches), including migrant ecclesiology, is shaped by culture. There is no expression of 'church' that is culture-free. Migrant churches realize this and often use it to their advantage. Many worshippers love their churches to be places where members can enjoy their home cultures, turning them into fellowships focused on preserving these cultures, and passing them on to their children.

Congregation two: A Zimbabwean international church

Five years into his work in Europe, Tumelo needed to reorganize and relaunch his ministry. Years of trying simultaneously to lead a congregation, learn about British culture, hold a full-time job (in addition to his church ministry) and raise a family left him in a constant state of burn-out. It had become clear to him that to grow the church, he would have to widen his reach.

Tumelo was not alone in this struggle. The majority of migrant churches are unsustainably small, with fewer than 25 members. For several reasons, they are not growing. The religious market for migrant churches in the UK has become saturated. Most towns will have multiple migrant churches, all of them working hard to attract a limited number of migrants in the local area. At the same time, other non-migrant (i.e., British-led) churches are keen to get their share of migrant Christians, often promising a more stable environment. Some migrants who have lived in the UK for longer tend to find British churches attractive, as they are more established and better resourced. They are more nuanced in their fundraising and less forceful in their collection of tithes and offerings – something that (African) migrant churches frequently emphasize, in spite of its divisive effect.

Unfortunately for Tumelo, by now several other Zimbabwean churches had emerged in Birmingham, such that he could only hope for a handful members. In addition, many of the Zimbabweans that he wanted to reach had settled in non-Zimbabwean churches in the city. Some of his own members left for other churches. Tumelo could no longer simply believe that Zimbabweans would come to his church because he was *the* Zimbabwean pastor in town. Several younger pastors and prophets rose up, challenging him for the role he had taken for granted. Many of these were better educated. Tumelo found it very difficult to stay relevant.

A few years into his ministry in Birmingham, the situation of Zimbabweans in the UK began to change. British political attitudes towards migration had become intolerant. Europeans, including the British, had become weary of migrants and wanted the numbers of foreigners settling in their countries reduced. Africans were greatly disadvantaged because most of them were considered economic migrants. Indeed, African migration to the UK in general started to dwindle. (Anti-immigrant sentiments continue today; migration remains a hot political subject.)

In this atmosphere, migrant churches often find it difficult to rent space for their services. Some British churches would rather keep their doors shut than share their premises. Tumelo knew of another Zimbabwean church in Birmingham that lost its place of worship because the owners decided they did not want to share it with 'those Africans who will mess up our kitchen with bad-smelling food'. Even when they are not looking for space to rent, many migrant churches struggle to build relationships with other churches in their neighbourhoods.

When Zimbabwean migration to Britain slowed down, the numbers of first-generation migrants (the constituency of Tumelo's congregation) began to dwindle. At the same time, several other countries opened their borders, leading many Zimbabweans living in the UK to relocate to Canada and other Western countries. Tumelo lost half his congregation. His leadership team scattered. The stress of this experience led to him being hospitalized.

In 2005, Tumelo decided to move his ministry away from focusing only on Zimbabwean Christians in Birmingham. He wanted to open it up to other nationalities, as this appeared to be the only way his congregation could continue to exist. The grand vision that had been hatched in Zimbabwe and South Africa had been found wanting in the streets of Europe. The desire to set Europe ablaze for Christ had fizzled out. What remained was a small congregation in Birmingham that no longer even identified as Zimbabwean.

This was the beginning of Tumelo's international church. It faced stiff competition from every other church in the area: Nigerian,

Congolese, Jamaican and British. Tumelo had to retrain for the ministry. Both he and his wife had gone back to school to get a theological degree, only to find that such a degree had no real practical components to train them for ministry in Europe. As Pentecostal African Christians, they struggled to find theological training in Britain that understood their background.

Despite the frustrations, Tumelo went on to acquire a Master's degree in missional leadership. His new training helped him to attract other African nationals to his church, de-emphasizing its Zimbabwean/South African origin. His new leadership team comprised people from ten African countries. The church definitely did not look Zimbabwean anymore. Tumelo's courage to make such a transition possible is commendable.

Congregation three: A church for the second generation

In its new format, Tumelo's regenerated congregation attracts many people from countries across sub-Saharan Africa. However, its primary constituency remains first-generation migrants. Tumelo is aware that the congregation lives with a real existential threat of not surviving its current membership. The congregation has no young members. In its 20 years of existence, it has not managed to hold the members' children, and neither has it been able to attract second-generation migrants from outside. Even Tumelo's own children have no interest in attending their father's church. They would rather go to a friend's youth church or to the British church in their neighbourhood, as it has a youth service.

This is currently the hardest challenge facing African and other migrant pastors in Britain: How do they disciple the generation of their children? Tumelo is rightly concerned that his children will grow up un-discipled or secular, and that the legacy of his ministry will be forgotten as soon as he retires. He is aware that migrant congregations tend not to continue after the first generation of migrants has passed on. When Tumelo reads stories of other migrant churches in

Britain, or visits churches started by migrants of the past generation (mostly from the West Indies), he realizes that if his generation of African pastors and leaders in Britain does not become more intentional, their children will lose faith and their churches will be empty in a few decades.

There is an entire population of second-generation African migrants who cannot fit in their parents' churches, but neither do they feel at home in other churches. Unlike their parents, who grew up in a culture where religion was the norm, these younger-generation migrants are growing up in a secular context, where religion is a foreign concept. They see religion at home with their parents in the many hours of prayer, the long Bible studies and other activities. But once they are out of their parents' homes, the second generation will switch not only their accents but also their outlook to fit in with a secular culture. Culturally, the younger generation are more British than African. To effectively disciple them, Tumelo's generation must engage them as they would people of a strange tribe. This is essentially a cross-cultural endeavour, akin to discipling their British neighbours. Tumelo's generation is quick to admit that this is something they are ill-equipped for.

Tumelo's solution has been to start a new youth congregation. He is currently trying to convince his daughter to become its leader. Tumelo believes that with a little mentoring, she will do well. If she indeed succeeds in running a youthful congregation, Tumelo will have ensured that even though his own congregation may not survive beyond his generation, the faith of the second generation will not fail. He plans to pass on everything to his daughter so he can support her fully in her ministry. This, he feels, is a noble end to his long ministry.

Conclusion: Towards mutual hospitality

Tumelo's story is the general story of migrant Christianity. His ministry in Birmingham – like many other migrant ministries – has faced many challenges that could have been better negotiated if he had sought out and connected with British people. Tumelo also has many gifts to share in the context of mutual hospitality, which would invigorate the faith of his neighbours.

The Bible comes to us with a hospitality imperative, especially in a world where to be an immigrant is tantamount to being a second-class citizen. Yet the Gospels tell of the Son of Man, who lived on people's hospitality. Christ was an immigrant, both in the act of the Incarnation (when he came to dwell with us) and as a refugee in Egypt. His ministry was provided for by his followers, especially the women. In accepting our hospitality, God (in Christ and through the ministry of the Spirit) models divine hospitality for us. Jesus sent his disciples out and commanded them not to carry a purse or a spare sandal, so that they could live entirely on the hospitality of others (Luke 10:4–9). This would, in turn, teach them to be hospitable. Later, when the Church emerged in Jerusalem, there was not anyone who lacked, for they shared everything (Acts 4:32–35).

Migrant Christianity is growing in Britain. Many new African, Asian and Latin American churches and ministries come into existence each year. Because these churches tend to have only migrant members of the same nationality, they fail to reach the two groups they need most to ensure their churches' survival: 1) their local British neighbours and their host community; and 2) their own children, who are growing up between African and British cultures. Consequently, many of these churches face serious dangers over the next two to three decades. Their children will leave their churches (as is already happening), and there will be no one to carry the work forward, especially as many migrant churches still have not found ways to work with their British neighbours.

However, British Christians seem to not pay attention to the migrant Christians in their neighbourhoods. In many cases, relationships between foreign and local Christians only go so far as exploring the rental of worship spaces. It seems that both foreign and local Christians are comfortable to live as if the other does not exist – to exclude one another from the expressions of their faith. However, exclusion and isolation only lead to the diminishing of life (symbolic

KEEPING FAITH IN THE DIASPORA

and otherwise) of both the host and the guest, or in this case, foreign and local Christians. To counter this, there is need for a continuous exchange of hospitality between the host and the guest.

Christian theology struggles to offer a coherent response to the 'problem of migration'. Many British Christians will agree that Christ was an immigrant, but they will blame migrants for social problems like unemployment. Yet it is impossible to talk about faith without thinking about migration. God's first call to Abraham was to migrate: *Leave the land of your fathers to a land that I will show you* (Genesis 12:1–3). It was in the process of migration that God revealed Godself to Abraham, that Abraham's faith was accounted to him as righteousness, and that God established Abraham as the father of many nations. Further, it was through migration that God visited Jacob, changed his name and promised him many nations (Genesis 28:13–15, 35:11). Thus, we learn from the Patriarchs that migration is indeed a theologizing experience. As God is drawn to people in migration, migrants could help us to understand God better. Immigrants themselves could lead a theological conversation, where the rest of us could learn of their experiences of God.

The African framework of *ubuntu* suggests that the fullness of life can only be experienced in communion with the 'other' – the stranger. In *ubuntu*, to be a person is to belong. Among my people in Malawi, this means to be hospitable and generous. *Ubuntu* is described in the dictum: 'I am because we are'. It is based on the human need for one another and for abundant life. At the centre of such a belief is the conviction that God breaks through to our world to connect us with strangers for purposes better known to God. *Ubuntu* suggests that migrant Christians need local Christians while, at the same time, local Christians need migrant Christians. In being hospitable to one another, migrant Christians and local Christians are actually engaging in worship. Hospitality, then, becomes a spiritual exercise that is done in reverence to God. In this mutual exchange, Christians encourage and energize one another, enabling each other to live life to the full and to serve God as God requires. Hospitality, as the Bible tells us (Hebrews 13:2), made it possible for Abraham to entertain angels.

CHAPTER 22

'Muhajir'

A Personal Journey of Art, Faith and Museum Objects

Hajra Williams

Born in the *muhajir* community in Karachi, Pakistan, I often asked
my parents to explain the term. They would state simply: *muhajir*
was Arabic for 'migrant'. Our community of Urdu-speaking people
had moved from India to help build Pakistan after partition in 1947.
Although we settled in the Sindh Province, where I was born, I was
not Sindhi, neither did I identify with the other regions that make up
Pakistan.[1] We were from India but were not from a particular ethnic
group, so *muhajir* was adopted as a common title. The word has an
important lineage: *muhajir* was applied to the people who accompanied
Muhammad from Mecca to Medina in 622 CE and were the first converts
to Islam. It is as much a poetic as a political word, with faith at its core.

My family moved from Pakistan to the UK – my father first in
the 1960s, and soon after, my mother, my siblings and I. After my
graduate studies at the Glasgow School of Art, I arrived in London in
1991 to begin a degree at the Royal College of Art. Just a short distance
from the Royal College, the Victoria & Albert Museum (V&A) became
a second home.

I gravitated most towards the Persian miniature paintings. In the
finely painted, elegant scenes of exotic interiors, lush gardens and
glorious figures, I glimpsed aspects of my lost ancestry and heritage

---

1   Punjab, Balochistan, North West Frontier Province.

in India. I felt a connection with the lives depicted in these scenes. Despite the passage of time and the ostentatious wealth on display, I recognized myself – not just the familiarity of the dark hue and features of the characters, but their clothes, jewellery and hairstyles, the henna on their hands and their mannerisms and gestures. As an artist, I felt a connection with the style of painting; it spoke to me of my own identity.

However, I often felt conflicted with the figurative aspect of these works of art. As a Muslim growing up in Glasgow, I was familiar with the injunction against depicting figures in Islamic art and design. In our home, figurative art was forbidden, not only on the walls as paintings but also on decorative items. At prayer times, we would turn family photographs face down so we were never, even accidentally, venerating a physical being other than Allah.

Despite my family's conservative attitudes toward figurative art, I was still drawn to the elements of miniature painting. To further my own artistic practice within an Islamic framework, I explored the V&A for inspiration. It was important to understand how these objects could exist as Islamic art and yet use figuration. In the process, I read authors who had studied the Hadith literature (a body of texts traditionally believed to be the actual sayings and practices of the Prophet Muhammad). When studied in detail, the Hadith literature, although vociferous against the use of imagery, seems to prohibit it primarily when it comes between the worshipper and God. In the Hadith, the Prophet's wife Aisha hung in her house a tapestry depicting images and scenes. The Prophet said, 'Draw back that hanging, for I always see the pictures before me when I am praying.' The hanging was then removed, cut up and made into cushions. The suggestion here is that images were forbidden only when used for devotional (rather than decorative) purposes (see Okasha 1981). I came to the conclusion that hostility towards imagery is due to the perceived relationship between images and idol worship.

As an artist, my own work consisted of jewellery inspired by the V&A's miniature paintings. As jewellery is a decorative form, designed to be worn on the body, I was able to justify the use of figurative elements. First, the mythical beasts, palace buildings and princely characters which were already stylized in the miniature paintings became even more abstracted in my work. Second, as the 'art' was worn on the body, it was decorative rather than an image that could be worshipped. In this way, I resolved the use of figuration in my own practice, but it was an issue that I had to revisit in my educational work with Muslim community audiences.

To outsiders, Muslim communities can feel closed and inward-looking, due to their traditional values, patriarchal structures, and lack of trust and communication with the wider society. Although my own family supported my art practice, I knew from growing up in a conservative, South Asian community that art education is often not valued highly. It is important to educate people about access to cultural venues such as museums. I believe that the religious and cultural events marked within a local community have a place in public venues. Celebrating faith in conversation with museum collections can serve to introduce diverse groups to museums in collaborative, informal and celebratory ways, and to initiate more meaningful interaction with the museum's objects.

The V&A's Indian collections: Opportunity in diversity

The Indian collections have been an important part of the V&A since its inception in 1857. They served as evidence of Britain's colonial authority over the Indian subcontinent, with London at its centre: 'a three-dimensional imperial archive' (Barringer and Flynn 1998, p.12). The objects were acquired as teaching resources and as aids for inspiration in promoting good design in a Britain undergoing the Industrial Revolution (Crill *et al.* 1990, p.12). The Nehru Gallery of Indian Art tells the history of India and its conquerors from 1500 to 1900, focusing on life at court and royal patronage. In 1990, as the new gallery opened, the Paul Hamlyn Foundation funded a museum education officer to work with South Asian communities, using the collections as the basis for outreach. Shireen Akbar, an inspirational Bangladeshi community worker, was appointed in 1991; I followed in 1997. This was a unique opportunity; there was no other role like it in the UK at the time. As a result, there was little knowledge and support, both within the organization and externally, for developing the programme. At times, I found it to be a complex and lonely undertaking. I had to navigate the politics and pitfalls of the V&A organizational structures, which were quite formal compared with the communities I was working with.

A common mistake is to treat South Asian communities as one homogenous group, rather than as people who are as interested in a diaspora identity that defines their separateness as much as their commonalities. South Asian communities tend to identify far more strongly by religion, region and language, and within a relatively contemporary framework, than by broader signifiers of culture and art. As the museum education officer, I had to develop my thinking around national identities (Indian, Pakistani, Sri Lankan and Bangladeshi), religions (Hinduism, Islam, Sikhism, Buddhism and Christianity) and languages (Hindi, Urdu, Punjabi, Sinhalese, Bengali, Sylheti, to name just a few). I also needed to consider generational differences and identities.

The museum engaged South Asian communities by developing education programmes in connection with the Indian and South East Asian collections, both permanent and temporary. This material would be used as a hook, with the aspiration that, over time, education activities would develop and digress into other areas of the museum's collections. Often, the exhibitions that attracted audiences by religion or region (for example, targeting Jains for the 'Jain' exhibition and Sikhs for the 'Sikh' exhibition) were victims of their own success. They were also a source of concern to me. It was difficult to strike a balance between enabling single-community identities to shine through without creating cultural silos.

The V&A's community education work was highly innovative and took place at a time when few UK museums were targeting specific ethnic community audiences on such a scale. It felt like a promising time to be working as an educator in the museum sector (see Anderson 1997). The Department for Culture, Media and Sport provided new access funds; lottery funding bodies changed their priorities from buildings to people; and trusts, foundations and sponsors made education a high priority in their giving. There was a feeling that museums could truly fulfil their potential as centres for learning.

The South Asian Education Programme

The Shamiana Tent (1991–1997) was an innovative project that targeted South Asian women's groups in London. The women brought much-needed diversity to the institution, while the project gave them an opportunity to express their creativity and to learn textile skills and sometimes English too. Women's groups visited the V&A for inspiration, then developed their sketches and drawings into textile panels. (The V&A gave specific dimensions, as well as a small budget to cover the cost of materials.) The project expanded to include other places in the north of England, Scotland, Ireland, Wales and internationally, with groups using their local museums for inspiration. The panels that the women stitched became biographies of their everyday lives, interspersed with the objects and stories they encountered in the museums.

In the summer of 1997, all the panels were brought together and exhibited in a Shamiana-style tent in the V&A garden. When the exhibition finished, various panels then toured other venues, including St Paul's Church in East London, the Slough Museum and the Kelvingrove Art Gallery and Museum. Eventually the panels were returned to the women's groups, who in turn gifted them to their local museum or community centre.

The participating museums learned as much about their audiences as the women learned about the museums and their collections. During the Shamiana exhibition, as during other specifically South Asian exhibitions, I noticed how much more representative of a multicultural society the V&A felt. The chatter of different languages, groups made up of young and old together, and different customs and clothes from the South Asian diaspora were all visible. The museum felt lively as these audiences interacted with and moved through the gallery spaces. Scale is important; one large community group arriving for a single visit, rather than the small groups or individuals that make up other museum visitors, has a great impact on the space.

This mass takeover was tangible during the V&A's exhibition The Arts of the Sikh Kingdoms (March–July 1999). As the project's lead educator, I developed a programme to address a broad range of audiences. Motivating factors included:

- engaging Sikhs and other audiences
- communicating the art and design traditions of the Sikh court
- enabling participants to engage in creative activity, in keeping with the V&A's mission as the national museum of art and design
- celebrating diversity
- promoting South Asian culture in a public forum
- communicating aspects of the Sikh religion
- encouraging understanding of Sikh culture.

For previous South Asian exhibitions, the V&A's practice was to encourage community groups to book targeted events, without ensuring that drop-in events were also accessible. In doing so, the museum had voiced contradictory concerns: on the one hand, that it would be difficult to predict interest from the community; on the other hand, that the groups attending would be too large to facilitate, or that they would face language issues and other barriers. I felt that this aspect of education provision should change, to be inclusive across the range of education activities. The challenge was to ensure participation, given the different needs of mixed groups in terms of age, gender, interests and size. We also needed to address health and safety concerns related to moving large numbers of people through the museum. One solution we devised was to hold popular events in the largest spaces, repeated two to three times during the day, to ensure as many participants as possible. Events included performances of *gatka* (a Sikh martial art), *bhangra* (Punjabi folk dance), demonstrations of miniature painting, embroidery, metal-inlaying, interactive sessions of *tabla* drumming, calligraphy and storytelling.

The initial consultation and outreach work with the Sikh community led to establishing a group of 40 volunteers to assist large South Asian community groups arriving at the weekend. Desks were set up at each of the museum's main entrances. The volunteers assisted visitors physically but also from a cultural perspective by giving talks in Punjabi. One happy by-product of this service was that although it was set up primarily for the benefit of the Sikh community, the volunteers were also approached by the general public. They enriched the experience of many non-Sikh visitors by offering insight into the beliefs and practices of being a Sikh.

It is important to stress the challenges of doing this work as a Muslim woman. I was aware of the irony: I was opening myself up to mistrust by representing the V&A, a very British colonial institution, in a role designed to do the opposite – that is, to engage South Asian communities. In addition, the diverse religious and cultural groups had allegiances of their own, and my very Muslim name (Hajra Shaikh) announced my religious origin before I even walked into a room. My role was to be an ambassador for the V&A while also advocating for South Asian communities and representing their needs to the museum. This two-way interaction required behaving ethically and professionally to ensure that both the institution and the community were fairly represented, leading to mutual understanding.

One comment I received from a senior member of the Sikh community was that their doubts about a Muslim education officer doing justice to a Sikh exhibition education programme had been unfounded. That I had gained the trust of this community is one of the highlights of my career. As a Muslim woman, I had to navigate complex relationships and traditional views on an ongoing basis. For example, most of the people I collaborated with on the Sikh education programme were men. Sometimes these were religious elders within the community; at other times they were younger, educated and professional. While curatorial expertise was more readily understood and respected, community representatives were less aware of my role as a museum educator. By working closely with communities from the outset, I was able to communicate the importance of education, outreach and collaboration.

Museums of belonging

A museum is an important civic space which can nurture a sense of belonging in diaspora communities. Personally, museums gave me the opportunity to learn about my cultural heritage and contributed to my development as an artist. I was lucky to learn directly from objects that linked me to a past and a place that I had migrated from, and also to an earlier history of my ancestors. In turn, I later had the good fortune to engage other people with the collections of the V&A. The South Asian programme was joyful, celebratory and ultimately concerned with learning. It was an opportunity for different faith communities to learn about themselves and each other, to participate in a public forum, and to take pride in their history and culture.

In our multicultural society, museum collections can tell shared and diverse stories. They are particularly important to migrant communities adrift from their homeland, who are seeking to assimilate and to contribute to a new country. Museums hold a promise of freely accessible knowledge. As the repositories of history and as the keepers of our material culture, they are unique places to learn about common humanity. They can teach us to respect and celebrate the differences which enrich us. Physical objects enable us to study and to develop an understanding about culture (our own and others') in a way that books and schools do not.

The challenge of fostering and sustaining diversity in the museum sector has been acknowledged for years. In the words of John Orna-Ornstein, former Arts Council England's Director of Museums:

There's an element of the emperor's new clothes about this. After years of discussion it's clear that only much stronger, braver action from all of us – funders, sector bodies, museums – will make an impact when it comes to real diversity. (The Museums Association 2016, p.10)

Ironically, my V&A career ended as priorities changed and leadership opportunities were actively denied. My experience has been that museums are too entrenched in their structures for sustainable change to come easily from within the organization. Many voices need to be heard instead of a few. Black and minority ethnic people need to sit at the boardroom tables not just as volunteers and participants, but as leaders and decision makers. Throughout my career, I was often the only South Asian person in the room. Although it was a great privilege to work with world-renowned collections and to represent my community, I would have wished for greater reflection in the sea of faces I encountered professionally. In the corridors of the V&A, I was once again a *muhajir*: solitary, adrift, displaced.

References

Anderson, D. (1997) *A Common Wealth: Museums in the United Kingdom.* London: Department of National Heritage (second edition,1999, published as *A Common Wealth: Museums in the Learning Age.* London: Stationary Office).

Barringer, T. and Flynn, T. (1998) 'The South Kensington Museum and the Colonial Project.' In T. Barringer and T. Flynn *Colonialism and the Object: Empire, Material Culture and the Museum.* London and New York, NY: Routledge.

Crill, R., Guy, J., Murphy, V., Stronge, S. and Swallow, D. (1990) *Arts of India:1550–1900.* London: Victoria and Albert Museum.

Okasha, S. (1981) *The Muslim Painter and the Divine.* London: Park Lane Press.

The Museums Association (2016) *Valuing Diversity: The Case for Inclusive Museums.* Accessed 03/01/19 at www.museumsassociation.org/download?id=1194934.

CHAPTER 23

The Montefiore Letters

Migrations of Jews to the Holy Land in the Early 19th Century

Sally Style

Over millennia, Jews have migrated to and from *Eretz HaKedusha*: the Holy Land of Israel. The early 19th century found several thousand Jews living there. This diverse population comprised Spanish and Portuguese Sephardi Jews and Arabic-speaking Jews, who had been there for centuries, and the more recently arrived Ashkenazi Jews from Eastern Europe. What were their motivations and hopes? How did European Jews fit in with the indigenous Jewish population and the other residents – the Muslims and Christians? Why had the Ashkenazi Jews left Europe to make the arduous journey to the Holy Land? What spiritual and practical concerns underpinned their migration?

In North London, a small room in the Spanish and Portuguese Synagogue offers some answers to these questions. The Montefiore Endowment Library contains the archive of Sir Moses Montefiore, including original letters by Jews of the diaspora, writing of their lives in the Holy Land.

The Montefiore letters

Sir Moses Montefiore (1784–1885) and his wife, Judith Barent-Cohen, were celebrities of the Victorian age. Renowned for their generosity, they devoted their lives to alleviating political and religious distress and to helping Jews around the world. The Montefiores, while both Orthodox Jews, were scions of separate factions: he was Sephardi while she was Ashkenazi. Their mixed marriage was one of the first of its kind. Judith was a compassionate and deeply spiritual person, who brought religious observance into her husband's life. Until the age of 40, Montefiore was a successful businessman, one of only 12 'Jew brokers' permitted to work on the Royal Exchange in England. He introduced gas lighting to the streets of Europe and was a founder of the Provincial Irish Bank and the Alliance Life Assurance Company. After retiring, the Montefiores embarked on the first of seven visits to the Holy Land.[1] There, Montefiore saw the abject plight of his fellow Jews and underwent a profound spiritual change. He swore to dedicate his life to charitable works, as required by some of the 613 *mitzvot* (commandments) in the Torah,[2] and to lead a pious, benevolent Jewish life.

The Montefiore Endowment Library contains documents relating to the Montefiores' work in the Holy Land, including censuses of the Jewish population and over 1200 letters addressed to Moses and Judith. These letters, written primarily in 1839 and 1849 to coincide with the Montefiores' visits in those years, provide insight into the minds and motivations of these 19th-century Jews. The letters are written predominantly in Hebrew with Aramaic, using a combination of biblical, rabbinical and liturgical Hebrew, at a time when the modern language was still to develop. The language relies heavily on ancient Jewish texts, demonstrating that many of the writers were knowledgeable and scholarly. The 613 *mitzvot*, incumbent on every Jew, form the framework for the correspondence. The *mitzvot* cited in the letters include: acting with righteousness; kindness to others; caring for the downtrodden and the poor, for widows and orphans; tithing 10 per cent of one's earnings to charity; freeing the enslaved; being fruitful and multiplying; honouring one's parents; living and

1   See Judith's travel diaries, which describe quarantine, plague, piracy and war.

2   The Torah, according to Orthodox Judaism, was handed to Moses by God on Mount Sinai during the Israelites' 40 years of wandering in the wilderness, on their journey back to the Promised Land. The Torah represents the fundamentals of Judaism; it contains 613 *mitzvot* which every Jew must observe. These enabled Jews to maintain their identity while living in exile in the diaspora, away from Zion.

studying the Torah; working the soil of the Holy Land; praising God as a congregation rather than as an individual; honouring the Sabbath. The *mitzvot* illuminate writers struggling to live as 'good Jews' who are religious, observe God's commandments, and who live in Zion.

Life was far from ideal in the Holy Land: Jews faced the privations of living as *dhimmis*[3] ('protected') under Ottoman rule in 1849, and under Egyptian rule in 1839, they suffered, hardship, violence and persecution; poverty and starvation; cholera epidemics; a catastrophic earthquake in 1837; and a swarm of crop-destroying locusts in the mid-1840s. The letters to Montefiore reveal the practical and spiritual concerns of Jews in the Holy Land and help to explain the motivations of Jews from Eastern Europe to migrate.

Why did 19th-century Jews migrate to the Holy Land?

The experience of religious persecution cannot be understated. For example, Russian Jews suffered violent pogroms, leading many to flee. They risked their lives on long, dangerous journeys in the hope (often erroneous) of finding a better life. The Montefiore letters reveal the theme of persecution as a common motivation – among others, described below – for migration.

Holy Land as homeland

Numerous letters reflect the importance for Jews to live in the Holy Land and to study the Torah there. The writers stated that they were now living on holy soil, as God commands; they wished to migrate for religious reasons alone.[4] A typical example is the 1839 letter by Yehuda Leib ben Yitzhak, who had arrived in 1830 to immerse himself in the dust and soil of the Holy Land. He informed Montefiore that he spent

3   Jews, like Christians and Armenians, officially had 'protected' status, but in reality lacked the rights of Ottoman citizens.

4   Zionism as a nationalist concept and movement did not crystallize until the 1880s. Contemporary scholars distinguish between the religious lovers of Zion, who were driven by the desire to live in the Land of Israel as God commands, from the largely secular, later Zionist nationalistic political movement (Silber 2008).

his days studying.[5] Such letters show their authors' belief in the Holy Land as the Jewish homeland from both a spiritual and historical perspective, following millennia of yearning for return. Some Jews argue that certain *mitzvot* can only be performed in the Holy Land, such as those related to tithing. It is incumbent on every Jew to give charity to the less fortunate. This could be achieved by growing a crop and, during harvesting, leaving gleanings for the poor in the corners of the field, as exemplified in the Book of Ruth and stated in Leviticus 19:9 (Lieber 1992, p.72). As Jews were not permitted to own land in Europe, the possibility of working the land and being able to fulfil these holy *mitzvot* must have been appealing.

The harsh reality was that most Jews living in the Holy Land could barely support themselves, given the hostile environment and conditions. Nevertheless, the letters to Montefiore show that charitable giving was intrinsic to Jewish life, as manifested in requests for donations to funds for orphans, bridal dowries and visiting the sick. The letters also reveal that giving charity and acting with righteousness were integral to the diaspora communities who sent money, via Montefiore, to Jews in the Holy Land.

Ḥalukah: Collection, funds and distribution

The centuries-old tradition of sending *shliḥim* (emissaries) to diaspora communities to collect funds to support Jews living in the Holy Land may have influenced Jews fleeing persecution. Financial help was essential because it was so difficult to scrape a living in the Holy Land – partly because it was understood that a Jew must be occupied in the study of the Torah, and partly because of the trials of living under Ottoman or Egyptian rule. The funding that the emissaries were able to collect was known as the *ḥalukah*, or 'the distribution'.

Numerous letters refer to the *ḥalukah* and the intricacies of distributing it fairly between the Sephardi and Ashkenazi congregations, and between community leaders and their less influential congregants. Several letters written in 1839, from various communities and officials in Jerusalem, acknowledged the arrival of funds and thanked

---

5   Core Collection, H575 letter 49d, 1839.

Montefiore for organizing it.[6] An insistent letter from a Russian congregation in Tiberias concerned the sharing of funding: money supposedly allocated for rebuilding their synagogue had not arrived, and currently they were forced to pray at those of two other congregations.[7] Leaders of the Ashkenazi congregation of Jerusalem wrote that life in the Holy Land was so difficult that only the *ḥalukah* prevented them from leaving and trying to make ends meet elsewhere.[8] The letters reveal tensions over the *ḥalukah* – between different communities and within congregations. Leaders of poverty-stricken communities, trying to feed and house their flocks in a hostile environment, sometimes became embroiled in accusations of corruption as they fought over funding. Their letters reveal desperate insistence that Montefiore should intervene on their behalf. The Sephardi congregation of Tiberias asked for Montefiore's intervention in 1839 in a dispute over unfair distribution of funds by the community leaders.[9] In 1849, a conflict developed in Jerusalem between the rabbis of two different congregations.[10]

The letters show heavy dependence on external financial help, both in the form of direct requests to the Montefiores, as well as through the general *ḥalukah*. In Montefiore, Jews had found an advocate, judge and advisor who (they believed) could protect them financially and politically. Due to his wealth and international profile, he could assume an important role in organizing and allocating the *ḥalukah*. This would have been attractive to Jews fleeing problems abroad, and it likely contributed to decisions to migrate to the Holy Land.

Practical assistance from Montefiore

Montefiore wanted to help Jews living in the Holy Land to support themselves financially, rather than relying on the *ḥalukah*. He sought

---

6   Core Collection, H574, letters 85, 86, 87a–e, 88a–c, 89a–c, 1839.

7   Core Collection, H576, letter 206, 1849.

8   Core Collection, H576, letter 10, 1849.

9   Core Collection, H574, letter 47a, 1839.

10 Core Collection, H587, letters 31 and 35, 1849.

to provide manual work for people unsuited to the study of the Torah. In particular, he was interested in setting up agricultural projects; his diary (1885) reveals his thoughts on the richness of the soil and the possibilities of growing crops in such a favourable climate (Green 2010, pp.120–121).

People wrote to Montefiore asking for practical help with a variety of endeavours, for example by providing funding for olive groves, bee-keeping, vineyards, cattle and sheep and goats, field crops, a mill.[11] Some migrants arrived from Europe with relevant skills, while others were novices and needed training. They asked Montefiore to fund their learning of a trade or area of agricultural expertise. Nine men of the Mizraḥi family described in their letter of 1849 how, several years earlier, they had left Europe to make a life in the Holy Land and encountered many difficulties in their efforts to establish a business. Now destitute, they appealed to Montefiore for help.[12]

Motives for appealing for agricultural work were often mixed. Sometimes people asked for practical assistance. Sometimes the appeal leaned towards the spiritual and biblical; the writers used emotive religious language to emphasize that they were living in the Holy Land and studying the Torah, as God demands. Some people cited the *mitzvah* of working God's holy soil. Appeals also stemmed from the hardship of living in a hostile environment. In a desperate letter sent from Safed, a man named Dov explained that he had sold barley to an Arab who was killed in an earthquake two weeks later. The Muslim authorities had taken the barley and Dov's customer's property. Dov had not been paid. He had sought help from the Consul and Muslim court in Acre, but it had proven impossible to gain any compensation for his loss. Desperately, Dov described how he had also suffered in the earthquake; his home collapsed and all his belongings were destroyed. At the end of the letter, he begged Montefiore to buy land for him where he could rear goats and sheep.[13]

---

11   Core Collection, H576b, letter 93, 1849; H575, letter 117a, 1839.

12   Core Collection, H576, letter 108, 1849.

13   Core Collection, H575, letter 56a, 1839.

Awaiting the Messiah

The letters to Montefiore contain prolific references to the coming of the Messiah. In Jewish tradition, there have been several periods in history when it is possible for the Messiah to come, according to interpretation of various religious texts. One of these years was 5600 in the Jewish calendar, or 1840 in the Gregorian (Morgenstern 2006, pp.23–49). Jewish communities in the Holy Land, and across the diaspora, approached the Messiah's coming in a variety of ways. The letters of 1839 can be read in the context of frenzied hope in the build-up to the Messiah's arrival. Shimshon Broder of Safed asked Montefiore for help, but not before addressing him as the 'light of Israel, the elevated general, comforter of the downtrodden, may he live until the coming of our salvation'.[14] With the Messiah expected the following year, this was not an unrealistic wish.

Likewise, several members of a congregation in Jerusalem sent a letter to Montefiore concerning charity for visiting the sick and providing bridal dowries for orphaned young women. In the opening paragraph, they wrote of their hope that he and Judith would see the rebuilding of Jerusalem (meaning the Temple) – a prospect only possible with the arrival of the Messiah.[15] Quoting from relevant parts of the holy books, writers from various congregations often ended their first paragraph addressing Montefiore and Judith with the words, 'until the Messiah comes', or, 'until Shiloh comes'.[16] The letters are peppered with other references to the Messiah, controversially addressing Montefiore with various alternative names for the Messiah[17] and referring to the 'Redemption of Israel'.[18]

Regarding the migration of the Perushi Jews to the Holy Land in the late 18th and early 19th centuries, there is another theory.

---

14   Core Collection, H575, letter 58d, 1839.

15   Core Collection, H575, letter 69a, 1839.

16   Core Collection, H575, letter 117b, 1839.

17   Core Collection, H577, letter 141, 1849 refers to Psalm 72:17 'yinon shemo', meaning 'before the sun his name will be magnified', a reference to the Messiah.

18   Core Collection, H575, letter 58d, 1839.

(The Perushim came from Vilna in Russia, modern Lithuania, and formed congregations primarily in Safed and Jerusalem.) Rather than trying to precipitate the Messiah's coming, they wished to be in the Holy Land in 1840, ready for the Messiah's arrival. After this, they believed, Jews would move into the *olam haba* (the world to come), where they would be resurrected in a valley near Jerusalem. People buried in the diaspora would have to 'transmigrate' by rolling underground to the Holy Land. By making sure they were already there by 1840, and buried if necessary, the Perushi migrants would avoid this unpleasant prospect (Lieber 1992, pp.39–40).

Letters to Montefiore appear to reflect this concern, albeit obliquely, in the following sentence: 'I have acquired four cubits of land in the Land of Israel.' A cubit is the distance from the elbow to the end of the middle finger on a person's arm; four cubits (a meaningful measure in Judaism) is approximately six feet – enough for a person's grave. The acquisition can be understood as preparation for events in the world to come. Numerous uses of this expression in the Montefiore letters suggest that some of the Jews in the Holy Land in 1839 and 1849, and their forebears, had migrated and established themselves in order to wait for the Messiah and be there in time for the Redemption.

Conclusion: Montefiore's legacy

The Montefiore letters show that the Jews of Eastern Europe, who migrated to the Holy Land in the late 18th and early 19th centuries, were motivated by a combination of spiritual, religious and practical reasons. The ethos of their religion demanded their yearning for, and return to, the Jewish homeland, the only place where certain commandments could be performed, and where they wished to study the Torah. Life in the Holy Land was not easy. It was unrealistic to attempt to live ideologically as a religious lover of Zion, without an income. The provision of the *ḥalukah*, the prospects of farming the land, learning a trade and being self-sufficient, offered with Montefiore's help, may have attracted some Jews to migrate to the Holy Land – particularly compared with the problems they endured in Europe. The belief in the redeemer, the Messiah, and his expected arrival in 1840 may also have motivated Jews from Eastern Europe to move to the Holy Land, in the hope of being released from the suffering of this world.

Yet more striking than any cold analysis of the motives for migration is the human message in these letters. Cries of desperation, begging Montefiore for help, leap off the pages. The insistent, emotive language can be heard as if spoken out loud, crossing the centuries to reach our contemporary eyes and ears. These voices from the past reveal the struggle to keep going in circumstances that we can only imagine from the luxury and comfort of our modern lives. Each letter reveals a moment in the life of its writer, giving insight into their culture and way of life. The letters show the immense difficulties and hardships endured by Montefiore's Jewish petitioners, not only in the Holy Land but in the places which some of them had left in the hope of finding a better and safer life. Today, migrants flee war-torn countries, desperately seeking refuge and security elsewhere. Like Montefiore's Jewish migrants, they hope for a compassionate welcome. The individual stories in these letters, speaking across 200 years, offer some understanding of the enormity of the decision to migrate to another home.

References

Green, A. (2010) *Moses Montefiore: Jewish Liberator, Imperial Hero*. Cambridge, MA: Harvard University Press.

Letters and Petitions, The Core Collection of the Montefiore Endowment Library. 1839 and 1849. Property of the Montefiore Endowment Library.

Lieber, S. (1992) *Mystics and Missionaries: The Jews in Palestine, 1799–1840*. Salt Lake City, UT: University of Utah Press.

Montefiore, J. (1885) *Notes from a Private Journal of a Visit to Egypt and Palestine, by way of Italy and the Mediterranean*. London: Wertheimer, Lea & Co.

Morgenstern, A. (2006) *Hastening Redemption: Messianism and the Resettlement of the Land of Israel*. Oxford: Oxford University Press.

Silber, M. (2008) 'Alliance of the Hebrews, 1863–1875: The diaspora roots of an ultra-Orthodox proto-Zionist utopia in Palestine.' *The Journal of Israeli History*, 27, 2, 119–147.

CHAPTER 24

Far from Home

Faith, Fellowship and Filipino Community

Filipino Community in Harmony, Action, Mobilization and Prayer

Since 1865, Sacred Heart Church has served the Catholic parishioners of Kilburn, northwest London. On an average Sunday, the church (affiliated to the order of the Oblates of Mary Immaculate) draws approximately 1700 parishioners for Mass, spread over four services. Once known as the most Irish area of London, today Kilburn is a vibrant, multicultural district whose diversity is reflected in the parish community of Sacred Heart. Inside the vast stone building, Kilburn's long-standing Irish Catholic population now worships alongside people from across the globe – of whom migrants from the Philippines and Eritrea are particularly prominent.

This chapter shines a light on one of Sacred Heart's most active communities. Filipino Community in Harmony, Action, Mobilization and Prayer (Filchamp) is a network of Filipino parishioners who gather regularly for fellowship and food and to welcome compatriots newly arrived in London. They play an active role in the life of the parish, particularly through their musical leadership for all regular services at Sacred Heart. In the following conversation, members of Filchamp gathered to reflect together on the importance of faith and fellowship, so far from home.

Finding faith in London

Lia: What time do you start working in the morning for your cleaning jobs?

Felma: Me, I start at eight. I have a daughter to prepare to go to school. So I work long.

Eduardo: I start at four o'clock in the morning. I wake up at two o'clock. That's why we need God more on our side during those days, during those times when you feel so tired.

Isabela: For me, without faith, I would not be able to stand my struggling. Only God knows. So my faith has really grown and grown up.

Nilda: Even our employer, if they know you're always in the church, they say: 'Oh, please, pray for me.' My boss, if she's looking for something, I'll just say: 'Okay, I'll pray to St Anthony.' And, thanks be to God, she found the things. That's why they say *faith can move mountains*.

Lia: You've moved from the Philippines to London. Very different countries, very different weather, very different cultures. How important has your faith been?

Nilda: It's very hard to explain it in English.

Maria: In the Philippines, I just go to church on Sunday, but when I came here, I'm here always. I just go to church – Saturday, Sunday, just to serve the Lord. I don't find this in the Philippines, to want to be in church also on Saturday.

Nilda: In the Philippines, we just go Sunday. That's it. But here, sometimes we stay here from Monday to Sunday for different activities of the church.

Isabela: We have to come.

Maria: Praise and worship.

Felma: My faith is stronger because of the community. Before, I don't have any time to come every week. But since I joined the community, my faith has become stronger. I have obligation.

Eduardo: Back home, you're always secure with your family; you'll be always with them. Here, you're alone, away from them. You miss them. There is no one else to talk to, except God. When you're away from home, you need to be in connection with God.

So just come to church! You'll find this fellowship here.

Now you can be comfortable with yourself. I come to Sacred Heart every Sunday because I've got brothers and sisters to talk to, to mingle with, to laugh with. I would be happy again. And then, the next week I would do it again, and again. So you just strengthened your faith.

Nilda: Yes, I think everybody feels that. Faith is very important to us because we're away from home. Now, this community is addicting to us.

Isabela: As a second family.

Nilda: We're always looking forward to the weekend.

Cultural comparisons

Lia: How does Sacred Heart compare to Catholic churches in the Philippines?

Isabela: There's a big difference.

Eduardo: In the Philippines, it's more conservative in wearing clothing.

Nilda: They're very strict in the Philippines.

Maria: Dress coding. In the Philippines, we cannot wear sleeveless.

Nilda: You know, sexy.

Maria: Cleavage.

Felma: Shorts are not allowed.

Nilda: Some churches, they are very strict. They still use veils for the women.

Isabela: Those are traditional Catholics.

Nilda: You can wear slippers, but shorts and sleeveless and cleavage, not okay. Not at all okay.

Felma: Here, it's modern.

Maria: But when you're serving the Body of Christ and you're wearing like that, that's not so acceptable.

Nilda: As well, the big difference is, here, it's very easy to talk to the priest, to enter the church. In the Philippines, you have to wait and you should have connections.

Maria: Some connection and bookings. Sometimes you should have money, yes.

Nilda: Here, it's very, very warm.

Isabela: The priest parish is so friendly to everybody.

Nilda: Supportive, yes. If there are any complaints, they entertain. In the Philippines, you cannot ask straight away with the priest.

Isabela: Yes, that's the big difference. But here, the priest, after Mass, they're going to the back and they congratulate all the people.

Language and home

Lia: What do you miss about the Catholic church in the Philippines?

Nilda: Choir, because they sing in Tagalog.

Felma: Our language.

Eduardo: You miss that. Every time we are all together, we speak our language.

Nilda: That's why we asked permission if we can hold a Filipino Mass here and they granted it. We have a Filipino Mass at three o'clock, every third Sunday of the month. The attendance is really good, 200 or something like that. Five hundred if we have a big event.

Maria: Participating, all, everybody.

Lia: What difference does it make when you're able to worship in your own language?

Isabela: It's easy to express. That's why. What you want to sing, if you're talking in English, there is something missing.

Nilda: Sometimes we're laughing because we pronounce the wrong words.

Eduardo: Everyone's going to be afraid that God might misunderstand it. So it's better to talk with Him in your language – to express that in your dialect.

Nilda: You try to adapt because you're an immigrant. But, to be honest, it's very hard for me to understand the English Mass, because of the way they talk when they give homily or read. It's very hard. Sometimes you just pray: 'Oh, Lord, sorry. I don't understand. Please forgive me.'

Felma: It's very hard, the Wales accent. If the priest is from Wales, it's very hard to understand.

Nilda: You have to train your ears. Thank God, today there's YouTube. You can watch in your own language, the Mass, the readings, everything.

Eduardo: But you still have to come to church, because you have to see your brothers and sisters.

The festival of Santo Niño

The Santo Niño du Cebú is a wooden statue of Jesus as a young boy, approximately 12 inches high and dressed in the style of a Spanish monarch. The statue, which was brought to the Philippines in 1521 by the explorer Ferdinand Magellan, is the country's oldest Catholic artefact. Devotion to the Santo Niño is a strong theme in Filipino Catholicism; replicas of the statue can be found in homes and businesses across the Philippines and throughout the diaspora. Every January, worshippers celebrate the Santo Niño in the festival of *Sinulog*, named for the ritual dance honouring the Christ child.

Nilda: The festival connects you to the Philippines.

Felma: All the Filipinos celebrate during the feast.

Eduardo: It's like a carnival. Like Mardi Gras. It's a big, big celebration.

Isabela: Santo Niño is the Child Jesus.

Nilda: Not baby. Child.

Felma: The statue of the Santo Niño is one of the most beloved and recognizable cultural icons in the Philippines.

Nilda: The statue, it belongs to the Filipino community.

Isabela: All of us during the feast day, we bring [it] to be blessed.

Nilda: Five hundred people all bring their statue, from small to big ones.

Maria: My statue is big. I brought it from the Philippines in 2009. He's flown in the suitcase – a big suitcase.

Felma: We do parade inside the church.

Maria: Yes, a procession.

Isabela: We go around the church, and then everybody follows with dancing.

Maria: We will dress like a Santo Niño, and we dance.

Nilda: The service is not in English, but there are so many different immigrants participating in that feast. They're looking for the souvenir, because we're always giving souvenirs.

Felma: Prayer cards with a Santo Niño image. A small image with prayer. That's our giveaway.

Nilda: It's very nice to bring your culture here. The immigrants, they recognize it. Even though they don't understand what we're doing, they're happy.

Felma: They can see the action.

Nilda: The immigrants here in the church are from different places. Any immigrants, they are very welcome to join us in this festival.

Eduardo: It's like spreading God's words or God's wisdom in us.

Felma: We like evangelized people to come in the church to develop their faith. That's why we are here – to show to them that we are celebrating the culture of Filipino communities and Santo Niño.

Nilda: This community was a very Irish community. That was 20 years ago. But now, it's different immigrants coming to the church. Not like before, when it was only Irish. But now I think the Irish are missing.

Maria: Yes, they go home. They are gone.

Nilda: Mostly immigrants are the ones who are coming to this church. Thanks be to God.

CHAPTER 25

Somali and New Scot

Faith, Migration and Community

Mohamed Omar

From Somalia to Scotland

I came to Scotland in 2001, with my single mother and my three sisters. I had just turned 15. We were, I believe, only the second Somali family in Scotland, and we were sent to Glasgow.

In the beginning, we came to London as asylum seekers. There was fear – not only our family's fear, but a Somali fear of Scotland. In 1989, a young Somali man was murdered in Scotland. For the people we knew in London, all they could associate with Scotland was that murder. People thought it was a dangerous, racist place.

But we settled in Scotland. My first impression was: *It's a very cold place*. It was quite a shock.

I spoke no English when I arrived. I knew 'How do you do?' We were sent to a part of Scotland where they had a strong Glaswegian accent. I must have seemed very slow when responding to people.

School was particularly good for me. There were students from Afghanistan, Iraq. Many people were also seeking asylum. It was an interesting time in Scottish history. Slowly, I adapted and made friends. Teachers were crucial. I had a bilingual teacher who introduced me to my very first book in English: *The Autobiography of Malcolm X*. I still have the book.

Finding community in the mosque

I didn't go to the mosque often when I first came to Scotland. But during the month of Ramadan, the father of the other Somali family took me with him to pray *Taraweeh* (a prayer performed during Ramadan nights). The *qutba* (a sermon that the imam reads at *Jummah*, the Friday prayer) was so different. In Somalia, you would hear the call to prayer when you were at home or outside, socializing. But in Scotland, there were no calls to prayer. The *qutba* was read in Urdu (the language of the main Muslim population) and also in English. I didn't understand English at that time, so I couldn't understand a word of it.

But with Muslims, we pray in Arabic. The Qu'ran is in Arabic. So that was how I could pray with others. It's the prayer itself, communication – a link between an individual and Allah, but also that commonality of being in a room and of embracing everyone praying to the same God. We went beyond language. Each individual has his or her own unique link with Allah. When praying, I could feel the sense of brotherhood with fellow Muslims.

The Muslim community – particularly the Pakistani community – helped with integrating Somalis who are Muslim in Scotland. There is this commonality of migrant experiences. They understood how it feels to settle into another country. There were people who would go out of their way to help, and not only in the mosque. For example, a gentleman in the corner shop would give us advice and a sense of orientation within the city. For my family, and generally for the Somali community in Scotland, the Pakistani community has been very helpful.

Scotland is very different from Somalia. After Ramadan, Muslims celebrate *Eid al Fitr* – the end of the fasting, which is obligatory for Muslims (for those who are able to fast). There's a big celebration. In Somalia, the entire community is celebrating, dressing up. The city is so vibrant. Whereas in Scotland, only a segment of society would celebrate. Everyday life, like school, would just go on.

Finding community in football

Football has shaped, and continues to shape, my experience of migration in Scotland. When I first moved to Glasgow, I was a teenager who did not speak English. But at the time, the one thing that I loved was football. It's a sport that I've been playing since I was a child in Somalia. So, in Glasgow, whenever I saw people playing football, I would play with them. That helped me to make friends.

Football goes beyond language. Not understanding English did not prevent me from playing football. When I came as a teenager, I played with my neighbours – with Glaswegians. That was great but also difficult. At that time, people were unsure about newcomers in the country. But football was a way of interacting with others.

When I was a teenager, playing with Glaswegians, I had to manage my time. Muslims pray five times a day. I had to take out time to pray on my own. I would have to just stop playing football and go home and pray. It's easier now. There's more awareness, in terms of people and groups from different faith communities.

As a teenager, I didn't have many Somali friends. Now there are growing populations of Somalis in Scotland. Now that I've been living in Scotland for so many years, every Sunday I play football with Somalis. It's a way to stay in touch with people from the same country. It's just people coming together.

It links us to prayer, as well. For example, on Sundays and during the winter, when it gets dark early, we pray on the football pitch. People are curious to see this. They wonder: *Why did they stop and pray?*

Finding interfaith community

Being Somali and Muslim, I think it's one. Islam and being Muslim are part and parcel of a Somali's life. With migration, Somalis find themselves in multicultural societies where they have huge opportunities to learn from other people and other communities. That's exciting. This is one of the reasons why I'm involved with the work of

Interfaith Scotland – an organization that promotes social cohesion through interfaith dialogue.

Interfaith work is important to me for a number of reasons. First, there is a huge rise of religious discrimination such as Islamophobia. In order to address this problem, people's relationships become very important. If there were more people getting to know each other from different backgrounds, we would reduce the level of conflict, misunderstanding and miscommunication. This is a journey that needs to be embraced by all segments of society.

Second, interfaith initiatives provide a platform for collaboration on issues of shared concern. While people of different religious backgrounds have different outlooks in life, we share the same space in everyday society. So, it is important that we collaborate to make it a positive environment for all.

Being Somali and Muslim can be monocultural, compared with, perhaps, Pakistan, where there are other minority religious communities. Moving to Scotland was unbelievably enriching for me, on many levels. In schools, in particular, you interact with people who are very different from you. I used to be an interpreter for newly resettled Somali asylum seekers, including young Somalis who went to Catholic schools. I would have conversations with the families that came from monocultural societies, about the similarities in the discipline of teaching between the two religions (Islam and Catholic Christianity).

Three years ago, I helped to establish an interfaith support group called the Weekend Club. Faith communities cooperate by helping isolated asylum seekers and refugees at the weekends. During the week, there are many other organizations that support asylum seekers and refugees, and there are many programmes that people can go to. But at the weekends, unless you have friends or things to do and you have financial resources to go out for coffee, it can be very lonely and difficult.

The Weekend Club recruits people from different faith communities to organize events. I worked with volunteers to go out and talk to their communities – to churches, mosques, synagogues and gurdwaras. Muslims, Christians, Jews and people of no faith are working together, showcasing their city. For the events we organize, we take a creative way of looking at migration and talking about it. We visit museums that are free in Glasgow, so people can then be self-sufficient and go on their own. We have also gone on trips to see the green spaces in Stirling and Bannockburn. Over 300 asylum seekers and refugees took part in the Weekend Club in 2016.

This experience showed me the importance of faith communities in standing up and joining together. It has been a huge success. Now the Weekend Club has been replicated in Edinburgh, as well.

I'm very proud of that.

Working for change

Scotland is a place where I can be myself. As a Muslim, I appreciate Scotland's strong equality legislation. When it's time for prayers, there are a number of mosques that I can attend to pray. I know that's a privilege. In some countries, there's not that luxury. In Scotland, you can be who you want to be, and the State supports you. Sometimes we take this for granted, but it's a very important right to have.

After my studies in law and international relations at the University of Aberdeen, I went to Germany to learn how human rights work in action. I did an internship with people from different countries. Through this, I was able to learn from their experiences and their projects.

In 2012, I started working for the Scottish government in health and social care policy. My lived experience of being a refugee (at school, university and in the civil service) helps me to understand the importance of this kind of policy. Currently, I work with the Mental Health Foundation to help deliver the New Scots Strategy – a government strategy for integrating asylum seekers and refugees from the day they arrive in Scotland. It's led by the Scottish government, but with non-governmental organizations working to deliver that vision.

Through the Mental Health Foundation's Refugee Programme, I co-convene the health sub-group, coordinating stakeholders to better support asylum seekers and refugees. As a policy and research organization, we put refugees at the heart of our work and highlight the issues that affect their mental health. Before refugees even arrive in this country, they suffer from many mental health difficulties related to their journeys. Their human rights are violated. When a person resettles, it can be really difficult for them to connect with other people and with existing services. They struggle with isolation, the language and cultural barriers. In addition, there's also the issue of mental health stigma. At the Mental Health Foundation, we are working to address this.

The goal is to make sure that society takes into account the importance of mental health for refugees. I like to think that I am a catalyst for change. I want to change the narrative around refugees – to highlight their voices and showcase their resilience and the contributions they can make to society when given support and opportunities. I am keen to ensure that refugees' mental health is mainstreamed, rather than only treated as an equality issue. We want the general public to understand that refugees' issues are as important as other societal issues, and that mental health has a huge impact on people's lives. This is what drives me – making sure that refugees have voices and are visible in Scotland, not only at the community level, but at the policy and strategic level. This is how we can ensure that society works for everyone.

CHAPTER 26

Home is Exile and Exile is Home

Jennifer Langer

August 2018. In the basement of the Covent Garden Poetry Café, another monthly Exiled Lit Café is about to begin. The bright yellow double doors are about to close, to shut out the rumble of London. When Exiled Writers Ink began its literary evenings in 2000, only a handful of writers attended. Now the Café nights are packed with refugees, students, writers, travellers and interested Londoners. We gather together in a newly modernized space, its plainness relieved by orange chairs and the splash of paintings on the wall. As the Afghan ruba player entices plaintive notes from his carved wooden instrument, the audience lapses into silence, some with eyes closed in ecstasy.

The theme tonight is 'From Absence to Presence'. This month, in partnership with the Syrian storytelling organization Hikayetna, our writers are of Syrian origin. Our first guest is poet Amir Darwish, who nostalgically describes his hometown of Aleppo before its destruction. Farrah Akbik tells us of her travels in Syria and of her love for the country, its people and its culture. Then we are stunned to hear that her beloved brother was killed in Idlib in January; she reads a poem in his memory. The lights are switched off and we watch two short feature films by Iraqi film-maker Koutaiba Al-Janabi.

The lights go on and audience members are eager to interpret the narratives. During the break, everyone heatedly discusses politics, literature, publishing and their latest activities. Some have been invited to participate in literature festivals in Spain, Italy and India.

Established in 1998, Exiled Writers Ink[1] brings together established, emerging and aspiring writers from repressive regimes and war-torn situations. The organization develops and promotes the creative literary expression of refugees, migrants and exiles, encourages cross-cultural dialogue, and advocates human rights through literature and literary activism ('Agit Lit'). The network provides a platform through performance, training, creative writing workshops, mentoring, translation, publications (including *Exiled Ink* e-magazine), live literature events, theatre, symposia and poetry competitions.

It all began when I edited *The Bend in the Road* (1997), an anthology of writing by refugees newly arrived in the UK. The anthology revealed diverse literary voices, providing insights not only into the pain of the refugee experience, but also into the complexity and diversity of the experiences and concerns of writers from different regions. Suddenly I was being contacted by a range of organizations requesting sessions featuring the refugee writers. When a large, enthusiastic group of exiled writers clamoured for their own organization, Exiled Writers Ink came into being.

While government and voluntary sector provision met practical needs, there was little opportunity for the creative expression and externalization of the refugees' inner, emotional and spiritual lives, and for sharing experiences. I remember Mir Mahfuz Ali, the exiled Bangladeshi poet, telling me in a rasping whisper that Exiled Writers Ink had provided him with a community of writers which was a haven out of his isolation. He had lost his voice in more ways than one. Riot police in Bangladesh had shot him in the throat during a protest, leaving him unable to speak. When he arrived in England, seeking both medical treatment and political freedom, he felt deprived of an identity because he had lost his mother tongue and felt invisible. Yet in 2013, Mahfuz won the prestigious Geoffrey Dearmer Prize, and in

---

1   www.exiledwriters.co.uk.

2014 Seren, the respected poetry publisher, brought out his first poetry collection *Midnight, Dhaka*.

In this chapter, I interweave the voices of Exiled Writers Ink poets and prose writers to explore the creative act of 'writing faith' in the diaspora. I explore diaspora as a space that allows the freedom to write cathartically for an understanding of the self in relation to religion and religious belief. Faith in the diaspora may be represented as a contested area of personal belief, versus the memory of the strictures of faith of the homeland. New encounters may lead to shifts in attitude.

Identity and exilic space

The state of displacement causes an enormous rupture in the self. Having been cast out by the home country or fled because of a longing for freedom, writers in exile are forced to confront the question of identity. They negotiate constantly with a conflicting sense of self, and so feel unstable and unable to find a place in the external world of exile. Afghan poet Hasan Bamyani (2007), in 'There/Here' expresses an acute sense of alienation, concluding that he is no longer a person.

The exiled Bosnian writer Himzo Skorupan (2005) phones his own home in his surrealistic poem 'Neither Here Nor There'; he is informed by the appropriator of his flat that he is not there. The poetic voice concludes: 'I am not really here, and over there, I am no more'.

Similarly, the Kurdish poet Kamal Mirawdeli (2005, p.276) confronts the disconcerting state of exile: 'You feel that your existential space has turned upside down...there is always this unavoidable inner odyssey which makes sure that you have no real presence anywhere.'

Devastation in the country of origin compounds the sense of alienation, stimulating the need for memory of the past in the desperate search for identity. Writing in exile, the barren soul is a dominant theme in Iraqi poet Ghareeb Iskander's (2016) collection *Gilgamesh's Snake and Other Poems*. Although it is a contemplation on the agony and pain of the devastation of Iraq, the poetic voice resolves that the stories of the past will not vanish or be erased despite being concealed from the eyes. Yet the oxymoron is that the past will be washed away, as his wisdom will be written on pages of water.

In my experience, most exiled writers express minimal affinity with the new external exilic space, portraying it negatively. This is due not only to their sense of destabilization, but also to their negative reception by the host community. Representing their inner struggles, bound with difficult experiences of immigration, detention and racism, the writers express an underlying tension and a reluctance to trust. Congolese poet and playwright Jean-Louis N'tadi (2007) wrote a bitter poem about being imprisoned in Campsfield Detention Centre, while prose writer Hasani Hasani from Zimbabwe cynically observes that the police round up those who have escaped from dangerous countries.

God and religion in the diaspora

Because of the instability of identity in the diaspora, some refugee writers call on their God to hear and help them. In his poem 'Cul-de-Sac', Kamal Mirawdeli (2002, p.88) finds himself in a nihilistic state and calls to God in despair:

O' God, O' God... I turn all my existence into a small entity
Lest I would lose sight of you
Lest a storm would blow
That would erase you from these waves.

In Exiled Ink's touring theatre production 'Breaking the Silence: Somali Women Speak Out' (Somali Women's Voices 2003), some of the women talk to Allah. They beseech him to restore their country and to end the suffering so that they may return.

In contrast, some poetic exilic voices repudiate the home country's established religion, of which they were victims. While words deemed subversive were stifled in the home country, exiled literary voices have generally erupted in the diaspora to speak out, to act as witness and call for help. They desire for the struggles in their country to be understood outside their communities. Indeed, the diasporic links between exiled Iranians are (to a large extent) based on their opposition to the Islamic state, so that Iranian exilic voices are strongly marked by their resistance to Iranian clerical rule: its imposition of morality and faith on the Iranian people; its control of women's destinies and bodies; its frequent violence; its human rights abuses.

Punishments for breaching or resisting religious rules are described by some Iranian poets. 'Death by Stoning', by Ziba Karbassi (2005, p.41), is a poem that is almost unbearable to read because of the shock, revulsion and sadness it evokes through the detail described by the victim's aunt:

> they said their skirts were filled with stones
> their hands were full of stones, their skirts
> everywhere stones were being rained down
> the world was become a world
> of stone

Ziba performs her poetry with tearful emotion suffused with the suffering of her people. Mehrangiz Rassapour (2007) has written the powerful poem 'Lash'. And at the end of a seemingly innocent poem by Ali Abdolrezaei (2005, p.16), about his crush on his primary school teacher, we learn almost parenthetically that she was executed. Abdolrezaei is castigatory about censorship by the theocracy in Iran:

> How could I write
> So that you would not censor it
> When silence is stamped on our mouths.

Recently, Exiled Writers Ink hosted a Café evening in partnership with Amnesty International, entitled 'Words for the Silenced'. It focused on writing about and from the point of those imprisoned in Iran for their opposition to the theocracy. Nasrin Parvaz (2018) read quietly from her memoir. Born in Tehran, she was imprisoned and tortured for eight years for her civil rights and women's rights activism.

These Iranian writers, who are vociferous in their condemnation of the regime and its values, risk endangerment even in exile. Other exiled Iranian writers resist criticism of the theocratic regime because of the potential repercussions on family members still living in Iran, and because of Iran's long, threatening feelers, which spread into the diaspora. Arguably, because of their negative conceptualization of the interpretation of faith in their homeland, for some Iranian writers the identity of 'Muslim' is anathema. Therefore, they refuse to define themselves according to faith but prefer to explore what it is to be human.

Similarly, Adnan Al-Sayegh's (2009, 2016) poems position the Iraqi poet outside organized religion. His cynicism towards it is characterized by disdain about the behaviour of its adherents. In the poem 'God's Money', he observes the hypocrisy of the religious man with his rosary who ignores the blind beggar with his palms outstretched. The poet condemns belief in a God inseparable from violence and bloodshed. In contrast, he articulates his belief through joyful word and song. He exhorts the religious zealots to hear their Lord in a flute. In his poem 'My God is One', Al-Sayegh accuses the major organized religions of lacking all faith. The poetic persona appeals to Al-Hallaj, a legendary 9th-century Sufi master, to deliver him from exilic despair.

Some writers reclaim pre-Islamic beliefs and myths. These are not merely cultural references but representations of nostalgia and manifestations of buried layers of memory. Describing her past in the poem 'There Me Here', the Kurdish Iraqi poet Nazand Begikhani (2002) draws on ancient Mesopotamian myths. She equates her past to a Goddess in the East and describes how Melek Taus, the Peacock Angel who is one of the central figures of the Yazidi religion, would hold the Goddess's hand to the dome of self-knowledge. Inanna, the Goddess of Love during the Sumerian period, would wait for her lover Dumuzy, who was responsible for promoting fertility.

Poetry can also express nostalgia for the religious rituals inextricably connected to family life and childhood. Choman Hardi's (2004) poem 'Fasting' refers to the month of Ramadan in Iraqi Kurdistan. She remembers the ritual of praying: washing hands, feet and forehead, sitting with her head covered at sunset, facing Mecca and waiting for the Imam's permission.

Similarly, the poetic articulation and longing for the ancestor worship practised in the home country in Africa is tantamount to an expression of nostalgia and loss. A palpable sensibility of mourning is evident in 'My Ancestors' Fire' by exiled Faziry Mafutala (2005, p.106) from the Democratic Republic of Congo:

> From my ancestors
> Who lived among the Bantu in the tropical rain forest
> Among the Pygmies in the deep bush
> I gathered the mysteries
> How the strongest ancestors sank in the sea.

It is with great sadness that the exiled poet realizes that his grandchildren will be ignorant of the power of the words for the ancestors:

> My grandchildren won't drink from the old calabash
> The first breath of humankind will drift away.

Writing and encounter

Exiled Writers Ink is one of the few cultural spaces where Muslim, Arab, Palestinian, Israeli and Jewish writers encounter each other. It is unsurprising that Jewish writers are involved in the organization, given their refugee and migrant ancestry and sensibility of otherness. In most of the Middle Eastern countries from which the exiled writers originate, there were established Jewish communities which are now absent and vilified. I was aware of the Arab world's demonization of Jews, inextricably connected to the ongoing Israel–Palestine context. So it was with trepidation that I first met an Iraqi writer when researching for my first anthology. However, I was gratified that on revealing my Jewish identity, he recalled with sorrow the lost Iraqi Jewish community, among whom he had many friends.

External perceptions about writing by Muslims affect their literary work, as the writers therefore attempt to counter the stereotypes. Frustrated by their misrepresentation and demonization as terrorists in the media, the Syrian Kurdish poet Amir Darwish (2015, pp.11 and 13) has written the bitter, satirical poem 'Sorry: An apology from Muslims, or those perceived to be Muslims, to humanity.' It lists the diverse and significant contributions that Islam (or the Arab world) has made to humanity, including algebra and couscous. The poem is presented as a mock apology to the West, yet it is telling that it concludes with Sufi verse by Rumi on the theme of higher love, suggesting that the liberation of the soul, in communication with the Beloved, surmounts earthly divisions. Unfortunately, 'Sorry' has been exploited and abused by Islamists as a propaganda tool, affecting the poet's peace of mind. He therefore no longer wishes to be associated with the poem.

In fact, Darwish's debut collection, *Don't Forget the Couscous*, is a love song to the Arab world: Syria, Kurdistan, Morocco, Palestine and his native Aleppo. It is a memoir of the failed Arab Spring and the civil war that has turned Syria into a 'fountain of blood'. And it is a bitter account of the demonization of Islam in the West, and the violent interference of the West in the Islamic world.

Exile may provide distance and new perspectives; it may even be transformative. Meeting and hearing the innermost narratives of Jewish and Muslim writers hopefully transforms the understanding of the 'other'. In her short story, 'There is a Fashion Show', Dursaliye Bedir (2002), attempts to understand the lives of the ultra-orthodox Jewish community of Stamford Hill, North London, where she once lived. Every Saturday morning, she observes the procession to synagogue. Her story ends: 'My dear Jewish neighbours, I no longer live in Stamford Hill but I think of you every Saturday. I miss you very much. Please don't disappear like those Greeks in Balat' (2002, p.161).

These are challenging times for both Muslims and Jews in the UK. As part of the Exiled Writers Ink symposium in 2017 at the School of Oriental and African Studies, University of London, we included a round table entitled 'On the Frontline: Muslim and Jewish

Writers' Self-Representation'. The session foregrounded less familiar paradigms of poetry by writers of Jewish and Muslim heritage. The intention was to unsettle what has become taken for granted in contemporary discussions. The poets Aviva Dautch, Reza Hiwa, George Szirtes and Nadia Fayidh Mohammed countered stereotypes, turning themselves into subjects through their discourse and individual poetic voices. Exiled Writers Ink now plans to form a collective of writers against Islamophobia, anti-Semitism and racism, to provide insights into the complexity of identity, faith and culture.

Literary expression becomes the Motherland

I sometimes ponder the incongruity of a Jewish woman leading Exiled Writers Ink. Yet my visceral feelings of outsiderness and difference have caused me to empathize with the marginalized of society, particularly asylum seekers and refugees. My own poetry reveals a concern with outsiders and victims such as the Herero tribe, Calais migrants and the Palestinians, among others. Equally, much is an exploration of my complex identity. Snatching at fragments of family stories, I strive to create a narrative and dream of a lost world. I was born of the history of memory of loss and of refugee roots. My parents were both Jewish refugees who had fled Nazi Germany for Britain, where they met. Eventually they learned that they were the only survivors of their respective families. My parents did not speak to me of their trauma, but in our living room there were photographs of their murdered relatives. I chose not to ask questions and shut off my mind about the way they had died.

As a child born in Britain, I felt a strange mixture of identities, with the German one predominating at that time. In the age before multicultural Britain, I became acutely aware of my parents' German origin, yet I was also aware of their ambivalent love–hate relationship with Germany, the perpetrator of unspeakable atrocities and genocide. Awareness of being Jewish was something that came late to me in my consciousness. My Jewish identity has evolved in a turbulent manner in the context of multiple, ever-changing challenges; the Middle East situation reverberates for Jews worldwide. I would not regard the Jewish ethic of *Tikkun Olam* (repairing the world) as playing a part in my poetry or my vocation to champion the words of those in exile. Rather, it is being the daughter of refugees – of being an outsider and of being 'other' – that drew me to empathize with the refugees of today and to establish Exiled Writers Ink. This, in turn, led me to edit four anthologies of exiled literature (1997, 2002, 2005, 2008) and to become a scholar of exiled literature.

As Exiled Writers Ink is an organization that is emphatically not predicated on belief or faith, my immediate assumption was that matters of faith were irrelevant, suppressed or marginalized. Yet the large network comprises writers with diverse religious roots. Faith is intertwined with the politics both of the home country and, increasingly, of the host country. The issue of faith is ever present, emerging both overtly and covertly in literary work and discourse by refugee, migrant and exiled writers. Faith may be deeply embedded in the culture from which the exiled writers originate, but retrospection in exile allows them to negotiate, affirm or even deny their religious affinity. For some writers, the old culture – inextricably linked to faith and memory – is absorbed and transformed to create a new perspective. Moreover, exiled writers may strive to contest and resist the demonization of their faith in the new land. Aware that the past cannot be restored, they create a new interpretation of their world, frequently invoking faith in its broadest dimensions.

Art is an act of the soul, and in exile the writers contemplate the past in order to understand it and re-interpret it for the present. Situated in the strange and estranging home of exile, it is literary expression that becomes the motherland, mystery and companion.

References and suggested reading

Abdolrezaei, A. (2005) 'Forough.' Exiled Ink Issue 4. London: Exiled Writers Ink.
Ali, M.M. (2014) *Midnight, Dhaka*. Bridgend: Seren Books.

Al-Sayegh, A. (2009) *The Deleted Part* (trans. M. Burgui-Artajo and S.Watts). London: Exiled Writers Ink.

Al-Sayegh, A. (2016) *Pages from the Biography of an Exile* (trans. S. Watts and M. Burui-Artajo). Todmorden: Arc Publications.

Bamyani, H. (2007) 'There/Here.' Exiled Ink Issue 8. London: Exiled Writers Ink.

Bedir, D. (2002) 'There is a Fashion Show.' In J. Langer (ed.) *Crossing the Border*. Nottingham: Five Leaves.

Begikhani, N. (2002) 'There Me Here.' In J. Langer (ed.) *Crossing the Border*. Nottingham: Five Leaves.

Darwish, A. (2015) 'Sorry: An apology from Muslims, or those perceived to be Muslims, to humanity.' In *Don't Forget the Couscous*. Ripon: Smokestack Books.

Hardi, C. (2004) 'Fasting.' In *Life for Us*. Hexham: Bloodaxe Books.

Hasani, H. 'A Life away from the Asylum.' Available at www.exiledwriters.co.uk/portfolio-items/hasani.

Iskander, G. (2016) *Gilgamesh's Snake and Other Poems* (trans. J. Glenday and G. Iskander). Syracuse: Syracuse University Press.

Karbassi, Z. (2005) 'Death by Stoning' (trans. S. Watts and Z. Karbassi). In J. Langer (ed.) *The Silver Throat of the Moon*. Nottingham: Five Leaves.

Langer, J. (ed.) (1997) *The Bend in the Road: Refugees Writing*. Nottingham: Five Leaves.

Langer, J. (ed.) (2002) *Crossing the Border: Voices of Refugee and Exiled Women*. Nottingham: Five Leaves.

Langer, J. (ed.) (2005) *The Silver Throat of the Moon: Writing in Exile*. Nottingham: Five Leaves.

Langer, J. (ed.) (2008) *If Salt has Memory: New Writing by Jewish Exiled Writers*. Nottingham: Five Leaves.

Mafutala, F. (2005) 'My Ancestors' Fire.' In J. Langer (ed.) *The Silver Throat of the Moon: Writing in Exile*. Nottingham: Five Leaves.

Mirawdeli, K. (2002) 'Cul-de-Sac.' In *Passage to Dawn*. London: Self-published.

Mirawdeli, K. (2005) 'Poetry and Exile.' In J. Langer (ed.) *The Silver Throat of the Moon: Writing in Exile*. Nottingham: Five Leaves.

N'tadi, J.-L. (2007) 'Campsfield House Hotel.' Exiled Ink Issue 8. London: Exiled Writers Ink.

Parvaz, N. (2018) *One Woman's Struggle in Iran: A Prison Memoir*. Market Drayton: Victorina Press.

Rassapour, M. (2007) 'Lash.' Exiled Ink Issue 7. London: Exiled Writers Ink.

Skorupan, Himzo (2005) 'Neither Here Nor There.' In J. Langer (ed.) *The Silver Throat of the Moon*. Nottingham: Five Leaves.

Somali Women's Voices (2003) Breaking the Silence: Somali Women Speak Out. Exiled Writers Ink theatre production

CHAPTER 27

Memory, Multiplicity, Home

Issam Kourbaj

These four images (*'Strike'*, *'Dark Water, Burning World'*, *'Lost'* and *'Another Day Lost'*) together form a narrative. Migration is a symptom of destruction. Because of the *Strike*(s) of barrel bombs, countless people are forced to flee Syria. *Dark Water, Burning World* reflects the trauma of leaving home and being *Lost*, physically and spiritually. *Another Day Lost* reflects the pain of waiting to return home.

Strike

Dark Water, Burning World

Lost

Another Day Lost

Image 1: *Strike*

Strike is a performance of the repetitive action of striking matches, as a response to airstrikes and barrel bombs that are killing thousands of innocent Syrians. It touches on the idea of building a nest by collecting sticks. However, there is a dark side: the nest is being burnt by bombs continuously dropped and dropped and dropped...

Many communities and cities in Syria have been devastated due to this daily destruction of the past, the present and the future. *Strike* draws on the feeling of living underneath these bombs, and what one feels on witnessing one's home, community and city turn to wreck.

Image 2: *Dark Water, Burning World*

This piece originated as a response to a small artefact from Syria, 2500 years old, in the collection of the Fitzwilliam Museum in Cambridge. A miniature model ship carries three goddesses. The minute I saw it, I immediately saw my project. The original piece is made of lead. I thought: *Lead and boats? It will sink!*

My first experiments were in lead, but that didn't last long. Then I noticed my bicycle mudguards. Mud/Guard: its function is to guard, but many of my fellow Syrians were *not* guarded by the dangerous, flimsy boats, made from cheap, poor-quality rubber. They might as well have been made from lead.

So I started making my artwork from mudguards and spent matches. Resin holds the matches upright, suggesting that in desperate times people bond, hold and support each other. Symbolically, I tackled the reality of colossal damage by burning these matches. The burnt parts might be read as a reflection on the trauma that women, children and men carry with them.

Image 3: *Lost*

Lost was inspired by images and stories by my collaborator, the poet Ruth Padel. One day, she called me from Lesbos to say: 'What can we do to commemorate the help given by the people of Lesbos to families escaping Syria?' She told me about the local newspaper editor who had helped pull refugees from the waves at night. Their stories were exactly like those told by Ruth's grandmother, who had been a refugee from the burning of Smyrna, in Greece, in 1922.

Many Syrians were arriving in Lesbos – some of them alive, some of them dead. The dead arrived with very little, except a piece of clothing. When the local residents had to bury them, they didn't know what to do or what kind of gravestone they should make. They were very considerate about the information they should reveal about the person they buried. So they wrote nothing on the gravestone but 'Anon'. They put toys they found in the sea on the children's graves.

To reflect on this tragedy, I started making 'gravestones'. I dipped pieces of children's clothing in plaster and I inscribed on them, in English and in Greek: 'UNKNOWN', 'GIRL' or 'BOY'. I included their age, the number of refugees arriving that day, and the date of burial.

I exhibited my gravestones at the Classical Archaeology Museum in Cambridge, a space filled with plaster casts of Greek and Roman sculptures. *Lost* was installed among these beautified bodies, next to *Laocoon* and *Children of Niobe*. *Lost* was curated in conversation with these immortalized legends, which were presented in plaster but are void and hollow inside. My plaster characters are unidentified, but with substance inside.

Ruth Padel's poem *Lesbos 2016* concludes this chapter.

Image 4: *Another Day Lost*

This piece was based on lyrics by the Lebanese Rahbani Brothers, describing the experience of time and exile The idea was to make a miniature refugee camp with thousands of small tents made out of repurposed materials (paper from discarded books and medical boxes). These camps would be encircled with burnt matches that function as a fence as well as a tally of the days which have passed since the Syrian uprising on 15 March 2011. Wherever I exhibited this piece, I tried to mark a day by burning a match at noon and adding it to the installation.

2015 saw *Another Day Lost* launched as a series of installations across five sites and curated by Louisa Macmillan as part of the London Shubbak Festival. On the first day of the festival, there were 1579 matches in every 'fence'. Another match was added for every day of the exhibition, resulting in a total of 1593 matches by the end of two weeks on display. The sites were scattered around London, mapping and loosely reflecting the geographic pattern of refugee presence outside the borders of Syria.

Another Day Lost has become a migrant in its own right. It has been exhibited on the upper deck of HMS Wellington Royal Navy warship, moored on the River Thames in London, shown in New York and Philadelphia, and displayed in Dubai to commemorate the fifth anniversary of the Syrian uprising. The twelfth edition was poignantly exhibited in Budapest, inside and outside a tent for the United Nation's Refugee Agency.

In conversation with Issam Kourbaj

Lia: How do you hope that your four images will challenge or provoke the readers of this book to think differently about migration?

Issam: Any form of art requires a speaker and a listener, a performer and an audience. So the responsibility is both mine and the viewer's. I put my artwork out there and let the viewer reflect on it, in the way they wish. We are all different; each of us reads things differently.

Although my images are referencing Syria, I would like them to be universal rather than local. I would like them to be about something whose meaning we all struggle with: home. Where it is? Where to find it – in front of or behind our skin? I strive to make artwork that has multiple readings. It's not a finished product, it's not a sealed object. It is a conversation.

In this body of work, I am particularly interested in getting the viewer to reflect on not only what's happening in Syria but in the world. We live in unstable times. Lives are on hold and many migrants are becoming 'citizens of a tent'. It is a global crisis that requires new thinking and policies.

Now, as an artist I don't have the answer, but I can construct a question through my artwork. I ask my viewer to be imaginative, sensitive and poetic. I strive to make my artwork as pieces of poetry that take the form of an object. When you are reading poetry, you will take something; I will take something else. We are different, and we need to celebrate our differences. Otherwise, if we all take only one thing, it reflects oneness or a mono-reality. And I am really interested in multiplicity.

Lia: That strikes me as a form of migration in itself, this journey from poetry to object, from oneness to multiplicity.

Issam: Yes. How we all seek meaning, of whatever object – it all depends on what we are alert to and what luggage we carry.

Lia: When you are at an exhibition and people come up to you to share how they experience your work, how have migrants, in particular, responded?

Issam: I gave a talk at St James's Church, Piccadilly, in London. At the end I said, 'I am going to finish my talk in memory of many of my fellow Syrians and all immigrants who lost their home.'

I lit a match and just kept silence for the length of that flame, until it died. It was a transcendental moment. The place was charged with emotion and people were sobbing. Many in the audience afterwards came to talk to me, to say, 'I am an immigrant. I have been there.'

Through my exhibitions, I have met many people who have lost their home. I felt they were touched by the simplicity of my tools, matchsticks, and the profound meaning of the light: the lighting of the match, the dying of it and the accumulation of the ashes – this is a powerful metaphor.

It was a shock for me to realize the impact of this performance. I come from a fine art, architecture and theatre design background. Emotion was not part of my academic landscape. In my recent work, as a practising artist, I am learning how to create an emotional landscape.

Lia: How would you describe your own journey of migration?

Issam: I come from the mountains in southern Syria, from a small minority called the Druze. I started migrating out of my hometown to Damascus, to study fine art. Then I migrated further, to Azerbaijan, to Baku to study Russian. And then further north towards St Petersburg (then Leningrad) where I studied architecture. A few years later I ventured westwards, before and after the demolition of the Berlin Wall.

I used to visit Cambridge regularly, travelling through Europe by train. I liked the scale of Cambridge, and I decided that I would like to make my home here. Half-home, semi-home – I don't know what to call it yet. 'Home' is a very complex concept. I'm still searching for it.

In my quest for home, I learned to respect 'the other'. I am a palimpsest. Each layer is a trace of different cultures I lived in, and people I connected with.

Lia: We have spoken previously about your resistance to identity labels. For you, what drives this resistance?

Issam: Labels fix things. There are so many labels that somehow solidify the liquidity of our spirit. We need to treasure this liquidity as a catalyst to connect with others. I resist labels, because defining my art by religion, gender or national identity is pointless. We should avoid pigeonholing people.

My artwork is dealing with my fellow humans who are forced out of their homes. What matters is if I am able to succeed in voicing their pain.

In the early 90s, I worked with migrants from many different parts of the world. I took them to the Botanical Gardens here in Cambridge. I wanted them to see the way flowers, shrubs and trees have been introduced from abroad. They are migrants coming from many different climates, and their original home is somewhere else. They live in harmony together and they work so hard to make new roots in the new soil. This is also the essence of our human nature. Wherever we are, we are always trying to create roots.

Lia: Yes. And yet the world has this desire to fix.

Issam: It is simply because we are living in fast motion. There is no space for contemplative thought. Labels are a quick fix, a temporary number or a name, just for quick classifications, quick pigeonholing. Done. I am not interested in that.

In the introduction to *Another Day Lost*, the first line is: 'We are all emigrants from our first home – the womb – and we carry with us, as a reminder of our journey to the light, a visible scar – the navel.' That is what links us as humans. We're all emigrant from that place and our lives are precarious and vulnerable. Because of fear, we seek protection. We create our own faiths, and we form our communities.

We are born alone and we die alone. But in between, to protect ourselves, we try to connect. The other day I learned something very beautiful: how the fishing net was created by somebody who saw a spider's web. This is what we do as humans. We learn from our environment, our nature and from each other.

The tragedy of our times is that people are consumers, not creators. In these fast, instant-fix times, we are less and less able to talk to each other or listen to each other or have time for each other.

Lia: I can imagine that there is a tendency for people to want to pigeonhole you, for example as a 'Muslim artist'. How do you resist that?

Issam: Many labels! 'Middle Eastern artist', 'Mediterranean artist', 'Arab artist', 'Muslim artist', and so forth. Labels are short-lived. I don't like to label others, and I don't want others to label me.

Though it might be coloured by its locality, art as a language is universal. We are coming from the earth, and wherever we travel we take that earth with us. In one of my recent installations on refugees, in Aldeburgh, I worked with sand. I really wanted to have different sands coming from Syria, Yemen, Afghanistan, from Africa, Asia and the Americas. But this is the magic about sand: it travels all around the world, and it has the DNA of all these places coming together. So, this piece of sand has multiplicity.

Particular labels – 'Syrian', 'Arab', 'Muslim', 'male' and so on – are far too quick. They are nothing but pigeonholing, which in my view is a lazy way out of using one's imagination. We need to take the time to know the other, on their own terms, rather than using labels that are ready-made, already explained, the mystery drained out of them.

Lia: As you know, this is a book about three big, interweaving themes: migration, faith and community. For you, how do these ideas intersect?

Issam: We migrate for different reasons. We are curious beings. We need to see the unseen, so we travel the world in search of connection with unfamiliar lands and unfamiliar communities. We need to wander beyond our physical homes, but always we need a piece to remind us of it.

I will tell you this moving story. It transformed me as person as well as an artist.

I went to visit my friends in Cuba, in Havana in the mid-90s. While there, they took me to a beach where locals brought their home furniture and whatever wooden pieces they might have. Though wooden furniture was scarce, they managed to find some, break it to pieces and construct boats from them. Many, unfortunately, did not make it to Miami. The boats were not seaworthy.

I was touched by the transformation of objects from being part of the home, into vehicles to travel by, to form another home. Somehow, the memory carried inside that piece of wood would be carried by you as an omen and would guard you on this painful journey. The word 'metaphor' is a boat itself, taking you from one place to another.

I do an exercise with my students at the beginning of each year. I ask them to empty their bags and see what they carry inside. Many of them, particularly from far away, bring with them something to remind them of home. Our bags have so much to do with our multiple selves. We all have a need to move, but we also need to have a small piece of where we are coming from – to take us to the next shore.

In my work as an artist, I am interested in transforming – or altering – a familiar object, to become an unfamiliar one and to generate new questions.

Back to your first question: What would I like people to take from my artwork?

Viewers and listeners should feel comfortable to project their own life into whatever art form they are experiencing. That requires braveness, because it's very easy to be imprisoned by the label that is given to you.

Lia: That's both a very generous but also a very challenging invitation.

Issam: It is only an invitation. I say to my students, when they go to exhibitions, that they should never start with a label, but experience whatever they are looking at and let it sink. In this way, when the artworks resonate, they start making their own stories about what they are reading, looking at, and listening to. To start with the labels, you only go there; it is a one-way system, too safe and limiting. Art, like relationships, requires time, openness and risk.

Lia: And it requires generosity, and a patience with the world.

Issam: I have a friend who makes very simple artwork. He draws multi-coloured parallel lines. He says something really beautiful:

If you invest time looking, you will be rewarded by something you will not know from the first glimpse.

Similarly, the artist James Turrell uses light as his medium and creates chambers called *Skyscapes*, where you are invited to view the sky from the window above your head. Though the sky is a familiar place to most of us, when it is framed, the colour, the clouds and stars are absorbed differently. This very familiar place becomes a spiritual one.

Lia: How would you describe the spirituality of your own work?

Issam: My way to making art started with calligraphy, Arabic calligraphy. My brother was the calligrapher; I was his assistant. He writes verses from the Qu'ran in very beautiful calligraphic fonts. There is something very spiritual about the way one letter comes to meet another letter, hugs the other letters. Transformation of an idea into language, or spoken words into written word, is a very spiritual journey.

Equally, as an artist I work with objects. I am listening to the spirit of that object, to the invisible voice of that object. When I meet a wounded, discarded object, it gives me great joy to shine a light on its unheard voice.

LESBOS 2016
Ruth Padel

I
The waves talk to their gods
the waves have their prey

the dead bump sideways
in gulleys gouged from grey fire

an arm a trailing bloom
sodden in the surf

where does the wave end
and water around it begin?

How do you separate
self from the other, edge from the flesh?

Shadows of ourselves
no more than a shiver on water

then another life and another
like the waves

and the dead face down
slamming the shore

II
Last night we waited again
we listened to the dark
beside bales of silver survival blankets
donated by the foreign charities

we listened to night-wind
the sighing of pine tree and tamarisk
slap slap of water on rock
slap slap of our hearts

this is where they come
and their stories our stories

my grandmother a girl

escaping the broken
howlings of heaven
the furnace and murder of Smyrna

this is how it begins
claiming a new place on earth
through waves like rings of a tree

rings of the centuries
blown furrows
over this sea

that has known
so many battles
so many deaths

slant to the foam
and stones
of our island's edge

III
And the families
the boy who went ahead to Europe
lost

the father
a forgotten hand
whose fingers feel for the dark

'Find the lowest star on the horizon'
she said to her firstborn
fifteen last year he set out alone

'Fix your eyes on that all night
and you'll be safe'
her bird–soul batters its way

crack-winged for Germany
impossible to penetrate

as the emeralds of Paradise

moon after moon
has gone by
waiting forking out more

and more money
for smugglers
for their excuses

the right time the right wind
surveillance no moon
wait a while longer

all for this terror
on the waters alone

Those facing backwards
see smudges of rose

like fire on the black-lace sky
That was our home.

The wave rolls over.
We feel it thrash

through the thin rubber skin
of the dinghy

how it hates
us and our life jackets

bought at blood price.
Not in our time, Lord.

Yes in our time. And the heart
tap-tapping its prison of bone.

Will this be the wave –
this mirror maze

of lidded muscle
fluted like the moon

a roaring of smithereen silver
slate-finned like a shark

spray-pelt and wave-crest
hour by hour denser and colder

sliding away to the spire and spine of a breaker –
that will shoot us

rocking and spilling
through the quilt of night on the windy sea

down to the blue cathedrals
or wash us up

on rocks
of a long-gazed-at shore?

IV
Where there was nothing
all night

where there was nothing
just grey mist

here is a shape
abandoned by Charon

steering through the small star-light
of cell phones

bursting on rocks
grit chipping lancing the skin

pull them out of the Styx
find the rhythm

wet to the bone
they hug one another

and shiver and they cry
sharp pebbles

whispering trees

our language strange no doubt

and our hands rough
slippery pulling them out

from the last tug of waves
to a sleepy burble of doves

wet faces
in dawn's crumpled blaze

lit for each other
as if water kept its shape

after the jug has broken
one shining petrified moment

before the shattered
pieces fall away.

CHAPTER 28

The Thread of Faith

Reflections on Academic Research, Faith and Creativity

Nazneen Ahmed

In memory of Claire Dwyer (1964–2019)

My mother is not a crafter. My grandmother, aunts and anyone who could have taught me all lived in Bangladesh, far removed from suburban Surrey, where I grew up. As a young teen, I taught myself to embroider, practising different methods from a little book of Anchor stitches. It has been the one craft I have returned to throughout my life.

Academia

From 2014 to 2017, I was the researcher on a project funded by the Arts and Humanities Research Council called Making Suburban Faith: Design, Material Culture and Popular Creativity in Suburban Faith Communities[1]. This project, led by two academic geographers, sought to identify the ways in which creativity manifests within faith communities in Ealing, West London. Through archival and ethnographic research and through creative participatory projects, we studied the ways in which faith buildings are adapted and designed. Our case studies included a 1930s Anglican church; a Sri Lankan Tamil Hindu temple; a Pentecostal church in a 1930s Art Deco cinema; a

---

1   www.makingsuburbanfaith.org.

multi-ethnic mosque in an adapted warehouse; a Liberal Jewish synagogue housed in a tin tabernacle; a gurdwara in a building once used by the Plymouth Brethren; and a diverse Catholic Church.

Through our work in these spaces, it became evident that textiles were an area of rich creative expression. We encountered hand-stitched banners and kneelers in the 1930s Anglican church; miniature saris used to dress the goddesses in the Sri Lankan temple; delicate white dresses worn for First Holy Communion at the Catholic church. We felt that textiles – with their rich, linguistic connections to identity and belonging, in threads, ties, fabric, weaving – would be a way to bring participants of different faith communities together.

Artist Katy Beinart led and designed the creative project, using textiles to explore ideas of identity, migration and faith. I researched the provenance of textiles in our case studies and recruited participants. In the summer of 2016, we assembled in the hall of the Catholic church, with approximately 20 participants from Christian, Hindu, Sikh and Jewish faith traditions. Participants shared work they had made previously, and it became apparent that embroidery would be the most effective medium for the research project. There were several highly-experienced embroiderers, but embroidery is also a craft that is quick to learn; it can be as simple or as intricate as required. It was simply happenstance, then, that I was already an embroiderer and could contribute to the project – not just as a researcher and interviewer, but as a maker.

Unfortunately, our project coincided with Ramadan, the busiest time for the West London Islamic Centre. It was not possible for the Muslim women participating in our case study to devote long afternoons to stitching in the church hall. How, then, could we represent the women of the West London Islamic Centre? How could we celebrate the beauty of Islamic creativity?

Faith

As a Muslim woman, my role as the detached ethnographic observer at the West London Islamic Centre had been gradually changing over the course of the project. I knew the women who worshipped there by name. I helped them set up for their weekly Qur'an study classes. I began, at one point, to worship with them.

The West London Islamic Centre was nothing like the tiny house-mosque I grew up knowing in my hometown in Surrey. That space had been entirely for men. There were few resources to invest in a building equipped adequately for men *and* women (indeed, for many years while they valiantly raised funds, they were only able to hold *Jummah* prayers for men in a Methodist church). Growing up in a town with a very small Muslim population (only a handful of predominantly Pakistani families), I never felt part of a thriving, active Muslim community.

Perhaps this is why ethnography into Islam has always been both natural and a challenge for me. I can make connections in mosques; I am familiar with their rhythms. Yet I also keenly feel guilt at not being a 'good Muslim', at being out of place. Islam and I have had a complex relationship. I do not know how to read Arabic, but I've fasted for Ramadan since I was 12. When I was 17, I went through a phase of wanting to cover my hair. My mother forbade me, telling me that modesty is about the mind, and that she didn't come to England for her daughter to become so conservative. For a few years after my father died, I became an atheist, disillusioned by the suffering I had seen him experience in his final weeks. I returned to Islam after a few years because I realized that I had lost more than my father by leaving it. Nevertheless, I am an imperfect Muslim – at the fringes, not fully within or without.

At the West London Islamic Centre, the women created a beautiful, inspiring space for themselves. They are a multi-ethnic group who communicate not in a diaspora language, like the Urdu of my hometown mosque, but in English, so that everyone may feel like they belong. They appreciate that not everyone has a solid working knowledge of Qur'anic Arabic, so they run classes where women can read the Qur'an in English or Arabic. They also run cake sales and fairs to raise funds for the mosque's redevelopment project (now complete), and homework clubs for younger girls. They beautify their space through handmade runners and tablecloths. From the very beginning, they made me welcome.

For months, I simply watched, made notes, and talked to everyone. But on Eid of the first year of the project, I touched my head to the mosque's green and purple carpet for the first time. It had been two or three years since I had prayed; I was nervous that someone would tell me I was doing it wrong. But something in me made me try. I felt as if I couldn't just observe that day. I was a Muslim; it was Eid. And while praying, there was something like relief. No one corrected me, or said I wasn't allowed to be there. I was just another Muslim woman in the row, connecting with her God.

From then on, when I was in the mosque at prayer time, I prayed.

Creativity in community

For the embroidery project, I realized that I was a part of the West London Islamic Centre. I could represent it, even if the women at the mosque were not able to attend the workshops. I could sew an Islamic contribution myself. I started with an English translation of the first words of the Qur'an: *Bismillah ir-Rahman ir-Rahim* (In the Name of God, the Most Merciful, the Most Compassionate).

I stitched while I sat in the West London Islamic Centre, listening to Ramadan-preparation lectures, attending Qur'an class. Women began to ask me what I was doing, admiring the work, passing it around, sharing their experience of embroidery and the mothers and grandmothers who had taught them to sew.

Once I had finished embroidering the English words, I realized I wanted to sew the Arabic. Even if its meanings and most of its sounds are closed to me, I love the Qur'anic Arabic script, with its delicate vowel markers peppering the page. The Arabic rendition of the first words of the Qur'an would look beautiful. But I can't write Arabic. So I asked the sisters, who directed me to the woman with the most beautiful handwriting. In time, she would become a very dear friend, who would cook for me, introduce me to her family and tell me her story.

She drew the Arabic onto fabric, and I embroidered it in the shade of fresh, vivid green that the Prophet (peace be upon him) said was his favourite colour. As I stitched, the Arabic would go through my head, just as it always does when I'm afraid, nervous or worried: soothing, calming, reassuring. The West London Islamic Centre sisters admired it when it was finished, running their fingers over the smooth surface of the satin stitch. I left tiny patches deliberately bare of stitches, where you can still perceive my friend's pencil lines. It was important to me that they remain visible: a marker of connection to the West London Islamic Centre and the collaboration that made the work possible.

It was not to be the only unexpected creative contribution to our research project. As the embroidery developed, I interviewed many of our research participants, not just about the project, but about the broader ways in which faith, place and textiles wove through their life. They made gifts of their stories to me.

I've always struggled with the notion of detachment that has classically typified ethnographic practice. Throughout my academic life, I have been harbouring a secret: I am, in fact, a poet and a writer of fiction. I do not simply listen when I hear a story, whether it's being told into a recorder, or on the bus, or by a driver in their pristine Uber. I feel the stories given to me; I see them coming alive in front of me, and I am changed by them. And then I have an almost desperate need to share them. To pass them on.

After I recorded these interviews, I found myself unable to just rework them into the strictures of academic prose, to take them apart as pieces to be dissected, analyzed and then locked away. I felt strongly that these stories needed to be honoured. They needed to be told with sensitivity, care, love. They needed to be shared, because within them was great nourishment, great power, great hope. The stories needed to be poems.

I started writing poems based on the interviews which had stayed with me, which came back to me at unexpected times, running through my head like prayers. (Before I went any further, or shared them more widely, I sought permission from my interviewees.) Two of these poems, 'Her Stories and Lebanon', are included here. As researchers, we had spent a great deal of effort analyzing and capturing the unique atmosphere of faith spaces. What would happen if I tried to do the same work, but in poetic form? More poems followed, including 'This is the House that God Built'.

When I started work on the Suburban Faith project, my creative life, my academic career and my faith were compartmentalized, separate things. Perhaps it was the way the project was designed to focus on creativity and faith; perhaps it was because we spent so much time getting to know people and buildings, coming to love them through the intimate lens of faith. Over the life of the project, those threads of my own life – creativity, faith, academia – wove themselves together to become a single, much stronger skein.

Further reading

Dwyer, C., Beinart, K. and Ahmed, N. (2019) 'The fabric of faith: A reflection on creative arts practice research.' In M. Berg and M. Nowicka (eds) *Convivial Tools for Research and Practice.* London: UCL Press.

Dwyer, C., Beinart, K. and Ahmed, N. (2018) 'My life is but a weaving: Embroidering geographies of faith and place.' *Cultural Geographies*, 26, 1, 133–140.

Dwyer, C., Gilbert, D. and Ahmed, N. (2015) 'Building the sacred in suburbia: Improvisation, reinvention and innovation.' *Built Environment*, 41, 4, 478–491.

Gilbert, D., Dwyer, C., Ahmed, N., Cuch, L. and Hyacinth, N. (2018) 'The hidden geographies of religious creativity: Place-making and material culture in West London faith communities.' *Cultural Geographies*, 26, 1, 23–41.

Her Stories

She left me a map in her stories
A trail of crumbs to follow.

London.
Ingutsheni.
Umsilaghazi.

Threads that tied her to different places
A road of stitches for me to follow.
Look up their history,
She told me,
And you will understand my story.

Germany.
Madras.
Bulawayo.

But her story is not written in the histories.
I search for her but she is not recorded there.
She was tied to all these places
In ways I cannot trace.

She left me her story in
In a bundle of knots
I cannot pick apart.

Which were her stories?
Which were histories?
They are for ever entwined.
Strands of the same skein.

Lebanon

While the bombs rained down around her in Lebanon,
She stitched.
When she was at school in Zimbabwe,
She stitched.
When her grandmother fled Turkey and sought refuge
In a Jerusalem convent
She stitched.

She pulls out piece after piece from their plastic wrappers.
This one, she tells me, is for Easter,
That one was made during curfew.

Trapped inside for a whole year,
She dreamed new patterns.
She brought them into being
By counting threads and spaces.
Her handiwork,
Precise and measured,
Even as bombs fell
And the walls shook.

There are hundreds of pieces of work,
Cushion covers, table cloths, coasters.
Made by her hands, her mother's, her grandmother's,
Each tying her to another place and time.

In Jordan, Dubai, Germany, London.
She stitched.
She stitched herself into place,
Making herself at home,
Making herself home.

This is the House that God Built

This is the house that God built
Smooth white walls and straightbacked pillars
Neem and peepal thrive where once a stern minister stood
Crushed marigold and parsley garlands damp underfoot
A gilded rainbow of gods
Their smiles warming worshippers
Sacred threads tying them to a faraway home

This is the house that God built
A warehouse tucked away from view
Cardboard box rooms stacked hastily upon each other
Full to overspill on jummah
A minbar lovingly laid in mosaic
The carpet patterned with rows of arches
At a diagonal to the walls
Rising from sujood too quickly
The world might turn upon its axle

This is the house that God built
The cool serenity of concrete and watercolour glass
The reredos gently faded into place
Humble wooden chairs bear
Squat bright cushions
Each handstitched and handstuffed
Dusted and darned
Even though people don't kneel when they pray anymore

How many hours of devoted work
To keep God's many houses.

CHAPTER 29

Poetry

Amir Darwish

Reprinted from Dear Refugee (2019, Ripon: Smokestack)

Dear Refugee

Be thankful to the roads,
Their stones as they lie before you to walk
Thank you not enough for the sky
Who always generous to show you
The moon while dangles its legs
Into your eyes
Say Thank you to nature, its rivers who feed
The earth to feed you
Be thankful to life and earth
When they nock open your heart.

We want to live

On a margin of a forgotten camp
With pain we want to live
With sadness
With agony
With traumas
We want to live
With or without food
We want to live
With thirst
With enemies or without them
We still want to live
Under a cut in a tent with every drop of rain at night we want
    to live
We want to live
At the long queues for clothes we want to live
With every step we take towards the journey of death
We want to live
With every tree we pass
With every pride swallowed, we want to live
With or without our children
We want to live
With or without our parents
We want to live
We want to live, simply because we love life.

What I left behind

I left that table with three books, a tea glass dirty
An ashtray
The TV remote still lost somewhere between cushions

A wall with a mixture of rotten green broken yellow light
Small window into an empty street
A white tissue travels lonely in a windy ruined alley

I left a pregnant apple tree
A sink full of pans, has remnant of favourite dish from last night
My plate among them with a tulip

I left half a bottle of red wine near bed
Money notes wrinkled
A belt with broken buckle

The art work in the corridor
The man in it hand on cheek tearful eyes
The forest behind him huge as the memory it leaves behind

I left a tape player once a lover gifted me
The Kurdish singer Mohammed Sixo on it screams
Oh the land Oh the land

I left my school desk with my name engraved,
The teacher who lectures me every time I bring a poetry book
Instead of syllabus book

I left the old corner shop
With a debt book
That has my name

Left the new shoe yet to wear
The yellow laces I bought
To go with it

My mother who stops by the door signals 'come food is ready'
I left a generous father who daily comes home with bags of figs,
    apples
And occasionally roast chicken in right hand
I left home.

Where I come from

From the earth I come
To the earth I come
From the heart of Africa
From the kidneys of Asia
From India with spices I come
From a deep Amazonian forest
From a Tibetan meadow I come
From an ivory land
From far
From everywhere around me
From where there are trees, mountains, rivers and seas
From here, there, from everywhere
From the womb of the Mediterranean I come
From a mental scar
From closed borders
From a camp with a thousand tents
From shores with Alan the Kurd I come
From a bullet wound
From the face of a lone child
From a single mother's sigh
From a cut in an inflatable boat about to sink
From a bottle of water for fifty to share
From frozen snot in a toddler's nose
From a tear on a father's cheek
From a hungry stomach
From a graffiti that reads, 'I was here once'
From another one a tree says 'I love life'
From a missing limb
Like a human with everything I come to share the space.

Continuing the Conversation

This book is only part of a far wider conversation about migration, community and faith.

Additional materials are available through the Susanna Wesley Foundation: a community of scholarship based at the University of Roehampton, which aims to equip faith communities and organizations through promoting dialogue, reflection, research and innovation.

www.susannawesleyfoundation.org/conversations/mapping-faith

List of Contributors

Nazneen Ahmed is a Southampton-based writer, researcher and historian. She is currently writing a fantasy novel aimed at readers aged 11 upwards.

Robyn Ashworth-Steen is a rabbi based at Manchester Reform Synagogue. Formerly a human rights lawyer, she is co-founder of Tzelem: The Rabbinic Call for Social and Economic Justice in the UK, and trustee of the charity We Stand Together.

Katherine Baxter is a London-based mapmaker, illustrator and Methodist lay preacher (www.katherinebaxter.com).

Sheila Curran is a practical theologian and a member of the Congregation of the Sisters of Mercy, Northern Province, Ireland. Until 2019, she was Justice Coordinator of the Association of Leaders of Missionaries and Religious of Ireland.

Aviva Dautch is a poet, academic and curator. She served as poet-in-residence at the Jewish Museum London from 2014 to 2016, and she received an Authors' Foundation Award from The Society of Authors in 2018.

Amir Darwish is a poet and writer of Kurdish origin, whose work has been widely translated. Born in Aleppo, he came to Britain as an asylum seeker in 2003. Amir holds advanced degrees in history, international relations, and creative and life writing. He is currently working on his doctorate.

Filipino Community in Harmony, Action, Mobilization and Prayer is a network of Filipino parishioners based at Sacred Heart Catholic Church in Kilburn, North London.

Rachel Godfrey is an interfaith and Jewish educator, Bar Mitzvah tutor and writer based at West London Synagogue, where she oversees the Scriptural Reasoning programme.

Yvonne Green is an award-winning poet, translator and writer who describes herself as 'an observant British Jewess' with family roots in Central Asia. She lives in North London.

Oliver Spike Joseph is a rabbi at New North London Synagogue. He works for Masorti Judaism, a young and progressive movement of Jewish communities across the UK.

Ivan Khovacs is an Anglican priest and senior lecturer in theology at Canterbury Christ Church University. He teaches Christian doctrine and practical theology, serves a parish church and is on the national commission shaping theological education in the Church of England.

Julie Khovacs is Priest Missioner at St Peter's Church, Eaton Square, in central London. Prior to ordination in the Church of England, she worked in healthcare chaplaincy in the Scottish Episcopal Church, and in special education in California.

Issam Kourbaj was born in Syria and trained in fine art in Damascus, architecture in St Petersburg, Russia and theatre design in London. Since 2011, his artwork has responded to the Syrian crisis, reflecting on the suffering of the Syrian people and their cultural heritage (www. issamkourbaj.co.uk).

Harvey Kwiyani teaches African Christianity and theology at Liverpool Hope University. He also leads Missio Africanus, a cross-cultural missions training initiative that equips African churches in Europe and North America for missional effectiveness in Western cultures. He is the founding editor of *Missio Africanus: The Journal of African Missiology*.

Jennifer Langer is a poet and the founding director of Exiled Writers Ink. She has edited four anthologies of exiled literature and is a Research Associate at the School of Oriental and African Studies, University of London.

David Mason is a rabbi based at an orthodox Synagogue in Muswell Hill, North London. He is Chair of the Haringey Multi Faith Network and serves as a trustee of the Council of Christians and Jews and the Forum for Discussion on Israel and Palestine.

Ibrahim Mogra is the Muslim Chaplain to Canary Wharf in London. He is an educator, a scholar and an imam in Leicester.

Michael Nausner is a theologian and minister in the United Methodist Church. He currently serves as Senior Researcher at the Church of Sweden Research Unit in Uppsala, Sweden.

Jacqueline Nicholls is a London-based visual artist, Jewish educator and regular contributor to BBC Radio 2's *Pause For Thought*. She uses her art to engage with traditional Jewish ideas in untraditional ways.

Pádraig Ó Tuama is a poet and theologian from Ireland. From 2014 to 2019, he led Corrymeela, Ireland's oldest peace and reconciliation centre. He lives in Belfast (www.padraigotuama.com).

Faiza Omar is an east African artist and the manager of 35 Chapel Walk in Sheffield (www.35chapelwalk.com).

Mohamed Omar is Policy and Development Officer at the Mental Health Foundation, where he leads a national project to increase refugee voices and visibility in mental health policy. Mohamed is a Fellow of the Royal Society of the Arts, and a board member of the Scottish Refugee Council.

Ruth Padel is an award-winning poet, Professor of Poetry at King's College London, and Fellow of the Royal Society of Literature (www. ruthpadel.com).

Alison Phipps holds the UNESCO Chair in Refugee Integration through Languages and the Arts at the University of Glasgow, where she is also Professor of Languages and Intercultural Studies, and Co-Convenor of the Glasgow Refugee, Asylum and Migration Network.

Hassan Rabbani is the Muslim Chaplain of Heriot-Watt University in Edinburgh. He received his traditional training at Al-Azhar University (Cairo, Egypt) and holds advanced degrees from Aberdeen University and the University of Glasgow.

Katy Radford works at the Institute for Conflict Research in Belfast. She is a Commissioner with the Equality Commission for Northern Ireland; Vice Chair of the Arts Council for Northern Ireland; and a member of the Executive Council of the Northern Ireland Jewish Community.

Sayed Razawi is Director General of the Scottish Ahlul Bayt Society. He is a visiting scholar at the Strathclyde Business School; Associate of the Project on Shi'ism and Global Affairs at Harvard University's Weatherhead Center for International Affairs; and a member of the European Council of Religious Leaders and of the United Nations Multi-Faith Advisory Council.

Sofia Rehman is a theologian and religious scholar based at the University of Leeds. She runs an Islam and Feminism Critical Reading Group in partnership with the Iqbal Centre for the Study of Contemporary Islam.

Lia Dong Shimada is Senior Researcher at the Susanna Wesley Foundation and Associate Chaplain of Whitelands College, University of Roehampton. She also runs a consultancy practice specializing in mediation and community dialogue. (www.liashimada.com)

Tawona Sitholé is Artist in Residence of the UNESCO Chair for Refugee Integration through Languages and the Arts at the University of Glasgow. He co-founded Seeds for Thought, an arts organization based in Glasgow.

Ric Stott is an artist and a Methodist minister. He collaborated with local partners to develop 35 Chapel Walk, a community art space in Sheffield City Centre. (ricstott.com)

Sally Style is the Montefiore Endowment Librarian Researcher and a Hebrew translator, based at the Spanish and Portuguese Synagogue in Maida Vale, London. She holds responsibility for the Endowment's manuscripts and artefacts related to Sir Moses Montefiore.

Hajra Williams is a museum educator, researcher and writer. She is currently conducting research, through the University of Brighton, on how South Asian communities in the UK engage with museum exhibitions.